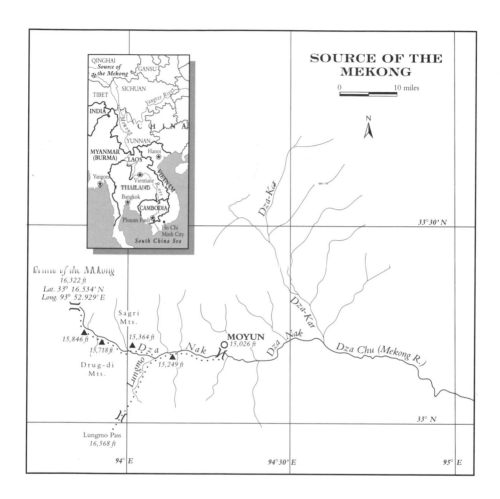

SOURCE OF THE
MEKONG

0   10 miles

N

QINGHAI
Source of
the Mekong   GANSU
SICHUAN
TIBET
Yangtze River
INDIA
C H I N A
YUNNAN
Hanoi
MYANMAR
(BURMA)   LAOS
Yangon
Vientiane
THAILAND
Bangkok
CAMBODIA
Phnom Penh
Ho Chi
Minh City
South China Sea

33° 30' N

Dza-Kar

Source of the Mekong
16,322 ft
Lat. 33° 16.534' N
Long. 93° 52.929' E

Sagri
Mts.

Dza-Kar

15,846 ft
15,364 ft
MOYUN
15,026 ft
15,718 ft   Dza   Nak   Dza Nak
Drug-di   15,249 ft   Dza Chu (Mekong R.)
Mts.

Lungmo

33° N

Lungmo Pass
16,568 ft

94° E   94° 30' E   95° E

THE LAST
BARBARIANS

THE LAST
*B*ARBARIANS

The Discovery of
the Source of the Mekong in Tibet

MICHEL PEISSEL

Henry Holt and Company   *New York*

Henry Holt and Company, Inc.
Publishers since 1866
115 West 18th Street
New York, New York 10011

Henry Holt ® is a registered
trademark of Henry Holt and Company, Inc.

Library of Congress Cataloging-in-Publication Data
Peissel, Michel, 1937–
The last Barbarians : the discovery of the source of the
Mekong in Tibet/Michel Peissel.
p. cm.
Includes index.
ISBN 0-8050-4534-1 (alk. paper)
1. Tibet (China)—Discovery and exploration. 2. Mekong River—
Discovery and exploration. 3. Horses, Fossil—China—Tibet. I. Title
DS786.P376 1997
915.1′50459—dc21   97–27534
CIP

Henry Holt books are available for special
promotions and premiums. For details contact:
Director, Special Markets.

First Edition 1997

DESIGNED BY PAULA R. SZAFRANSKI
MAPS BY ADAM MERTON COOPER
PHOTOGRAPHS BY THE AUTHOR EXCEPT WHERE NOTED

Printed in the United States of America
All first editions are printed on acid-free paper. ∞

1 3 5 7 9 10 8 6 4 2

To Jacques Falck and Sebastian Guinness

We shall not cease from exploration
And the end of all our exploring
Will be to arrive where we started
And know the place for the first time.

—T. S. ELIOT

CONTENTS

⌘

AUTHOR'S NOTE

⌘

Tibetan is a written phonetic language. The spelling of Tibetan names respects archaic phonetic traditions; as a result, to use classical Tibetan spelling can be very misleading for everyone but scholars. I have therefore transcribed Tibetan names using the rendition of their modern pronunciation as adopted for over two centuries by Western travelers. On rare occasions, when necessary for precision's sake, I have added or used the Tibetan spelling of certain place names.

It appears unwise to use the often-fanciful spellings found on Chinese maps, which would acknowledge the rewriting of town names in the wake of a strongly contested military takeover. Furthermore, the transcription of Tibetan names into Chinese often produces quite unrecognizable results.

THE LAST
BARBARIANS

1

DREAMS AND REALITY

⌘

On the seventeenth of September, 1994, at 6:30 P.M., riding a small black horse in the company of Dr. Jacques Falck, the Honorable Sebastian Guinness, the Chinese mountain guide Ling, and a Tibetan muleteer, I reached a natural amphitheater from which oozed and trickled three little streams, streams that united to form what some twenty-eight hundred miles downstream is known as the "mother river" of Asia. We had discovered the source of the Mekong—an act as banal as it proved to be magical. There was little or nothing to see. The true importance of our discovery was all in the mind, for we had reached one of those rare sacred places where myth and reality meet, where the dream world and the true world become one.

I was there leading our small party, a man of fifty-seven, because ever since childhood I had been unable to distinguish between dreams and reality. As a result, I never really grew up, and as the years went by

I became increasingly involved in projects that required putting aside reason in favor of passion. This form of rashness led me all over the world in quest of those lost horizons that we believe exist out there somewhere, just beyond our reach, and which we all secretly crave.

With each new expedition I had come to realize that dreams very often come true.

It was the second of September when Jacques Falck and I boarded the flight from Paris to Beijing. An airplane ticket to the unknown looks very much like an ordinary ticket, yet I knew that before I would need the return stub I would be a different person.

I will try here to record the events as they happened, well aware that to write about them is to travel all over again in one's head, straying down the mysterious paths of memory in which past, present, and future intermingle with fact and fiction. Inevitably I will wander off course, because nothing is ever as simple as it appears, and one's perception of even the simplest of facts is disturbed by one's memories.

Excitement, as opposed to boredom, is, I feel, the motivating factor of most of my journeys. It is not that I am often bored; it is that I am afraid of being bored, a feeling that swept over me for the first time at the age of eight. I was then living in tame old England, the middle child of a middle-class family in the middle of Britain. My life was already crammed with the boring routine of school, a nightly bath before dinner, and early to bed.

The only excitement I got came from the stories that my nanny read to me, drawn from the Victorian lore that was then deemed acceptable and proper. Those were still the days of empire, the British Empire that circled my globe in pink and was interrupted only here and there by the pathetically smaller French Empire in blue-gray. A French boy living in England, I managed to take pride in both. At school I rooted for France, a land I did not even recall, having left it in my mother's arms to join my father, a diplomat stationed in London, at the outbreak of World War II. Later, at school in France, I rooted for Britain. In the meantime, the only excitement I had was in hearing accounts of the great Victorian explorers who, for queen and country, were allowed to stray from the rigid decorum of their habitual routines to joust with the unknown.

My heroes were Scott, Mallory, and others who died for the sport of it all, their lives nobly wasted in quest of that undescribable and, today, unfashionable thing called *glory*.

Today people seek fame and fortune rather than glory, but I was seeking neither as I took my seat on the China Airlines flight from Paris to Beijing. That such a flight existed would have amazed Dutreuil de Rhins, the French explorer who had set out from Paris to discover the source of the Mekong exactly a century before me, never to return.

"Is there really anything left to explore?" my friends would ask. I was well aware of the paradox, that in our age of space travel there should be anything on earth left undiscovered. All my life I had been called an explorer, a dubious title that I hated and that made people smile kindly and look down on me as something of a simpleton.

Yet I *am* an explorer. The name itself conjures up visions of the past: although Neil Armstrong and the other astronauts have every right to be considered the greatest explorers of all time, somehow nobody thinks of them that way. Most people think instead that explorers are old-fashioned or completely obsolete because there is no need for them anymore.

To explore or to discover, when applied to geography, has a very specific and slightly racist meaning. Did Columbus discover America and explore the New World? In our age of belated remorse, some people would say no, that Columbus did not discover America, because it was already known to the Indians.

What does "to discover" actually mean? In political terms, it has been defined traditionally as the first publication by a European of the existence of a place, people, plant, or creature—the notion of European having been generously extended of late to include Americans and Japanese.

The discoverer, therefore, is the first explorer to publish and publicize what he's found, not just the first to find it. Thus, the Vikings may have reached America "first," but they failed to publicize the fact except among themselves, in the Icelandic sagas. Perhaps they failed to appreciate (as Columbus did later) that what they had discovered was a "New World." When Amerigo Vespucci realized that it was and coined the phrase, the entire territory that had been discovered was given his name.

There are many places on earth still to be explored, and many undiscovered plants, insects, mammals, and reptiles, not to mention viruses and bacteria. But few people were willing to take my word for it, and I had a lot of trouble persuading anyone that the source of the Mekong, Asia's third-largest river and one of the world's most famous, was one of those places.

"You're joking." When I brought up the subject, people tended to laugh in disdain and walk away. And it was even harder in the end (and it took longer) to persuade the world that we had really discovered the source of the Mekong, once we had done it.

In our day, when the globe can be photographed by satellites and overflown by planes and helicopters, it makes perfect sense to ask if there really are regions that have never been explored.

The answer is that the unexplored lies where satellites can't see and planes and helicopters can't fly, or in politically forbidden territories that have been closed for centuries.

Among such forbidden territories are vast tracts of the former Soviet Union, where neither foreigners nor nationals were allowed to roam under a ban that had existed since the time of the czars.

Another such region is greater Tibet, a vast area three times the size of France or Texas, which has been closed to outsiders and further protected by the highest, most impassable mountain ranges and plateaus on our planet.

Even as satellites fly over these regions, they can't distinguish small terrain features, such as the flow of little rivers and streams that form the headwaters of the great rivers.

The Amazon and New Guinea have been a paradise for explorers and pseudo-explorers for centuries, and both regions are better known than many would have us believe, because they have long been wide open to exploration.

On the other hand, the highlands of greater Tibet were closed for hundreds of years by order of the Tibetans themselves, and have remained closed under Chinese domination.

A strict ban on travel to certain parts of Tibet has been maintained since 1982, when the first tourists were allowed in by Chinese Communists. The ban is necessitated not only by the remoteness of many of these areas but also by the presence, in some regions, of ferociously independent warrior tribes, among them the Khambas and the Goloks, with whom the Chinese have a long history of conflict and animosity.

Of course I knew all this because Tibet had long since become my second home.

As I sat aboard the plane heading for Beijing I tried again to count how many times I had set out for that part of the world.

I will never forget my first journey. I was only twenty-two, and I had flown out of Boston, where I had been studying at the Harvard Business School. With me was the French anthropologist Alain Thiollier. There being no jets in 1959, the flight took two days to reach New Delhi and made stops in just about every capital en route. Moreover, the cost of it was so high—nearly twenty times today's fare—that I had seriously considered taking the still much-used alternative route, by sea, from Marseilles to Bombay, the route of the empire builders and of all the early British colonialists and explorers.

Captains John Hodgson and James Herbert were among those who went that way, sailing around the Cape of Good Hope in 1817 (the Suez Canal not yet having been built in those days) on their way to discovering the "Cow's Mouth," the source of the Ganges, the holiest of all Asia's rivers. The mouth turned out to be in the ice cave of a glacier at the foot of Mount Gangotri, a majestic pyramid of a peak that marks the nearby frontier between India and Tibet.

I visited this cave in 1980, at the end of a bizarre expedition on which I had tried to get to the source of the sacred Ganges by shooting up its rapids in a hovercraft. When the hovercraft broke down, my companions and I ended our quest on foot through towering granite gorges, past other caves where for centuries pilgrims had come to die on the banks of what they considered the mother river of life. When we got there and stood inside the "Cow's Mouth" ourselves, it was a moment of some emotion. At the time we were the first foreigners allowed by India to visit the place in thirty-three years.

The discovery of the source of the Ganges in 1817 triggered a long series of searches to find the sources of the Indus, the Brahmaputra, and the Sutlej, India's three other great rivers. Finding their sources proved much more arduous, however, because they lay beyond the great Himalayan range inside forbidden Tibet.

At about the same time as the discovery of the source of the Ganges, in disguise and driving a flock of sheep, William Moorcroft and Hyder Jung Hearsey crossed over into Tibet and became the first Englishmen to investigate the shores of sacred Lake Manasarowar at the foot of Mount Kailas, the holiest of all holy mountains, the epicenter not only of the Buddhist world but of the Hindu pantheon as well.

Moorcroft was a happy-go-lucky doctor turned veterinary surgeon, who had become rich practicing in Oxford Street and had then lost his fortune in an attempt to industrialize the manufacture of horseshoes. And so he set off for India. Bored with his job as veterinary surgeon to the East India Company, he set out to explore Lake Manasarowar but failed to identify exactly the nearby sources of the Indus, the Sutlej, and the Brahmaputra.

After this first expedition, Moorcroft explored Ladakh, or "Little Tibet," in the western Himalayas. On his way there he met a prudish young Frenchman, Victor Jacquemont, who later stated that "Moorcroft's principal occupation was making love with the natives." But Moorcroft was a true gentleman—not a Victorian creep—and his natural interest in women was as nothing compared with his courage and love of scholarship. From Ladakh he headed for Bokhara, the most secretive city of central Asia at the time, but he died of an undiagnosed illness on this journey just after having reached his goal. Fortunately for us his detailed notes survived, brought back by his faithful native assistant.

Following in Moorcroft's footsteps were several young British officers, one of whom, Edmund Smyth, came to be considered the discoverer of the source of the Brahmaputra. He had traveled to Ladakh with Lieutenant John Speeke, who later discovered the source of the Nile. So it was that what we might call "river fever" began to spread.

In every culture and civilization considerable importance is attributed to the sources of rivers. Herodotus, the father of geography, was obsessed by the idea that the source of the Nile and the source of the Dnieper "were a mystery-unknown." It fascinated him and many others that rivers could be flowing from unknown regions, bearing down to the sea the water of secret origins.

To every man there comes a moment when, looking at a river, he lets his imagination wander to where it all began, to the place few see but all envision. In our days of fast cars, bullet trains, and the Concorde, we are slightly less fascinated by what the ancients saw as the mysterious perpetual movement of the waters of rivers. But historically the quest for the sources of rivers paralleled the quest for all knowledge, the search for all origins, the same quest that today still motivates philosophers and scholars to ask *how* everything began.

I admit I had been curious about the sources of rivers, but not terribly so. I knew of the great controversy between Burton and Speeke over the source of the Nile. I had dreamt of the source of the Amazon, imagining it to be the remotest of all. (In fact, it was discovered only in 1953 by a Frenchman named Michel Perrin. But this I found out later.)

Flying out to China I was not very much concerned with the Amazon—or with the Mekong, for that matter. My principal worry was how my companions and I might get along, and how all three of us would react to the altitude of Tibet's highest plateau, the true roof of the world.

By definition, the sources of rivers are generally found at the highest elevations of any given region, and so it is that the source of the Mekong as well as the sources of the Yellow River, the Yangtze, and the Salween, four of Asia's largest rivers, are all located on the highest and remotest portions of the world's highest plateau, a plateau that is today part of China's Qinghai Province, which roughly covers the old Amdo region of the once-independent greater Tibet.

In the late nineteenth century many explorers sought to enter forbidden Tibet, some of them in search of the sources of Asia's great rivers. There was, in fact, something of a rush to try to find the sources of the Indus, the Brahmaputra, the Yellow River, the Yangtze, Salween—and the Mekong. By the beginning of this century, the sources of all those rivers had been found except for the Mekong.

Although no explorer had ever been to the source of the Mekong, satellite photographs had given us its approximate location and enough data to know that it was the innermost and the remotest of them all.

Seated next to me on the China Airlines flight, Jacques Falck would have appeared to a stranger as tall, heavy, even clumsy looking. He is, by any standards, strange, if not downright bizarre. A scholar in every sense of the word at thirty-eight, he still looks like a schoolboy with dull brown hair that points in every direction, the kind of boy you hated for always being the first in his class. Serious through and through, with a frown on his face as he answers even the most trivial question with long, well-thought-out scientific explanations, Jacques is a man unto himself. I had been taken with him ever since I had met him ten years earlier in Spain.

It was a paradox that he, a medical doctor fascinated with the selective antibacterial properties of specific antibiotics, preferred to be thought of as a filmmaker, but his true passion was making films, an activity to which he dedicated more time than he did to medicine. In fact, he kept his work as a doctor to a strict minimum, substituting for surgeons on holiday when he needed the money. All told, he simply found looking through the eyepiece of a movie camera more interesting than looking down a patient's throat.

For Jacques films were no less serious an operation than, let's say, amputating a leg. To judge from his more or less constant frown, it was hard to believe that he actually derived any pleasure from filming—or from life in general, for that matter. But every now and then an ironic smile, a fleeting glimpse of his genuine but well-hidden sense of humor, would betray itself on his scholarly face.

Ever since he had explained to me at our first meeting the detailed chemical composition of the emulsion of color slides, I had been convinced that I needed Jacques at my side in all of his various capacities of filmmaker, medic, and scholarly companion. My decision to take him along in 1988, in a giant pre-Columbian dugout canoe down the coast of the Yucatán, had been made without asking him whether he could swim. Fortunately, he could. He was also an accomplished yachtsman of the scientific kind, who analyzes the fibers of ropes before he pulls them and has studied meteorology down to the last millibar.

I now worried how he, as clumsy as he is meticulous, would fare riding ponies in Tibet: he admitted he had never ridden any kind of horse. Maybe he was the wrong man for this venture, in that he had never been to high altitudes, either. Yet somehow I knew he would wear well—or die gallantly—with a Victorian indifference to hardship in the tradition of Scott, who died a heroic, yet lucid, death on his way back from the South Pole. In 1989, Jacques had been an excellent second-in-command of a wretched little Viking boat in which I had foolishly decided to cross the whole of the (now former) Soviet Union from the Baltic to the Black Sea. He had rowed and filmed without complaining up the Dvina and down the Dnieper, a total of fifteen hundred miles; at the end of it, to our mutual amazement, we were still on speaking terms.

Of course, this was another expedition altogether. We were then at most three hundred feet above the Black Sea or the Baltic; now we would be over fifteen thousand feet above sea level for the duration of our journey—a journey that not only was considered impossible by many, but had been proven so by the fifteen-odd expeditions that had preceded ours and all come to grief, failing to reach the source of the Mekong.

I remember thinking that at least Jacques could see to it that we didn't die unexpectedly from such high-altitude sicknesses as pulmonary edema. No sooner were we seated on the plane from Paris to Beijing, ironically, than he began to explain, in a morbidly dreary voice, the origins of the foam that invades the lungs as a result of reverse osmosis, the first symptom of that deadly affliction whose sinister name was to haunt our journey.

When, like me, you think you are twenty-seven but you read in your passport that you are close to fifty-eight, it feels good to have a doctor along. "Bring something against heart attacks," I had said jokingly, but I later made sure he had because, after a year of immobility in Paris, I was hardly in shape, even if I had been to Lhasa for a four-week stay in May in an effort to prepare for our journey.

Just as Jacques was tall, gray, and serious, Sebastian Guinness was short, rosy-cheeked, and jovial.

He was an excellent rider of pleasant disposition, but what mattered most was that he spoke Chinese and had been on two previous expeditions to Tibet. He was the son of good friends, and I had known him as a child.

At the last moment my sponsor had backed out, and I had had a mere two weeks to recalculate everything. I had to pay Jacques's way, but Sebastian kindly had volunteered to foot his own bill, allowing us to carry on, thus saving an expedition that had taken me two years to organize. As far as we could tell, we had the first permit ever granted by the Chinese allowing foreigners to travel to the highly restricted area where the source of the Mekong was to be found.

I had obtained this extraordinary permission thanks to *Equus caballus*, or the common horse.

Ever since Moorcroft broke into Tibet uninvited and in disguise, pushing a flock of sheep before him, foreigners have been unwelcome there, and for good reason. For over two hundred years the only foreigners seen by most of the inhabitants of Asia were colonial troops, out to seize political power and dominion over local commerce.

The British swept across India and the French across Indochina, and the Russians gained control over the Near and the Far East from the Black Sea to the Pacific, from Azerbaijan via Mongolia to Manchuria.

Only Tibet and three other countries escaped the greed of the white man: Nepal, whose people gave the British a thrashing in 1815; and Bhutan and Afghanistan, which were protected by fierce warriors of their own and by high mountains.

Buddhism had worn down the warring spirit of most Tibetans, so they defended themselves, instead, by slamming the door against all travelers, be they priest, merchant, or suspected spy. By closing their frontiers they hoped to escape being colonized.

It is useless to demur on how pompous the British were in colonial days, especially in the colonies themselves. They were, unarguably, as pompous and arrogant as I was as a child, looking with pride at how the white man had come to control or, more delicately, to bestow the benefits of his civilization upon the world's primitives. To recall the shimmering egret feathers in the tall white topees of the British viceroys is enough to understand how deeply vexed they were when mysterious monks from Tibet and Bhutan scorned British power by (for instance) returning their letters unopened.

Worse, Sir Ashley Eden, representative plenipotentiary of the British Crown, dressed in full regalia, feathers and all, had actually been spat upon in Bhutan. War followed immediately, of course, but then the British forces had been severely defeated, just as they had been in Nepal. As for the Afghan Wars, after the massacre of the British fleeing Kabul, colonial troops on the "Northwest Frontier" had made little or no progress in a conflict that was to stretch from 1839 until 1937.

Thus, in the West, the mystery of the region was laced with fear and needled by the insolence and mockery of Tibet and her neighbors. It just "wasn't on" for natives to defy the humorless Victorians who, after the Indian Mutiny in 1857, had replaced the more congenial members of the British East India Company, or John Company, as it was also called.

To discover the source of the Indus and the Brahmaputra, the British had had to rely on adventurers. And where the British couldn't go in Tibet they sent native secret agents to map the land for them clandestinely.

For my part, I had used *Equus caballus* to gain access to Tibet's forbidden territories. Since the Chinese were even less keen than the Tibetans to allow foreigners to roam freely around the country— much less to have a look at the garrisons they had set up to pacify it— a lot of work was required to allow me to travel to restricted areas.

Years before in Cadaques, in Spain, I had first mentioned to Sebastian's cousin Loel Guinness, a keen polo player, my idea for an *Equus caballus* project. I myself am a keen but lousy polo player, and well short of the financial means to play the game, as much as I love it, but I have always been interested in horses, and for eighteen years, between occasional polo games, I indulged heavily in the slightly archaic and currently very unpopular sport of hunting wild boar and stags on horseback.

When I pointed out to Loel that the word *polo* was a Tibetan word meaning "ball," and that *rTa-polo,* "horse ball," was a Tibetan game imported via Baltistan into British India, he was surprised, to say the least. He then became enthusiastic when I suggested to him somewhat later that it would be interesting to seek out and study the various Tibetan breeds of horses.

Historically, foreigners in Tibet had been too busy studying the Buddhist monasteries and their monks to bother about the horses they encountered. On the whole they considered them to be rough, vulgar ponies, like all those they had encountered on the borders of the British Empire; this I knew to be untrue.

Horses exist everywhere around the world, but, whereas we can trace their origins through fossils to a doglike, clawed creature, we know very little about the provenance of our modern horses. On the one hand there are the wild equids—zebras, asses, and the Przewalski horse—and on the other hand, all the tame, domestic horses, in two types: the rustic horses and the man-made breeds. The rustic horses and ponies are breeds that mate freely according to whim.

Do all domestic horses have the same origins, from the Shetland pony to the Arabian thoroughbred? In a word, nobody knows.

Thanks to help from Loel's foundation and to his enthusiasm, in 1992 I was able to organize my first "equine expedition" to Tibet in search of various breeds of Tibetan horses.

It was then, quite by accident, that I found in horses the unexpected "open sesame" to the last secret regions of Tibet, where I believed I would also find the source of the Mekong. For the sensitive Chinese government, there was apparently nothing political in horses, and I was allowed to enter regions normally closed to foreigners; thus it was that I was now able to consider exploring the upper reaches of the Mekong River.

This explains how, on September 2, 1994, I found myself seated next to Jacques Falck, off to try to find the source of the third-most important river in Asia. It all seemed a little bit too grand and too extraordinary to be true. I felt like getting up and explaining all this to the stewardess, but of course I did nothing of the sort.

I hate airplanes in which one cannot sit in the front seat, and find modern air travel about as exciting as riding an elevator. Yet in a matter of hours I was crossing a distance nonstop that had taken Marco

Polo two years to traverse. As I munched on tasteless chicken, beneath me unfurled the carpeted grasslands of the Ukraine, followed by the basin of the Volga and the deserts bordering the dehydrated Aral Sea. Then came the sands of Bactria, leading to the orchards of Samarkand and Tashkent and on to Chinese Turkestan, the Taklamakan desert, and then, just north of Tibet, to the Gansu corridor of the Silk Road, better known in China as the Horse Road. It was there that I had ridden the Silk Road post pony, the Chakori, a small vivid little beast, born to amble and carry fat merchants between Urumqi and Lanzhou.

We were to meet Sebastian in Beijing, where he was flying from the United States via Tokyo.

As we were winging our way toward Beijing, it was hard to escape the magic of the name. My heart beat faster as I got off the plane, even though this would be my fourth touchdown in the Chinese capital. My mind crowded with images of dreamland China, coolies and mandarins, the tinkle of bells and the banging of gongs, everything poetic—but unfortunately far removed from what actually greeted us. There were lines of taxis fighting for customers, billboards advertising Korean television sets, foreign exchange desks, hotel pushers trying to whisk you away to the Sheraton, the Holiday Inn, the Swiss Hotel, the latest German Palace, or simply to the Novotel or the more modest Taiwan Hotel for overseas Chinese, all claiming to be downtown, although most are miles apart in what seems the most far-flung city in the world. As Pico Iyer has written, one really travels in one's head, and for me, superimposed on the Peking of Marco Polo, the Cathay of all marvels, was the Beijing of Mao and the People's Liberation Army, whose soldiers had caused the shedding of so much Tibetan blood. *That* Beijing was the capital of the enemy, the Beijing that had, in 1972, banned me from China, and whose embassies had written to the world press calling me a liar, to discredit my book on the Tibetan freedom fighters.

My love of Tibet had caused me to cross swords with China before, but that China now seemed nearly as far back in the past as the land of Genghis Khan: the China of drab, dark-blue masses, besotted by a cult of Mao bordering on the ludicrous, his name hammered into everything in a trancelike litany, quoted by the Red Guards up to fifty times a page in every article—the same Red Guards who had burned, dynamited, and pickaxed every Tibetan monastery they could get near, thereby doing away with the last traces of ancient libraries already partially gutted by the People's Liberation Army a decade earlier.

In Tibet the Cultural Revolution had turned into the blindest folly, an orgy of vengeance, fueled by the genetic fear all Chinese seemed to have for the "barbarians" on their western frontier.

Driving into Beijing from the airport in 1994, one could see everywhere that the destructive hysteria of the years before had now been channeled into a building boom. The new fanatics sang the glory of Mao no more, but worshipped instead the gods of greed.

In Beijing, the future is today. It took over an hour for a taxi, laden with our kit bags, to make it to the walls of the Forbidden City, weaving its way between yellow Japanese minitaxis and cyclists to the glass front of the fifteen-story Peace Hotel in the true heart of the city.

Arrogance is the favorite weapon of an old civilization that scorns all others. In China today one experiences in reverse the humiliation the Chinese suffered at the hands of the colonial powers. Its ports, at Hong Kong and Shanghai, taken by unfair treaties, the Chinese were deeply hurt in a manner Westerners have trouble understanding. Steeped in their ancient dignity, to have to suffer the dictates of dog-faced barbarians was a fate that surpassed all cruelty, especially for the highly educated, who ascribed so much importance to saving face.

To understand China in the West, one has to appreciate that for a very long time, it might as well have been another planet, a planet floating in a void. To the east stretched the limitless, empty horizons of the Pacific. To the west, behind the double barriers of the Great Wall and the Himalayan ranges lay the no less limitless horizons of the steppes of Mongolia and Tibet, empty horizons possessed of a crucial distinction: *They* were the realm of the barbarians.

However short the miniskirts of Beijing today, however bright the neon signs in the streets, nowhere can one forget the Great Wall. Not just because the shops are called the Great Wall *this*, the Great Wall *that*, but because the Forbidden City itself is a visual reminder of that serpentine giant, the greatest monument in the world to fear: an atavistic fear that still lies present deep down in the hearts of a majority of Chinese, a fear of the barbarians who, for thousands of years, as far back as memory can stretch—which in China is further than anywhere else on earth—came out of the nameless steppes of central Asia to swoop down and conquer China.

As we drove past the great gates of the Forbidden City along the north end of Tiananmen Square, I pointed out to Jacques that above the formidable bastion of the imperial enclave, the highest monuments on the city's skyline were two giant Tibetan *chortens* (shrines), ever-present reminders of the barbarians at the gate, reminders that Tibetan Buddhism was, until 1912, the official creed of the Manchu emperors, and reminders, finally, that Tibet and the Dalai Lama are still a very sore point in the minds of the Chinese.

Invasions in Europe came from the east, and in China they came from the west. If one were to pinpoint where they came from exactly, one would point on the map to the very place we were headed: the heart of the highest plateau of central Asia.

When Sebastian sailed across the hotel lobby, half a ton of brand-new kit bags in his wake, I suddenly realized we were all there, all of the members of the smallest and least impressive expedition I had ever led. Excluding myself, whose own less-than-striking countenance I could not see, the twosome of Jacques and Sebastian was not what you would call imposing. To be charitable to them, they looked for all the world like Laurel and Hardy out of their element. There in the ugly beige marble lobby of the Peace Hotel in Beijing, I was struck, once again, with the fact that I had talked myself into yet another impossible venture.

Had I been encouraged by some august institution and backed by the same, I would have had an excuse. But it was all my own doing, this idea of trying to find the source of the Mekong, a place that everyone before me had failed to find, on a river for which I didn't give a damn. There was really nothing in it for me except a measure of glory, perhaps, that shining nothing of a currency, as useless today as it is out of date.

That evening I held a conference, which is to say that I had an intimate chat with my two friends. I briefed them on the operation before us. We would have to wait two days in Beijing before taking a flight to Xining, the capital of Qinghai Province.

I had advised the QMA, the Qinghai Mountaineering Association, of our arrival, and they would greet us at the airport.

I explained to Jacques and Sebastian that we couldn't linger in Xining because of a concern I had that had soured our departure. A few weeks before leaving Paris I had been visited by a woman whom I took to be an innocent and sweet young lady. She told me that she had read all my articles on how, in 1993, I had identified a remarkable new breed of horses in southern Qinghai. I, in turn, had told her of my new plan to find the source of the Mekong. Then, to my amazement and dismay, just before we left I received a fax in which she said she had obtained funds to ride "my" horse in Qinghai, and that she and a companion were also going to find the source of the Mekong. She had, in fact, made a public announcement to that effect. I was furious and upset, for although I held no proprietary rights in the matter, this person had stolen my project outright and had used my research to further her own ends. I called the young lady to say how upset I was, only to have the bitter facts spat back at me: I didn't own the source of the Mekong.

Once again I would have been better off keeping my mouth shut. Now, not only did we have a potential rival in our quest, but she and her companion were due to arrive in Xining eight days after us.

I said to Jacques and Sebastian that I thought it unlikely that they would secure permits to the restricted areas. Yet, whatever I said, there remained a threat that we would be beaten to our own goal. The threat was a constant source of irritation until it was superseded by an even worse menace from another quarter.

In the meantime we set out filming Beijing and shopped for last-minute supplies of film stock, camera bags, gloves, sunglasses, rope, and other small pieces of equipment.

2

BEYOND THE MOON

⌘

As we repacked our bags to fly from Beijing to Xining, a region that was once part of greater Tibet, I couldn't help thinking back to the first expeditions that tried to reach the source of the Mekong.

It all began in June of 1866 in Paris, four years after the discovery of the source of the Nile, when the Société de Géographie created the Committee for the Exploration of the Upper Mekong. The American Civil War had just ended, and the United States was still suffering from its aftermath. By contrast, in France, Napoléon III was at the height of his power and was transforming Paris with Baron Haussmann into the beautiful city it is today. That very year, Jules Verne published his book *From the Earth to the Moon*, but it would have been hard to believe then, I'm sure, that man would actually set foot on the moon before finding the source of the Mekong.

France had long lagged behind Great Britain in the race to expand its empire. Having just colonized Indochina, the French were determined not to let the British spread east of Burma. In their never-ending quest for new territories, both countries relied heavily on the services of a new breed of independent and erudite gentlemen explorers, such as La Condamine, Mungo Park, and Alexander Humboldt.

The Marquis of Chasseloup-Laubat, minister for the navy, was president of the Société de Géographie, and it was he who named the young elegant naval officer Doudart de Lagrée president of the Committee for the Exploration of the Upper Mekong, created "because we don't know where this river takes its source." The charter of the committee made the following statement: "One can say that the Mekong is unknown. This great river, the largest of Indochina, one of the most important rivers of the world, presents great prospects for exploration." The report then specified that the leader of the expedition should, above all, "establish the course of this river . . . concentrating on seeking information as to where lies its source . . ."

The French had good reasons to back an expedition up the Mekong. One of them was that the French explorer Henri Mouhot had gained celebrity for traveling up the lower Mekong and discovering in Cambodia the spectacular ruins of Angkor Wat, a place certain newspapers called "the Versailles of Asia." What stung the French was that Henri Mouhot had been backed in his explorations not by the French Société de Géographie, but by the Royal Geographical Society of Great Britain. Of course there was an excuse for this minor outrage: The young Mouhot had married a granddaughter of the great African explorer Mungo Park and lived on the English Channel island of Jersey. Sadly, though, Mouhot had died of fever, at thirty-five, on his second journey up the Mekong. No doubt to save face, Doudart de Lagrée, the newly appointed leader of the Mekong expedition, was asked to locate Mouhot's grave and to raise an official French monument over it.

At the time, another aristocrat, Vice Admiral de la Grandière, was governor of the small, relatively new French colony of Cochinchina, as French Indochina was then called, a colony whose capital at Saigon was still a sleepy little town. It was from Saigon that the vice admiral saw de Lagrée's party off. With de Lagrée were seven men manning two gunboats and a second-in-command named Francis Garnier. It took the party all of a week to locate Mouhot's grave, three miles from Louangphrabang, where he had been buried seven years before. Lagrée built a small monument on the site and wrote back to Mouhot's family (with a copy to the press) that "Mouhot had acquired the esteem and affection of the local natives to such a degree that the king of Laos had kindly given the materials for erecting the modest monument upon the spot where the young man had died."

Little did Doudart de Lagrée imagine that within less than a few months, he himself would be dead, his expedition a disaster.

They ran into trouble almost immediately. First came the foaming falls of Sambor around which the boats had to be hauled, then the terrible rapids of Khone near the present border between Cambodia and Laos. Struggling forward the party encountered yet more white water, as the Mekong showed its true force. Exhausted, one after the other, the explorers fell ill. Francis Garnier, delirious with typhus, suddenly got up screaming and threw himself into the river, to be fished out just as he was about to drown.

With every member sick and their boat stuck, the expedition abandoned the Mekong and entered Yunnan in an effort to save themselves by returning home across China. Garnier recovered from his fever and eventually made it to Shanghai, but Doudart de Lagrée died somewhere in Yunnan, and the site of his grave remains unknown to this day. Thus, the Mekong had thwarted the first in a long series of expeditions to its source.

Nearly twenty years elapsed before two other expeditions were mounted in the hope of finding the headwaters of the great river. By then it was clear that the Mekong did not, as everyone hoped, lead into China, but into the unexplored wilds of neighboring Tibet, which was, as everybody knew, closed to foreigners.

None of this deterred Georges Eugène Simon, a French naval captain who, like Lagrée, sailed out of Saigon in the spring of 1893. With better success than their predecessors, his party made it up and around the fearful rapids, but after having traveled twelve hundred miles they had to turn back halfway along what is today the Burma-Laos frontier. The leader was given a hero's welcome. He had explored much new territory, but the source of the river had eluded him. In fact, it lay yet another twelve hundred miles from the farthest point he had reached.

Unknown to Simon and to nearly everybody else, a year earlier a small expedition, headed by a man named Dutreuil de Rhins, accompanied by Joseph-Fernand Grenard, had left Paris for Tibet via Samarkand. Its objectives were vague, and the journey, a very long one, was to last three years. The two Frenchmen crossed the whole of Russian Turkestan, their way paved by the Franco-Russian alliance signed that year. Leaving Russian territory, they entered Chinese Turkestan before veering south across the Karakoram into Ladakh, which had recently been incorporated into the Indian state of Jammu and Kashmir.

With little in the way of funds and only a few ponies and local porters, the expedition then proceeded back into Chinese Turkestan, crossing the Taklamakan desert on the old Silk Road before turning south again in a bold bid to enter Tibet from the northwest, across the high plateau of Qinghai. Eventually the Frenchmen were turned back from reaching Lhasa at Nakchu-ka, and so decided to set off east across the high unexplored Tibetan plateau in the direction of western China. On the way they explored part of the upper course of the Salween River and then decided to head northwest along yet another unexplored route.

Having crossed a high pass in the Tangla range, the explorers found themselves on a marshy plateau crossed by a meandering river, the Dam Chu (*Dam* meaning "marshy," and *Chu* meaning "river" in

Tibetan). They believed the river to be the longest branch of the Yangtze, the longest river in China, but the fact that they had guessed right was confirmed only a century later. Leaving the Dam Chu, they reached a pass sixteen thousand feet high on the ninth of April and recorded it as the Dza Nak pass, or the Black Dza pass, *Dza* being the Tibetan name for the Mekong and the Dza Nak being the longest of the two branches of the upper Mekong. Although the ground was covered with snow and the streams were iced over, the party jumped to the conclusion that the small river running down from the pass, a river we now know as the Lungmo, was the westernmost branch of the Mekong and, therefore, that the Mekong's source must lie just beneath the pass somewhere under the snow. They followed the Lungmo down to the main headwater of the upper Mekong and rather hastily congratulated themselves for having discovered the source of the great river.

The leader of the expedition was never able to make his claim, however, because two weeks further down the trail he was brutally murdered. Or so goes the official version. The story, as later told in detail by the surviving Grenard, is a tragic account of a misunderstanding between the arrogant local Khamba tribesmen and the expedition members.

Exhausted, after having crossed most of Tibet's highest and most barren plateau, the party was down to a half-dozen ponies when, on reaching the village of Tong-bou-mdo, they found that two of their horses were missing. Investigation revealed hoofprints alongside the boot prints of a local Tibetan leading out of the corral where the horses had spent the night. Rather haughtily and without thinking, Dutreuil de Rhins rounded up some villagers and had his men seize one of their horses, proclaiming that it would be returned if and when their own horses were found.

Such high-handed posturing might have worked nicely in some French colony, but the Khambas of the Jeykundo area, famous for their warlike disposition, took immediate offense. On the morning of the fifth of June, 1894, when their horses were not returned after several hours, the French party set off, Grenard in the lead, the "bor-rowed" pony behind him, with Dutreuil de Rhins in the rear. Slowly they climbed out of a narrow valley opposite the village. The vil-lagers, seeing them leave with the hostage horse, fired warning shots in the air. When the caravan continued on, they took aim for real. Several ponies were hit, then Grenard heard his companion cry out. Backtracking under fire he courageously went to the side of Dutreuil de Rhins, who had been hit in the belly and was ashen, clutching his stomach. Under a hail of bullets Grenard tried to get some of the porters to make a stretcher but they ran off. In vain Grenard alone tried to carry his companion, but then reluctantly he bade him farewell, as Dutreuil de Rhins muttered deliriously, "A glorious day . . . what a waste . . . what a waste . . ."

Back in Paris Grenard repeated their claim of having found the source of the Mekong, but he was not very persuasive, as under April snow it had been practically impossible to locate a precise source. Grenard went on to become a diplomat and ended his career as ambassador to Belgrade in 1927. He never tried to validate his claim nor did he protest this statement about the Mekong in the famed eleventh edition of the *Encyclopaedia Britannica* (1910): "Its sources are not definitely settled, but it is supposed to rise on the slopes of the Dza-Nag-Lung-Mung in about 33° N, 93° E."

And so, beyond the turn of the century the mystery of the source persisted. Tibet continued to forbid entry to foreigners so strongly, in fact, that in 1904, aggravated by the isolationist arrogance of the Tibetans, the British decided to invade just to get some sort of reply from the thirteenth Dalai Lama, who had continued to return unopened the letters of the arrogant Viceroy Lord Curzon. It was Curzon's obsession with the idea that the Russians might try to occupy Tibet that led the British to march on Lhasa. Upon their withdrawal shortly afterward, Tibet closed its doors ever tighter until in 1910, China invaded, only to be booted out by the Dalai Lama two years later.

Needless to say, these events did little to help explorers enter Tibet, although during the brief British invasion cartographers were rushed into western Tibet to check on the sources of the Indus, the Sutlej, and the Brahmaputra.

For information on the rest of Tibet's vast unmapped expanse the British had to rely on the sporadic reports of their secret agents. These famed "native explorers," Indians of Tibetan origin, roamed Tibet disguised as monks or merchants and carried with them prayer wheels filled with blank paper to which they consigned their notes at night. Inside their canes were hidden thermometers, which they dipped in boiling tea kettles to get altitude readings. These men were known only by their code initials. Although they paced much of central Tibet, counting each step on fictitious rosaries, only one of these remarkable agents, Kishen Singh—known simply as A. K.—traveled across Amdo/Qinghai into the barren northeast, where lay, presumably, the sources of the Yangtze, the Mekong, and the Yellow River. The year was 1882, and even he failed to reach any of the rivers' sources. As a result the map of Tibet issued by the British was approximative at best and still full of blanks and mistakes. Sixty years later the Chinese themselves had no better maps, and even they used British maps when claiming territory from India after they seized Tibet in 1950.

Flying North West China Airways from Beijing to Xining, the capital of Qinghai, I peered down at the rim of the great Tibetan plateau. Barren brown chaotic ridges, cut as if by a mad plowman, rose ever higher beneath us.

The formation of the high Tibetan plateau is nothing if not unique. It all began some sixty million years ago, a very long time, indeed, even for paleontologists. In those days the continents were fragments floating around the globe, having just broken off the two great continents of Laurasia and Gondwanaland.

For reasons ill understood linked to neotectonics, the Indian plate, or continent, moving northward across the Thetys Sea, collided with the underbelly of the Asiatic plate. This collision was not a sudden impact but nevertheless a most tremendous crash that resulted in part of the Indian plate slipping under the Asiatic plate, forcing it to rise. The result of this terrible crunch was that, after inching its way skyward (a process not yet over), the great Tibetan plateau reached a mean altitude of fifteen thousand feet. It still gains in places over four inches a year. Under this plateau the earth's crust has been found, by Sino-French scientific expeditions that began in 1980, to be double the thickness elsewhere around the globe, some fifty miles instead of the normal thickness of approximately twenty miles.

The plateau reached its present height only about two million years ago—not very long ago as nature goes. Animals existed by then, and before the plateau reached its full height it was, according to fossils, quite a nice warm place to live. No more.

The highest and largest mountainous plateau in the world, the Tibetan highlands form a unique continent in the heart of Asia, a continent with its own particular animals, plants, and climate. It is so high, the plateau could well have been covered with glaciers and snow like Antarctica were it not for the Himalayan range. Fifteen hundred miles long, the Himalayas mark the surface impact line of the terrible crashing together of the continents. Culminating with Mount Everest at twenty-nine thousand feet, the continuous range is higher than the plateau and serves as a rain trap, stopping the clouds of the Indian monsoon to the south from crossing over and falling as snow over Tibet. Were the Himalayas not there, the high plateau would be but one huge ice cap. As it is, it is a frigid, dry desert at high altitude, a land where it snows, hails, and rains only sparingly during the short summer, when precipitation quickly melts and evaporates under the burning rays of the high-altitude sun. Due to the flatness of the plateau, the resulting water forms innumerable lakes, marshes, and bogs that are nearly impossible to cross in summer, the high-water season. As a result, the best season to travel is during the eight-month-long winter, when the lakes and rivers are frozen and the bogs dry or frozen—and therefore easy to cross. But therein lies the catch. If one travels in winter, like the ill-fated Dutreuil de Rhins, one cannot hope to find the source of the rivers under the ice and snow. The only logical solution to the problem, or so we hoped, was to travel in late summer, just before the winter sets in. And that was why we landed in Xining on the sixth of September, 1994.

Soldiers in khaki, alongside grim-looking officials in blue, filled the small modern airport only just opened to civilians, a reminder that Qinghai was, and still is, a penal colony for all of China. Here, starting in 1955, the Chinese began to settle a number now upward of three million people, most of them political exiles and prisoners sent out for indefinite terms of "reform by labor."

As we waited for our conspicuous baggage, I was delighted to spot in the crowd Mr. Wang Tsun Yi, the young man who had been my guide in Tibet the preceding year. With him and Caroline Puel, a diplomat and journalist expert on Chinese horses, I had spent seven weeks exploring on horseback and by jeep the remotest regions of southeastern Qinghai. It was there that I had begun to prepare our present assault on the source of the Mekong.

Wang had proven most enthusiastic and helpful and, even though he had admitted that he was with the Public Security Bureau, the political police out to keep an eye on us, I hoped he would accompany us again. Fun-loving, and always ready for a good drink, he would be a welcome companion as far as I was concerned.

By the time we had collected our fifteen kit bags and loaded two waiting Mitsubishi short-wheelbase vehicles, however, Wang announced that he would not be traveling with us, and then turned toward a diminutive schoolboy of a young man with well-combed greasy hair and introduced him as Mr. Ling Haitao. Mr. Ling, not he, would be our "guide"-cum-policeman.

"Welcome, Mr. Psl," young Mr. Ling broke out. "We will do all we can to make your journey a pleasant and memorable one. Anything you need, you ask me."

I took an immediate dislike to Mr. Ling, which soon justified itself as we discovered his brittle autocratic personality.

Sebastian and I, to be fair, shared a rather debonair attitude toward life, one that for all his seriousness Jacques also possessed in a funny sort of a way. Ours was a venture more akin to those leisurely Victorian explorations than to the disciplined, ecologically minded, humorless, dead-earnest modern-day expeditions.

To tell the truth I hate sports, which I put down with disco dancing as a waste of good energy and an unnecessary evil. When I indulge in nightclubs and such sports as polo, it is always with a feeling of guilt that the energy involved could be better spent riding off somewhere into the unknown, where the outcome is less predictable and much more interesting.

Ling was a sadly modern, narrow-minded young Chinese Communist with none of the undisciplined humor of the Red Guard or the intelligence of the old soldiers of the Long March. Humor he took as a personal insult, and his duty as a matter of deadly seriousness. For him we were about to travel deep into enemy territory, the enemy being all Tibetans. Ours, he explained with a deep frown, was a truly dangerous enterprise.

In a way, of course, he was right, and we would not have been there had not the terror inspired by the Tibetans of the region we were headed for kept outsiders away for centuries.

If the geographical and climatic characteristics of the high plateau of Tibet pose adverse conditions for travelers, they are a small obstacle compared with the political considerations.

As far back as the late Stone Age, according to a recent discovery by Chinese archaeologists, nomads have inhabited the high plateau.

Their life today seems to be little different from what it was thousands of years ago, except, perhaps, for the fact that their original stone tools have been replaced by modern steel implements.

These nomads are still divided into hundreds of tribes, each with a well-delineated territory. Like herders elsewhere, these tribesmen are obsessed with their territorial rights and very suspicious of all foreigners, even of their neighbors. Foreigners inevitably are taken for cattle rustlers, people out to steal their livestock—so much so that few dare wander into the pastures of neighboring tribes without special permission from the local chiefs, a permission practically impossible to get without first risking a trespass.

I was twenty-two when I discovered that the world knew very little about Tibet beyond what was known about its monks and their religion. Religion has always been a blind behind which the Tibetan people have been hidden. Even today, when one evokes Tibet it is nearly always in relation to the Dalai Lama and the lamaist religion. The true Tibet, made up of real people, has remained inaccessible.

Ever since I first became interested in Tibet, I was attracted to the nomadic warrior tribes of Kham, as eastern Tibet is called. In my mind, they seemed to be the last free men on the planet. As the years went by I became familiar with how they had fought the Chinese Communists and had eventually forced the Dalai Lama himself to join them in the struggle.

My professor of Tibetan civilization in Paris, Rolf Stein, had spent years studying in ancient manuscripts the names of these tribes, tribes whom he himself had encountered at Tatsienlu, the eastern gateway to Tibet and the doorway to Kham.

The earliest Chinese chronicles called all these men Kiang, lumping them together regardless of their true origins. The warlike nomads had constantly harassed the Chinese, frequently invading China itself, most recently in 1929.

"Wild and accustomed to living by loot." Thus they were branded by exploring Europeans such as Pierre Migot, who found himself naked on the summit of a pass, his clothes down to his underwear stolen by local nomads. Not even the Dalai Lamas trusted these ferociously independent tribesmen. That said, the present Dalai Lama himself is from Amdo, the home of—among others—the Goloks, the fiercest of them all, although His Holiness is from the extreme northern part of Amdo, near Xining, a region of farms as opposed to pastures.

Xining is the capital of Amdo/Qinghai. At seventy-two hundred feet in altitude it is located just south of the Silk Road and just east of Koko Nor, the largest inland sea of Asia, a great turquoise saltwater lake the size of Corsica. Xining has always been an important crossroads for caravans: From here set out two trails that link the Silk Road with Tibet and with Chengdu, the capital of Sichuan, China's most populous province.

Xining was first mentioned in the West by Marco Polo, who referred to it in his memoirs as Sin-ju, and, although a town of considerable importance, it escaped the attention of Westerners for centuries thereafter. We owe the earliest good description of it to the American diplomat and scholar William Woodville Rockhill, one of the few Western explorers of Tibet who spoke both Chinese and Tibetan. He set out in 1888 hoping to reach Lhasa from the north, having been preceded along that route by two French missionaries, Huc and Gabet, who traveled all the way to Lhasa and back from China in 1846. The account they left of their journey was so unpretentious, so naïve, and so vivid that in a way it shamed the pompous Victorian explorers who came after them, such as the Russian Przewalski, whose imperialistic anticlericalism moved him to try to negate the fact that the innocent missionaries had succeeded where he failed thirty-five years later. Przewalski bestowed his unpronounceable name on the wild horse of central Asia, but his efforts to discredit the two French missionaries somewhat tarnished his reputation forever after. This famed Przewalski horse was first encountered by the Scottish doctor John Bell during a visit to central Asia in the service of Peter the Great from 1719 to 1722. It was the Russian geographer, however, who brought back specimens of the breed, which has since died out in the wild, but which flourishes still in zoos and on special farms around the world.

Rockhill was as unsuccessful at reaching Lhasa as Przewalski had been, but a measure less pompous, and his account gives us our first scholarly and informed description of the tribes of eastern Tibet.

My small party and I left the bustle of the airport and drove into Xining proper. I couldn't forget that in 1933 near Xining, in a village called Tagster, lived a certain horse dealer whose sons were to bring him unimaginable fame and satisfaction. The eldest son of the horse trader was identified as the reincarnation of the abbot of the region's most famous monastery, Kum Bum, that of the one hundred thousand images of Buddha. Kum Bum was the holy birth site of Tsong Khapa, the great reformer of Tibetan Buddhism and the founder of the Gelug pa, the yellow hat sect of the Dalai Lamas.

The holy oracles of the region having pronounced the horse trader's son the lama of Kum Bum, his family moved some twelve miles closer to Xining and took up residence in the great buildings of the monastery.

In 1928 Xining became the capital of a largely fictitious Chinese province called Qinghai, whose governor was a self-appointed general called Ma Pu-feng, a Chinese Muslim warlord.

In fact, Ma Pu-feng ruled only the northern part of Qinghai, in that he was constantly at war with the nomads of the south, principally with the feared Golok tribe and the inhabitants of a mysterious kingdom called Nangchen, whose existence had escaped the attention of most explorers. The remotest, largest, and most secretive of the many little kingdoms of the much-feared Khamba tribes, Nangchen was incorporated by mapmakers into Chinese Qinghai. According to my maps, the source of the Mekong lay somewhere in Nangchen.

Two years after the great thirteenth Dalai Lama died in 1933, the State Oracle of Tibet suggested that a delegation of monks be sent to northeastern Tibet to look for his successor. And as amazing as it may seem, it was in the family of the same poor horse dealer from Tagster (whose eldest son had by then become head of the Kum Bum monastery) that, in 1938, they found the reincarnation of the fourteenth Dalai Lama—the present Dalai Lama, currently in exile in Dharmsala, India.

In 1939, Ma Pu-feng demanded one hundred thousand Chinese silver dollars to allow the new Dalai Lama to go to Lhasa. Upon receiving the amount stated from the Tibetan government, the warlord abruptly changed his mind and asked for an additional three hundred thousand silver dollars before he would release the young god-king.

As we drove into the modern Chinese city of Xining, I searched in vain for anyone looking remotely Tibetan; everyone around me was Chinese. Today Xining has nine hundred thousand inhabitants and a high pollution rate from the smoke of its hundreds of factories, most of which, it is believed, are manned by political prisoners.

In Xining we were the "guests" of the Qinghai Mountaineering Association. In Communist countries where officially no private enterprises exist, one cannot do anything unless one is sponsored by an official governmental organization. I had discovered this in the former Soviet Union when I decided to take my Viking boat overland (rowing and sailing the major rivers) from Riga to Odessa. In Russia the Soviet Peace Foundation had been my chaperon. In China I had opted for the obscure QMA, which had provided me in 1993 with the necessary official status to perform my first survey of southern Qinghai in search of horses.

Once again the QMA was ready to assist me—for a price—by granting me the official permits to go, this time, deeper into the forbidden territory of the southern nomads to look for the source of the Mekong. No member of the QMA had ever been in the area, except of course for Mr. Wang, whom I had taken south the preceding year. But now, alas, he was not coming with us.

In Xining we were hustled into a modern twenty-story hotel, the local skyscraper, where as we lay down for a short rest before sorting our bags, I contemplated the future of our project. Without Mr. Wang we would have our work cut out for us to get the support we needed. I knew that the QMA members were more interested in the money we were paying them than in helping us actually find the source of the Mekong. This was evident in everything Mr. Ling had to say. He treated us as if we were some sort of tour group just out to have a pleasant holiday. The fact that three cases of Pepsi were just about the only provisions he had packed, and that he had neither adequate tents nor reasonable clothes for travel by pony, clearly showed that he was not quite aware of what he had gotten himself into.

All this was most worrying, but not half as worrying as the news that Mr. Wang now broke to me.

"Ten days ago," he announced, "a party of Japanese set out up the Mekong along with a group from the Chinese Academy of Science."

The news made my heart sink. In spite of the fact that I like to think myself uninterested in setting records, I had not organized this expedition to be number two. I went to sleep with visions of our reaching our objective exhausted only to run into a big gang of Chinese and Japanese scholars having a party. The thought was unbearable, so unbearable that I chased it from my mind.

Now there was a double threat to our venture, the French party arriving in a week and the Asian scholars. To cheer up I kept repeating to myself that my primary interest in the region was in the horses and in the exploration of the mysterious kingdom of Nangchen.

My research into the history of Nangchen the previous year had convinced me that Nangchen was no doubt the last of the truly unexplored old Tibetan kingdoms.

I have always had a special affection for lost kingdoms, and, in fact, I owed much of my small reputation as an explorer to having been the first to place on the map the little kingdom of Mustang in Nepal. Thirty years had elapsed since I had fought my way alone across the Himalayan range via the deep Kali Gandaki gorge headed for the walled city of Lo Mantang. The year was 1964, and thousands of Khamba guerrillas who had fled Tibet and crossed Nepal were still fighting the Chinese and had made Mantang their new headquarters. From there they crossed over into Tibet to attack the Chinese convoys heading for Lhasa.

Tibet was then strictly beyond the reach of foreigners, and since the CIA was secretly helping the Khamba guerrillas in Mustang, no one was allowed to go there but the Khambas themselves.

My claim to fame was in discovering that Lo Mantang was, in fact, the capital of a tiny kingdom called Lo or Mustang that had been independent for nearly five hundred years. It was so remote and inaccessible that its very existence as an independent region had escaped the notice of even the best of Tibetan scholars.

Compared to Mustang, the kingdom of Nangchen was enormous—6,500 square miles, in fact—or so I reckoned from my journey to its ancient capital of Nangchen Gar the preceding year. Should our river expedition fail, I reasoned, a trip there would prove a satisfying fallback exploration.

"We wish to leave tomorrow morning," I said to Mr. Ling, who seemed puzzled by our haste. "All right, Mr. Psl, but you must first go to the bank and pay us."

I agreed. I never knew exactly who got the money that I paid to the Qinghai Mountaineering Association—now, for the second year in a row. But I paid a high price for two four-wheel-drive vehicles, their fuel and drivers, along with local food.

3

THE FINAL SOLUTION?

⌘

In our room on the twelfth floor, overlooking the gray buildings of the sprawling Chinese city of Xining, we pored over our various maps. The most detailed was the 1:500,000 satellite map of southern Qinghai, which gave the topography only a few place names.

Then came an equally imprecise map used by pilots, the one-million-scale map, or ONC G-8, to be precise, which had a strange, white square on it marked "relief data incomplete," followed by the amusing notation "maximum elevation believed not to exceed 10,000 feet." The blank area depicted was close to where we were planning to go, and we knew that all of it was above thirteen thousand feet. More amusing still was the fact that here and there on the map were little black squares marked "nomad camps," as if it would be of help to lost pilots to use movable nomad tents as points of reference. On the other hand, a note saying "Aircraft infringing upon

non-free-flying territory may be fired on without warning . . ." probably kept planes away in the first place.

Comical as it was, this map proved useful because it gave a fairly
precise idea of the topography. The Mekong River, however, was
shown petering off in every direction in little blue dotted lines.

My other maps were less topographically accurate but bore more
names, though none that were the same from one map to the other.

"Have you any good maps of the region?" I asked Mr. Ling hopefully, well aware that he didn't. The Chinese are very secretive about
maps of the Tibetan highlands, and of Qinghai in particular, because
it is here that they have based the principal launch sites and tracking
stations for telecommunication satellites and, possibly also, the silos
for their nuclear missiles. Some people whisper that Qinghai is home
to atomic test sites, but officials point out that the Lop Nor desert of
nearby Xinjiang is the official testing ground.

Maps were, in a way, what our whole expedition was about. The
maps of the world, it seemed, had all taken it for granted that the
source of the Mekong was at the site identified by Dutreuil de
Rhins, in spite of all the subsequent denials and challenges. It was
now up to us to draw a new and, one would hope, definitive map.

For this purpose we were equipped with a Global Positioning
System, a GPS, a little electronic, hand-held calculator with an
antenna that contacts one or another of the twenty-one geostation-
ary satellites that circle the globe and, in a few seconds miraculously
calculates one's exact latitude and longitude, and even one's altitude.

This modern technology would be priceless for drawing our map
but of little use in finding our way. Early explorers to Tibet had had,
for the most part, no problem finding their way, because they traveled the well-worn caravan routes, whose resting places have always
been known to all. But few explorers dared to stray from those routes
because of the risk of getting lost. Three years before, one of the
members of the Qinghai Mountaineering Association wandered
away from his camp alone and was never seen again.

"His body was never found," Ling commented dryly when I asked him about the tragedy.

One of the best map rooms in the world is housed in the red-brick headquarters of the venerable Royal Geographical Society, the temple of exploration, located on Kensington Gore in the heart of London.

I contacted the Royal Geographical Society in preparation for our expedition. Mr. Collins of the map department promised to do a special investigation to determine whether I might not be mistaken and someone had, indeed, already discovered the source of the Mekong. Three days later I received the unequivocal reply, a precious piece of information that confirmed all my other inquiries:

"There is no indication that the source has been precisely located."

Xining is seventy-two hundred feet above sea level, which is a relatively low elevation similar to that of Mexico City. Nevertheless, arriving from Beijing, which some claim is twenty-six feet *below* sea level, we were immediately exhausted by the change in altitude. After finishing off with Sebastian the first of the two whisky bottles we had brought along for comfort, I tried in vain to sleep.

My brain was afire as I contemplated what might lay ahead, and once again I asked myself how on earth I had gotten myself involved in the drudgery of yet another near-impossible venture.

The truth is, there seem to be two people inside me: a nice, rational self and a malicious demon.

I suppose everyone is somewhat the same, the difference being that when most people grow up, the naughty child in them vanishes or fades into the background, leaving the reasonable adult in command.

In spite of my gray hair, somehow it seemed the devil was still in full control. I was thrilled that we were heading for the unknown, right into the very unmapped heart of the most forbidden and remote territory of the Tibetan highlands. Secretly, I yearned for as much trouble as possible, imagining my companions all dying on the journey so that I might return a lone hero. I would beat the Chinese and Japanese to the source of the Mekong, come what may. With this resolve, I finally fell asleep.

When I awoke the next morning, the feeling of exhaustion caused by the altitude was sobering. I was puffing and blowing and bent in two, my lungs making a peculiar squishing sound as I pulled on the low boots that were to be my only shoes on this journey.

I shaved and carefully packed the black kit bag that was from now on to hold my little universe—not just a change of clothes, but my film, notebooks, maps, and those few photographs that in remote parts would remind me that out there, far beyond the jagged horizons, I had children, the only really valid reason for me to want to get back.

Bags are the nightmare of every expedition. Each night, when one is exhausted, they have to be opened and unpacked, and every frigid morning they have to be packed up again. This routine goes on, day in and day out, and, since bags shrink at night, what fits in one day won't fit the next. Sleeping bags just grow bigger and bigger.

Alas, in the proletarian People's Republic of China, I had no recourse to the British-trained sherpas who were attendant upon my first expedition to the Himalayas in 1959. Twenty-two years old and still a democrat in those days, I had trouble at first with the bearers' custom of kissing my feet in the morning and insisting that they tie my shoelaces. Yet that was what they did, and any effort to stop them was considered an offense. But now there was no question of being helped by my guides. Ling was as censorious as a boys' school prefect and would certainly kiss nobody's feet, let alone lift a bag. Having hauled my own bags down to the lobby, I was greeted by the rest of our party, two chauffeurs and a young cook.

First things first. After a hasty Chinese breakfast of cold omelette and spongy, saltless, cold dumplings, we were whisked off to the bank at 9 A.M. sharp. Here we were forced to give up a large amount of our ready cash in dollars just in case we didn't survive to pay on our return. In exchange I received a thin rice-paper voucher, in Chinese, which would soon disintegrate.

We were nearly ready, but I still wanted to buy a ball of string (unavailable among the nomads), razor blades, drawing paper, sweets, and a few other odds and ends. All the shops were closed, however, and we left without these essential items.

Driving the streets of Xining seemed very similar to driving through a suburb of Beijing. The same police standing on the same red-and-white-striped pedestals from which they directed the same traffic of khaki jeeps, white-and-red buses, and blue trucks, their registration numbers stenciled large across their tailgates. All this traffic was intermingled with bicycles and rickshaws and pushcarts, and, occasionally, with a horse-drawn flatbed wagon piled high with Chinese cabbage. On either side of the street rose little stalls crested with ideograms proclaiming the professions of the shopkeepers. I found it restful not to be able to read them, those playful signs that I took to be little more than dancing children. I wondered if the illiterate were not possibly the happiest people in the modern world, impervious as they are to the constant assault of political and commercial propaganda and to aggressive police orders like Stop, Slow, Beware, No Entry, Dead End, Danger. The undecipherable Chinese characters, elegant and meaningless as they were to my untrained eye, may, in another sense, prove the downfall of China: Because of them, it takes eight to ten years to learn how to read the newspaper, with the result that the Chinese are illiterate, compared with the barbarian Tibetans, whom they scorn. The Tibetans are fortunate to have a simple phonetic syllabary with twenty-nine letters, one written vowel (*A*), and four vowel accents that are used in combination with them. It takes a smart young Tibetan three years at most before he can read elementary texts, and so nearly everyone in Tibet knows his *ka kha ga nga*, the Tibetan version of the ABC.

· Tibet owes its alphabet to its first famous historical king, Songtsen Gampo, who became ruler of Tibet in A.D. 634 at the age of thirteen. A mere boy, he raised a huge cavalry from among the nomads by distributing banners and buttons. In no time thousands of sturdy Tibetans swore an oath to obey him, and aided by his chief minister, Tongsten of Gar, also a great horseman, he set out at the head of his cavalry to conquer the world as it was then known to Tibetans—which is to say, all of Tibet's neighbors: Mongolia, China, Bengal, northern India, Nepal, Baltistan (Bolor), the four garrisons of Chinese Turkestan, and the great Samarkand. He established the Tibetan language over this vast territory, and then, having sent scholars to India to obtain an alphabet tailored to Tibetan sounds, he introduced the Tibetan alphabet, one derived from the Sanskrit (Indian Gupta) alphabet.

Upon attacking China, the great Tibetan king, notwithstanding the fact that he had already taken a Nepalese princess as his bride, asked the emperor for a royal Chinese princess. To appease their cumbersome and aggressive neighbor, the Chinese handed over Princess Wen-tch'eng. Popular songs in China still recall the hardships and sorrow of the beautiful princess, forced to leave China against her will to go into the wilds. The Tibetans paint a slightly less grim picture. Far from being the barbarian the Chinese took him to be, the Tibetan king and his court in the valley of Yarlung (southeast of Lhasa) had surrounded themselves with Hindu, Chinese, and Persian scholars. They had goldsmiths of international repute make them refined vases, jewelry, and other objects of great luxury. If one were to judge from the size and magnificence of the tombs of the early Tibetan kings, which were built around golden inner chambers and looked after by "the living dead," servants of the deceased, the palaces of the living king must have been fabulous.

According to one story, it took the princess two years to reach Yarlung. On the way she slept with Tongsten of Gar, Song-tsen Gampo's chief minister, and had a child by him who died. Upon the arrival of his Chinese princess bride, the great Tibetan king accepted her. He then converted Tibet to Buddhism, the religion of both his wives. Scholars were sent to India to invite monks to come to Tibet, and in a spot known as Ra-sa, "the goat's land," a monastery was built by Nepalese artisans that would soon become the holiest shrine in Tibet and be rebaptized Lhasa, "the land of the Gods." This early shrine is the famed Jokhang, the cathedral of Lhasa that still stands today in the heart of the holy city.

All this is to say that the antagonism between China and Tibet goes back to ancient times. For fourteen centuries Tibet and China have lived side by side, alternately as mortal enemies, rivals, and—on occasion—cordial trading partners.

Listening to Ling, we realized the present was a period of enmity. For Ling the Tibetans were ignorant and evil. To the Tibetans, the Chinese, particularly the Communists, were pigheaded and conceited pagans.

As we left Xining we followed the huge barbed-wired brick walls of countless "penal factories," each with armed guards in little turrets. Running parallel to the road was a railroad track, the famed trans-Tibetan line whose construction was hailed as one of the great achievements of Mao's positive thinking. Originally the line was supposed to go all the way to Lhasa, but, as it turned out, it stopped in the middle of the most deserted portion of eastern Qinghai at a place called Golmud. Experts from all over the world were called upon to figure out a way to push the line farther into the mountains. But there was no way to proceed without tunneling, and, because the mountains of this part of Tibet consisted of a loose mixture of earth, shale, and ice that melted on being exposed, boring tunnels was declared impossible. Thus it is that Golmud, a place meant to be a whistle-stop, remains today the end of the line, some seven hundred miles short of Lhasa.

Yet the railroad does serve the purpose of funneling to the many factories of Xining the rare metals and minerals in which the Tibetan highlands abound. For centuries Tibet was famed for its gold-bearing sands, but today it is lithium, lead, antimony, and other rare metals that are extracted for greater profit. There is still plenty of gold, however, and the latest gold rush has been on since 1980.

Every spring close to one hundred thousand people from China, mostly from the Xining area, set out on tiny two-wheeled tractors linked to two-wheeled covered wagons laden with panning equipment and head southwest to the region of the source of the Yangtze River. Here gold dust abounds.

In the spring of 1993, along the very road we now traveled, I had encountered thousands of these gold diggers chugging out onto the great freezing plateau to make their fortunes. It is a gold rush that the Communist government can neither halt nor control, for gold fever in China is a very old and established disease. The Chinese people, much more than Europeans or other Asians, are what one might call "business-minded." They are similar to North Americans in this respect, great entrepreneurs always seeking to make a yuan, and if they can, a buck. In this attribute they differ radically from the Tibetans, who despise petty commerce and have maintained instead a society of warrior agriculturalists similar to that of continental Europe in the Middle Ages.

Looking at the pointed straw hats of the peasants working in the neatly drawn fields fringed by poplar trees, we found it hard to believe that this was Tibetan territory and that the Tibetan language was still the "official" language of this Chinese province, insofar as every Chinese sign was supposed to be translated into Tibetan script.

Of course what we were witnessing was the Chinese-style "final solution" to the Tibetan problem, the mass introduction of Chinese settlers intended to drown out the Tibetans, a scheme largely successful in this part of Amdo, where the people of Tibet had now become a small minority in their own land. As our guidebook put it, somewhat crudely: "The province [of Qinghai] is a sort of Chinese Siberia where common criminals as well as political prisoners are incarcerated."

Less than twenty-five miles out of Xining the trees began to disappear as we left the main road and railroad track to Golmud on our right and turned left and started to climb. In a few miles all trees had vanished, as did one barley field after another until, in low gear, we began climbing between grass-covered hills. Slowly we rose up to the Sun and Moon Pass, which marks the northern edge of the great Tibetan plateau. The pass is 12,468 feet high, and we were panting for breath as we stopped and tried out our GPS for the first time since reaching China. It took some time for the machine to locate the satellites and make its preliminary calculations.

"It is here," Ling explained, "that the Chinese princess shed tears as she set off to marry the king of Tibet." We now received a very Chinese version of early Tibetan history, of how the barbarians had abducted the fair lady and how she had cried all the way to Lhasa in the arms of Gar, the minister who had enlivened her journey. We looked with awe at the scene that stretched before us. As far as we could see, which was very, very far in the crisp, bright, high altitude, there loomed chain upon chain of mountain ranges linked by a seemingly endless stretch of sparse grass, giving way here and there to sandy, dunelike patches of desert.

Camels were very common in this region as a means of transport, and it was on such beasts that the two French missionaries Huc and Gabet had ridden, just as Przewalski and Rockhill had after them.

Our mechanized transport was less romantic, to be sure, but because of it we hoped to be able later to travel on foot farther into the unknown than our predecessors had ever reached.

As we stared ahead into what travelers have described as a "dreaded void," I looked at Jacques and Sebastian, curious to know what their reactions might be.

"Well here it begins, I guess," Sebastian said. Jacques was busy filming.

Although I was still uncertain as to the impact of the high plateau on my companions, its effect on me was clear. I took one deep breath and was filled with bliss. I was home again, at long last, and in no time reminded Mr. Ling that from now on it was I who spoke the native language.

As we stood there getting our bearings, a man rode up over a nearby crest draped in a great sheepskin gown; beside him were the large black masses of a dozen yaks. We had entered a new world.

When I was small I couldn't understand why everybody didn't live on the sunny beaches of tropical islands, and why the Eskimos had not all moved to Florida. It was a mystery to me why Greeks, after having made their fortunes, would elect to return to the rocky, barren, sun-bleached islands where they were born. How is it that the Scots love haggis and the French snails, and that Tibetans are happy in a climate and landscape that makes others shudder?

But now I knew. I understood that beauty has to do less with looks than with love. And love is a question of time.

Shah Jahan, the great Mogul emperor who built the Taj Mahal, said when describing the delightful tree-shaded lakes of Kashmir, "If there is a paradise on earth it is here, it is here, it is here. . . ." Maybe he was right, and most foreigners, by the same standards, would describe the great Tibetan plateau as "hell on earth" unless for them it was a land of sweet memories, the desert and the void and frigid ranges populated by the smiles of friends and the glitter of stars so much more brilliant and real than those in the rest of the world. That's the way it was for me.

It took me a long time to understand that in the open desert one's interior landscape becomes sharper and much easier to read, as if the desert were a limpid screen upon which one's thoughts can be projected.

Tibetan folklore and religion, with colorful good and evil deities, provides the loneliest of nomads with ample scope for the play of his imagination.

For all too many of us in the West, Tibet is no more than an exotic word that conjures up images of strange, red-robed monks, of jagged peaks and the abominable snowman. Few appreciate that Tibet is not just a country but a civilization that spills across geographical boundaries to form a vast cultural and linguistic family, a holy Tibetan empire of sorts.

Tibetans, one should remember, are the only people among those of Europe, Africa, or Asia who can walk two thousand miles in a straight line and be understood in their mother tongue all the way. Today, fourteen centuries after King Song-tsen Gampo came to power, his language, writing, and "lamaism," the religion he helped spread, are still the means of communication and worship for almost the entire territory that was once his. No other empire has lasted as long on such a vast scale. The empire of Alexander lasted a mere five years, that of Napoléon two decades, the British Empire two centuries, the Roman barely five.

In concrete terms this meant that from now on, fifty miles out of Xining, I would encounter the same customs as those of faraway Ladakh.

Somewhere deep in my heart I feel truly Tibetan, connected in spite of myself to a certain basic humor and a broad-minded approach to existence. Tibetans are a friendly, no-nonsense sort of people, without any of the pomposity that comes from being British, or any of the affectation associated with the "superior" Chinese. Tibetans are just straightforward, fun-loving optimists.

How much of their attitude toward life is due to their culture, how much to their religion, and how much to their tough way of life is hard to say. What is evident, as Hugh Richardson points out in his *Short History of Tibet,* is that "Western visitors so diverse in personality and objective as the Jesuit fathers Francisco D'Azvedo...and Ippolito Desideri..., the British emissaries George Bogle and Samuel Turner..., and the Indian Civil Servant Sir Charles Bell... all agree in describing the Tibetans as kind, gentle, honest, open, and cheerful."

Scholars believe that this attitude was common to Europe in the Middle Ages, in the days when all things were either black or white, when people were good or evil, and both behaviors were accepted as normal. People lived with greater intensity and passion, for good or ill, because in those days in Europe, the future always seemed uncertain, as it does today in Tibet.

What has happened in the West is that our technicians and scientists have put an enormous effort into predicting the future and thereby reducing the uncertainty that was the daily lot of previous civilizations. The telephone and other means of communication—maps, weather forecasts, planes, medical checkups, statistics, indexes, news bulletins, et cetera—are all designed to lessen our anxiety about what lies ahead.

In Tibet when somebody walks out a door he might as well have disappeared for good. There is no way to know where he is going (no maps), or when he will come back (no phone), no way to contact him (no addresses or mail): not even his name is much use because all Tibetans share a few first names (Tsering, Dawa, Nyma, and so on), and hardly anybody knows the names of people's homes and villages, the only means of identification that are specific to an individual.

All this breeds an intensity in human relations. In the absence of newspapers, all information is relayed during chance encounters. When two Tibetans meet they exchange not just gossip but everything they know or have recently seen or heard: the price of barley in the next valley, the cost of yaks and horses, the health of distant friends and relations. Every encounter thus becomes an important moment in the knitting-together of a far-flung society without the aid of newspapers, radio, television, or telephone.

Tibetans are well aware of the great size and scope of their world. They all know and care about Ladakh and the Tibetan districts of Ganan in China's Gansu Province, although they are fifteen hundred miles apart.

Stepping onto the plateau I felt at home, as if I were once again in Mustang, Zanskar, or Bhutan. All my earlier Tibetan experiences came flooding back, and even though the Amdo herders spoke with a strange accent, we were instant friends because of our shared appreciation of the land they lived in.

I looked at the road, which headed south as straight as a dart and cut the landscape in two, along the ancient trade route linking Xining with both Tibet and Sichuan.

The control of such vast and mountainous lands was conceivable only to a horse-riding people.

A tomb found recently on the edge of the Black Sea contains the skeletons of small horses whose teeth bear the irrefutable signs of the bit, fixing at 6000 B.C. the earliest known date at which man first domesticated the horse. Just how important it was for man to be able to ride a horse can best be judged by thinking how important airplanes are to us today. Seventy years ago, before the coming of the commercial airlines, the world was a very different place. It took seven weeks to two months to get to Australia from Britain. America and Europe were at best seven days apart. And since time is money, travel over large distances was for most people prohibitively expensive.

Just as planes changed the geography and in many ways the politics of the globe, so did horses. Moreover, along with domesticated horses, there arose a different breed of man, the cavalier—a mounted elite that had the upper hand over ordinary people. Except in China, a notable and sizeable exception, around the world society was divided between those who rode and those who got about on foot, between cavalry and infantry. Nobles were cavaliers and their vision of the world expanded accordingly.

Today, surprisingly, the possession of horses is still very much associated with social prestige in the West. There is the hunt club society, and the very different cosmopolitan polo set. Then there are those involved in show jumping and dressage, a different group from the sulky and trotter crowd; the breeders and thoroughbred racers; the cross-country horseback riders and, finally, the would-be cowboys who put on costumes of a weekend and ride "Western style"—all compose separate and often antagonistic social groups.

Tibetan society, on the other hand, would not exist at all were it not for horses. Every Tibetan has in him the mentality of a cavalier. Accustomed to travel, assured of a certain dominance over nature, and open to external ideas, his innate broad-mindedness is in direct proportion to the vast horizons that spread out before him from birth.

We who, for the most part, live in cramped and overpopulated cities, have developed a certain antagonism to our fellow man, whom we are just as likely to consider an enemy or a rival as a friend.

In sparsely populated Tibet, human relations are quite different—people are generally thrilled to meet each other, to talk and to share.

I say "generally" because as the road sped south we were heading straight for the Amne Machin range, the home of the Goloks, who, more than anyone else, had rendered access to the source of the Mekong all but impossible. The word *Golok* has always spread fear in the hearts of Tibetans and abject terror among all foreigners, Chinese or Europeans, who dared venture into their parts of the high plateau.

"I can't wait to meet a Golok," Sebastian said, and I admitted I had been equally keen to have a look at these men whose reputation had been conveyed to me from as far away as America. I had read that a Golok queen had had seventeen husbands, and that they ate human flesh. They were said by some to have killed thousands of Nationalist Chinese seeking shelter in their territory; others said they had killed ten thousand Communist troops. Rather than cross Golok territory, caravans preferred to make huge detours. The few caravans that dared enter their lands, an annual two-way tribute mission between the Dalai Lamas and the Chinese government among them, did so only under heavy escort. Yet the Golok sharpshooters were so effective that even the annual caravan was discontinued in the 1800s and replaced, for a while, by a triennial affair.

In July 1993, I had crossed Golok territory. Three months later the press announced that the Goloks had distributed pamphlets calling for a free Tibet. The army was called in and hundreds were arrested, but the rebel spirit of the Goloks remains undaunted.

The first three hours of our drive across the Tibetan plateau were tense in that we hadn't yet gotten used to our white-gloved driver, a handsome man of about thirty, who looked far more mature and responsible than Ling.

Ling was visibly nervous. This was his first time accompanying foreigners, and he confessed that he had never been south of Xining, previously having been a schoolteacher there. We began to suspect that he had, in fact, studied and failed at the police school for interpreters, from which my previous guide had come. In spite of his fears, it was obvious that he wanted our journey to be a success. He was overly eager to please—the only problem was that he didn't seem to have a clue as to what our objectives were. When I mentioned the source of the Mekong he answered vaguely, "Don't worry, whatever happens you will have a pleasant time. Our groups are always very pleased." In vain I tried to explain to him that we weren't a group of tourists out to have fun, that this was my third visit to Qinghai, that I was here to study Tibetan horses and locate the exact source of the Mekong River. He looked at me with a pained expression and then answered patronizingly, "Don't worry, you will really enjoy yourself."

"Tonight we sleep at Madoi," Ling announced. Madoi is a Chinese garrison guarding the upper Yellow River, which is known in Tibet as the Ma River, or Ma Chu. The Yellow River, or Hwang Ho in Mandarin, is the second-longest river of China after the Yangtze. Its huge basin is the cradle of China. Like the Nile, its annual floods fertilize and irrigate millions of acres. As such it is a symbol of life for the Chinese. Since very early times its source was the object of special veneration by the Chinese emperors. Where exactly the source lay no one was sure. In fact, the earliest maps of China, drawn with the help of French Jesuit astronomers and mathematicians in the eighteenth century, show the Yellow River as taking its source in the Taring and Oring Lakes, an assertion later contested because some claimed that both these lakes are salty.

It seems that the source of the Yellow River actually lies in a grouping of marshes known as the "plain of the Stars." It is here that every year in the name of the Chinese emperor a white horse and seven white sheep were to be sacrificed in the seventh moon, with a corresponding announcement in the *Peking Gazette*, as follows:

"The worship of the source of the Yellow River at Odontala and the two snow-clad mountains of the Alang-Nor and Amne Machin was duly performed in the prescribed form. . . ."

But unfortunately, according to the American explorer Rockhill, the money for the sacrifice was more often than not pocketed by corrupt officials, who found their own uses for it.

Was the source of the Mekong the object of a similar devotion? I wondered.

I knew that Madoi, the town we were supposed to reach that night, lay on the other side of the Amne Machin range, the home of the Goloks. It seemed to me quite improbable that we could travel that far on our first day.

Having driven a couple of hours across a near-desert stretch of the high plateau, we stopped to lunch in Gonghe, a modern oasis town with green fields and groves of poplars. Here again the population seemed mostly Chinese, yet in the crowd I picked out a few Tibetans in homespun wine-red gowns, accompanied by women showing off well-greased pigtails studded with turquoise. They walked around with a slow gait as if strangers in the bustling Chinese city. I couldn't resist approaching them to speak Tibetan. It had been a full year since I had last spoken the language. As before, I had trouble making myself understood by the Amdo Tibetans, whose dialect is very different from most of the others of Tibet.

I inquired where we could buy the broad-brimmed felt hats that have become the hallmark of Tibetans for over a century. Originally they were imported from Italy, and are efficient at protecting the wearer from sun, rain, hail, and snow.

I was led to a state-owned general store with its habitually poor array of goods: enamel basins, flashlights, cotton undershirts, plastic cans and buckets, flowery red and blue thermoses, and, more interestingly, sweets of every variety, on which I promptly stocked up. In one corner was a whole array of various Chinese brandies next to cans of preserved fruits and tinned pork.

To one side we found great bolts of woolen cloth used by Tibetans for their gowns, and a stock of the felt ten-gallon hats we were looking for, in beige-black and in dark green, the color I chose. We all three now looked part of an Asian spaghetti Western as we marched proudly down the dusty main street under the ferocious, high-altitude midday sun. My GPS said we were twelve thousand feet above sea level, an altitude confirmed by my thumping heart and the great difficulty I had had climbing the stairs to the first floor of the government department store. After all, just twenty-four hours before, we had been at sea level in Beijing.

Ling, the two drivers, and our cook had located a Muslim restaurant, where we were offered spicy dishes of beef and noodles, which we washed down with cups of tea made by pouring boiling water over lumps of crystallized sugar mixed with large berries of uncertain origin and what looked like tea leaves and orange blossoms.

From now on, until we jumped off into the wild, we would stop to eat in Muslim teahouses, of which there were a great many, as the Muslims had followed the Chinese into Tibet to service the Chinese garrison towns and make their living as shopkeepers. The Muslims have a rather difficult time of it because they hate the Chinese, but not nearly as much as the Tibetans hate them. On the one hand, they have never forgiven the Chinese for the terrible massacres carried out against them between 1862 and 1878, and, on the other, the Tibetans think the worst of them, even to the point of believing that they serve human flesh in their restaurants, or so I've been told on numerous occasions by horrified Tibetans. This mistrust of Islam goes all the way back to Song-tsen Gampo himself, who fought the early Muslims in faraway Samarkand, then much later, at the beginning of the last century, when the Muslims of Kashmir attempted to invade Tibet.

As Christians, we felt an affinity with the monotheist Muslims we encountered, but what mattered to us more than that was the fact that the food they prepared was excellent and cleaner than what we could get in the local Chinese or Tibetan teahouses.

I didn't linger long at the table and was able to sneak out before the end of the meal and have a long conversation with a Tibetan monk I found in a side-street market. He confirmed what was already evident—that here, as in many other parts of Qinghai, the Chinese had moved in "like bugs." He asked me if I had any pictures of the Dalai Lama, but I didn't.

Happy at having entered Tibetan soil at last, I watched the straight road slip by as we headed south for Yushu, formerly Jeykundo, alias rGal-kun-mdo, the Chinese district capital of what had been until 1957 the ancient kingdom of Nangchen. Ling was insistent that we should sleep that night at Madoi, but we still had very far to go.

As we left Gonghe the paved road gave way to dirt. In parts it was bordered by walls of dried mud that snaked for dozens of miles along each side of it, the remains of failed efforts by the Chinese in the more fanatical days of Chairman Mao to fence in and settle the elusive nomadic inhabitants of Qinghai.

The road narrowed just as we were struck by the first of many hailstorms. In what seemed a matter of minutes the clear blue sky clouded up and suddenly it hailed so hard that it was difficult to see, while our vehicle sounded like a steel drum pelted with gravel. In no time the green-brown plateau turned a wintry white, and the hills became snow-covered mountains. Why does it hail so much on the roof of the world? Meteorologists have yet to come up with an answer. What is certain, though, is that hailstorms in Tibet are fearful affairs, wiping out entire herds of yak, and killing humans caught away from their tents, their only protection on the high plateau. Hail is so feared that the holiest and most sought-after monks and shamans in Tibet are the sacred "hail men," who are supposed to be able to ward off hailstorms. Hailstones the size of eggs are frequent, as a result of the considerable variations in temperature at these high altitudes.

"Bitten once by a snake, for ten years afraid of a rope" was the Chinese proverb that Ling thrust at me when I explained how dangerous such hailstorms could be. I told him of a hair-raising experience I had survived in southeastern Tibet. I had been in the front seat of a truck when it had started to hail so hard that the surrounding mountains became instantly white. Then for some reason the accumulated loose hail began to slide down the mountain slopes in an avalanche of mud that swept away the road in front of us. The driver slammed on the brakes but hit the mud at the very moment another mud slide hit the rear of our truck. Those in the back jumped out, among them a Tibetan woman. It was pelting hail as I ran from the truck's cabin. The hills and mountains around us were all running, crashing down in a thousand rivulets. Looking up we could see large hailstones and rocks bounding down at us. We all ran out to the flat dry bed of a nearby stream, thinking that we would be safe there. No sooner had we reached the streambed, however, than a crashing sound made us look around to see a three-foot wall of liquid mud carrying bushes before it as it rushed toward us. We had just enough time to dodge the wave and scramble up a mound to which the Tibetan woman had directed us before the steeper hillsides around us collapsed into the raging, mud-filled torrent. Protecting ourselves from the hail as well as we could, we saw our truck buried and the road disappear entirely. We were fortunate not to have perished in the disaster. It took us three days' walking to get away from where we were stranded, and I learned later that the road was down for two years afterward.

There was no question about it. I was afraid of the proverbial rope, and more than concerned as the hailstorm seemed to be traveling along with us. We were now in sight of the Amne Machin range. Jagged gray rocks soared nineteen thousand feet above sea level, supporting sparse snowfields. According to the nineteenth-century

French missionary Huc, the Goloks who make their home here were given to eating the hearts of their victims; they were Buddhists, but with "a divinity of banditry." Huc and his companion Gabet had set out from Xining to Lhasa in 1845 with the Chinese emperor's ambassador and three hundred soldiers in escort. But they dared not take the direct route across the Amne Machin range for which we were headed. They chose instead to travel west to avoid the Goloks, who had, the preceding year, attacked an official caravan traveling up from Lhasa and kidnapped and killed an emissary of the Dalai Lama.

So much has been said about the Goloks as bandits and also as patriots that I am always intrigued upon meeting them, as if something in their faces will explain their reputation.

In all my journeys I myself have been robbed only once, and in rather odd circumstances. I wasn't attacked so much as inspected. My camp was simply invaded by Khamba guerrillas—too many to oppose—and they, with smiles on their faces, opened and examined my trunks, taking what they saw fit. They stopped just short of thanking me, and they were polite enough, besides, to give me a sort of Surgeon General's Warning "that any resistance would cause serious injury." I felt that the only proper thing to do was to collaborate and open my own bags for their picking.

This episode left me with a strange impression, one very different from the ersatz violence of television to which I had become accustomed. Crooks, I now knew, didn't necessarily look like crooks, but were generally normal people whose profession simply differs a little bit from the norm. In southern India, there are criminal tribes whose entire livelihood is theft. During the days of empire, the British were forced to create special courts for them, as they could not be judged by the general standard. Isolated in their mountains, at the constant mercy of yak rustlers, the Goloks would be naturally wary of foreigners and seek from them the material possessions they had no other means of acquiring: guns and gold, pots and pans. I doubted, however, that their monks actually endorsed crime, in spite of the proven existence in Tibet of "criminal monks," who went about

doing everything upside down—eating excrement, engaging in violence, and so on—to hammer in the great precept of lamaism: "Life
is an illusion of the senses and therefore meaningless; truth and the
absolute lie beyond our human reach."

In my journeys I had met many of the fiercest Khamba fighters,
men branded like the Goloks as criminals. For the most part they
had been tall, ferociously handsome, and amiable people. By contrast
the Goloks were not impressive. Short, with small round faces, they
seemed banal, even harmless.

It was nearing six o'clock when we drove into the first Chinese
garrison inside Golok territory.

The road was lined on both sides with one-story earth-brick
stalls and shacks. While our drivers went to buy diesel fuel, I approached a group of Goloks on the side of the road. A young man
with long hair stood beside a woman and two girls. As I talked to the
man, one of the girls squealed with delight at the hair on the back of
my hand. Laughing and amazed, she called her sister to come and
see. I was one of those "dog-faced" barbarians she had heard about:
a hairy monster, even though I didn't have a beard. We all too often
forget that European men are an exception among the people of the
world, in that we are, indeed, hairy-faced. Today, Europeans are less
conspicuous in Asia than they once were, with their huge and rather
ugly thatches of hair around their mouths—the dog faces that
shocked and disgusted so many Asians. To them, only our women
were human-looking, in spite of their funny, pointed noses.

"You should not speak to these people, Mr. Psl," Ling warned
me as I joined him in a teahouse. "They are ignorant, dangerous, and
cannot be trusted." At first I thought that he said this because of the
Goloks' reputation, but soon I discovered that his wariness extended
to all Tibetans.

It was late when we got back to the cars and began our climb into
the heart of the Amne Machin range, so little known that in 1949 an
American pilot named Clark was able to persuade many geographers
that it contained a peak higher than Everest. His conclusions were

based on reports by pilots who had strayed there during the Second World War, but who had clearly erred in their altimeter readings.

The Goloks, who had for so long been feared as bandits, were to become in many ways heroes in Tibet's unsung struggle for independence. When Mao came to power in 1950, his first speech was to announce that China's main duty was to "liberate" Formosa and Tibet. No one has ever quite understood whom he intended to liberate Tibet from. In those days there were only a handful of foreigners residing in the country, most of them missionaries settled on the borders of Kham and Sichuan. As for the Goloks, they had never been anything but their own masters. In fact, when fleeing the advancing Communists, a detachment of Chiang Kai-shek's Nationalist Chinese entered Golok territory in the eastern sector of the Amne Machin range and were ruthlessly cut to pieces. Likewise the People's Liberation Army suffered terrible casualties when they first moved into the land of the Goloks. It took ten years and the massacre of thousands of tribesmen before the Chinese considered this area safe. In 1986, several tourist groups were even allowed to tour the range on horseback. Yet in September 1993, as mentioned, the Goloks distributed a massive number of leaflets calling for the expulsion of the Chinese and demonstrating that they were not reconciled to defeat, after all.

It was dark when we reached the foot of the 17,060-foot main pass through the mountains. In vain I tried to convince Ling that we should stop and sleep before pushing on for Madoi, which still lay far ahead. To drive by night amid the hail and the rainstorms could prove a very dangerous enterprise.

He refused to listen, arguing that it was more dangerous still to stop in Golok country and that, in any case, we were expected by the police at Madoi, and they would send out after us if we failed to arrive as expected.

As if to reinforce my argument, it suddenly began to rain so heavily that we could barely see beyond the hood of the car. Water washed over the road, and I was afraid that we might at any moment be engulfed by a landslide.

Slowly, in the dark, under torrents of rain, we headed onto the upper reaches of the plateau, plowing our way through mud, our vision confined to the narrow beams of the headlights illuminating the wind-driven rain mixed with hail.

It was close to midnight when, against all expectations, having barely escaped breaking down, we finally made it to the walls of the barracks at Madoi. Everyone was asleep, and it took a long while to find anyone to let us into the cell-like rooms of the local government guest house.

Panting, we lay down in our sleeping bags on top of wooden beds like tables. We were exhausted from the lack of oxygen and from fourteen hours of bumping our way south. We had covered 280 miles—over half the distance between Xining and Yushu—a journey that would have taken fifteen days or more forty years ago.

How I hated these sinister garrisons, perpetual reminders of our forcible collusion with the enemy. If only we could be without escort, or were allowed to have Tibetan escorts. A small consolation lay in thinking that we would soon find ourselves off the beaten track.

My strategy was simple enough: We would try to go as far as we could by jeep, and then transfer to horses and follow the bed of the Mekong to its very end; this, in spite of the fact that our maps were vague and contradictory, and they all disagreed as to how far and by what course the roads extended.

Quite apart from the prospect of our getting lost, we faced another equally disquieting peril. Lack of oxygen has two slightly contradictory effects on the body. It produces a feeling of euphoric light-headedness and at the same time a sense of total exhaustion. Turning over in my sleeping bag left me panting, and the halting remarks of my companions revealed they were as tired as I was. Jacques had a headache, and possibly to cheer us up or to get rid of it, he continued to elaborate on pulmonary edema and all that stuff about foam in the lungs. He also explained why he had not brought along those miracle plastic inflatable chambers invented to save mountaineers. All you have to do is put the victim of pulmonary edema inside the plastic body bag and pump up the bag, except that, as Jacques explained, the device could be as harmful as it was supposed to be helpful, and it could, in fact, kill the user if pumped up too much. We dozed off, finally, as Jacques elaborated on the chemical composition of the diuretics that he hoped would save our lives instead.

I coughed just to see if I had any foam in my lungs and fell asleep to visions of hundreds of miles of straight roads zipping by. . . .

4

THE ROOF OF THE WORLD

⌘

It was raining when I awoke to take stock of the "golden prison" in which we had slept. It comprised six rows of barracks huddled behind a great wall. Between the buildings, in pools of mud, small black pigs snorted as they played around. Several Chinese in dark blue Mao suits lingered gloomily here and there. Were they prisoners or police? I couldn't say, but I thought they could quite probably be both—exiled policemen. Madoi was certainly no promotion for anyone used to the bustle of, for instance, downtown Shanghai.

At 14,760 feet, Madoi is close to being among the highest settlements in the world, the record going to the town of Wenchuan (16,732 feet), located in western Qinghai. Madoi certainly qualifies, on the other hand, as one of the most sordid. One long cement road, bordered by penitentiary-like walls, intersected two equally grim side

streets, along which were located a petrol dump, a desolate state the-
ater or propaganda hall, a large satellite dish linking it with headquarters in Beijing and Xining, three shops, two Muslim eating
houses, and a very large cemetery in honor of the Chinese who died
here, no doubt "liberating" Qinghai from itself.

As we waited in the freezing dawn for a semblance of breakfast,
Sebastian and Ling and I had the opportunity to talk with a Chinese
"civil servant." Nearing sixty, the man was from Shanghai and had
been exiled here some thirty years ago for political reasons. When
asked if he planned to return to Shanghai, he announced that he
would love to but could not, that he had become accustomed to the
altitude and the cold healthy air and felt he would surely die if he
went back. Lacking the antibodies to survive the bacteria of the lowlands, Chinese who have spent a very long time on the Tibetan
plateau do run a serious risk if they give up their exile. Thus it is that
many find themselves obliged to serve life sentences in Qinghai—
ironically, for reasons of health.

Having arrived by dark of night, we were shocked by the scenery as
we drove out of town onto the small dirt road. Gone were the green
pastures and rugged mountains. I felt a strange inner desolation looking out upon the higher reaches of the bleak Qinghai plateau. Around
me stretched a huge plain dotted with low, rounded, sandy hills partially covered with dry scrubby grass, and among which a thousand
mirror-like ponds reflected the immeasurable sky above. Here, close
to the source of the Yellow River, the land was a flat watershed, with
rain collecting in pools and ponds merging into mostly salty lakes.
Unfolding before us was a preview of the bleak no-man's-land for
which we were headed, a windblown world shunned even by the
nomads themselves.

It was hardly surprising that somewhere nearby lay the mythic
source of the Yellow River, for this was clearly one of the poles of
the earth, the summit before the sky—the last step up and, if one

turned around, the first one down heading to the sea. Here in marshes and bogs, lakes and ponds, percolated the water of the roof of the world that would slowly run down to form the great rivers that irrigate the whole of Asia.

As we drove I became increasingly fascinated with the endless vistas of pools and lakes vibrating in the heat waves of the morning sun. I understood how one could easily get lost here, not just because of the sameness of everything, but because of the deadly bogs. Lacking in any definite drainage, the water of the high plateau, where it didn't form a pond, created labyrinthine marshy wastelands.

The preceding year, while on my quest for the horses of Nangchen, I had been galloping across what seemed like a grassy plain when our Khamba guide shouted for me to bear to the right. I did so but failed to pass the word in time to my companion, Caroline Puel, who was galloping happily ahead of me down the center of the valley.

I watched when her horse suddenly began to flounder and sink in what appeared a stretch of solid grassland. In a distance of four paces her horse was immobilized, with mud nearly up to its stomach. It took a long time to haul it out without breaking its legs. These bogs are extremely hard to detect, in that they don't support a distinctive vegetation. Although I had chosen, this time, to travel in September, after the rains, to avoid these pitfalls, it had been raining continuously, and the dry season, if one in fact existed, was not yet in sight.

As we drove among the lakes here and there bespeckled by flotillas of ducks, of which the most spectacular were a Tibetan variety with pheasant-like golden feathers, I suddenly sighted to our left a small herd of kiang. I made the driver stop and flagged down the second vehicle, pointing toward the animals.

Jacques slipped out of his seat and set off slowly to stalk them with his camera.

The kiang belongs to the family of wild equids, which includes all the various types of zebras and the rare wild asses of Africa and

Asia. In Africa, one subspecies of wild ass, *E. a. atlanticus,* has just become extinct, and the two others are officially endangered. In Asia wild horses are more abundant. They are divided into two groups, the *Equus hemionus* and *Equus kiang.*

The Hemionus comes in six varieties, ranging from the Syrian wild ass to the Mongolian and Gobi dziggetai. They are different from the African wild asses in that they produce a sterile offspring when crossed with domestic donkeys.

The kiang are a subspecies of wild ass, of which so far only three types have been roughly identified, due to a lack of any formal study: the eastern kiang, which inhabits the region we were traveling in; the southern kiang, found south of the Brahmaputra River; and the western kiang, found in Ladakh. They are all native to the Tibetan plateau.

I spent several days without success tracking down kiang in the wild regions of eastern Zanskar in 1981. I had had to wait until 1992 to see my first animals in the wild while crossing western Qinghai in winter. Man-shy, the exotic creatures are forced down to lower altitudes in the cold season. We now had before us seven kiang who seemed not at all upset by our presence.

For over half an hour we observed them as they alternately walked and galloped in single file. At fourteen hands (fifty-six inches) they were as tall as the local saddle horses. They had a very light and long fleecy yellow winter coat with three brown oval patches each; one along the neck, one over the body, and one covering the rump and the thighs.

As Jacques approached them, they shifted their position, slowly rising to a crest over which they eventually galloped out of sight. Once kiang were seen in the thousands, but since the Chinese People's Liberation Army began to kill them for food their numbers have substantially decreased.

We found this encounter a good omen as we carried on ever deeper into the maze of lakes and hills, occasionally catching sight of a snow-crested peak in the distance. We were now fully launched onto the plateau of Qinghai, a territory that has proven more difficult to explore than the remotest jungles of the Amazon and New Guinea. At some point four hundred miles from where we were lay our goal.

Crossing two more passes, we ran into trouble when the road turned into a pool of mud and we joined a long line of government trucks buried up to their axles. A bulldozer was attempting to move the trucks, but it seemed hopeless, as each attempt simply plowed the mud into worse traps, in which the vehicles inevitably sank again. Rocking and pushing our jeeps, we managed to blaze a trail on the side of the road and finally to move some three miles to the head of the line of paralyzed vehicles.

Once again, we encountered solitary black tents, as yaks in the hundreds roamed the plateau like bison on the plains. Occasionally we caught sight of a distant rider rounding them up like cattle. We were in the "Wild West" of Asia, the land of Tibetan cowherders. The horses here were related to the fine breed with enlarged lungs that I had studied the previous year.

Horses are very much like people: They all look alike until you get to know them. I have acquired over the years an "eye for horse-flesh," as the colonial phrase goes. From a distance I can size up the finer points of a horse's conformation. It's a sort of sixth sense, but one that can be acquired and improved. Since my meeting with Sebastian's cousin Loel and my first "horse hunting" expedition in 1992, I had become obsessed with Tibetan horses.

Horses, not dogs, are man's best friend. But what does that actually mean? What is the difference between a wild and a tame horse?

The answer is a strange one. Tame animals tend to be smaller and to live shorter lives than their wild brothers, and tame species tend to look infantile and neotenic—that is to say, less advanced in their development, having proportions like those of young animals, with larger heads and clumsier bodies than wild adults.

Who first tamed horses, and how and where was it done? We really don't know. The more important question is: Which horse was the first to be tamed? Today all the horses in the world are tame, with the exception of the "wild" Przewalski horse, which itself exists now only in captivity.

Although closely related to the domestic horse, the Przewalski horse has certain substantial differences of appearance, character, and also chromosomes. It has 2n=66 instead of 2n=64 chromosomes, yet it can mate with domestic horses and produce fertile offspring. In matters of appearance, its neck shows a marked break in its curvature, whereas its tail has short donkey-like hair toward its roots, as opposed to the long hair of domestic horses. The nose of the Przewalski is white, like those of asses and donkeys, and last but not least, it has a very pugnacious character.

Some scholars believe that our modern domestic horses derive from crossbreeds of the Przewalski, but others strongly disagree. As we drove on, little did I imagine that in the coming year we would discover a living fossil, an unknown breed of Tibetan horse that might help solve some of the mystery surrounding the earliest domestic horses.

What is certain is that domesticated animals changed man's world. The oldest stone carvings found in the Tibetan highlands of Ladakh depict men, accompanied by dogs, shooting ibex with bows and arrows. These earliest inhabitants of the highlands were hunter-gatherers whose best friend and ally in tracking down game was the dog.

Later came the domestication of cattle and horses; nobody knows which came first, but it seems likely that sheep were first, then bovines or cows, and horses last of all.

As we drove across the plateau I kept my eyes peeled in hopes of seeing a giant wild yak, its huge stature making it the tallest of the bovine family. I had once had a strange encounter with wild mountain yaks in Bhutan, but they are smaller than the giants of the high plateau, which I had never seen.

It was 1968. My party and I had been climbing for two days up the 13,320-foot Ruto-la pass, one of the most rugged passes in cen-

tral Bhutan. Dwarfed by giant Douglas firs, hedged in by rhododen-
dron bushes, I was happy to emerge at last into a vast clearing where
I decided to pitch our tents for the night. No sooner had we arrived
than a small herd of magnificent yaks crashed out of the forest and
invaded our camp. Impressed by their size and their striking jet-black
robes, I immediately went for my camera. Full-blooded yaks are rare
in Nepal and Bhutan, and I had not yet been to Tibet. "Whose yaks
are they?" I asked. "They belong to the king." I took the reply at face
value and understood that the king would have only the best of animals. I was dressed in a bright red down jacket, and seeing a yak close
by I gave my camera to Tsering, my Tibetan companion, and asked
him to take a photograph of me and the yak; whereupon I
approached the giant beast, then turned my back to him to face the
camera.

Alas, I have lost the photograph of the yak and me, the beast
huge and black and me small, in bright red with a blissfully ignorant
smile. The yaks did indeed belong to the king, like the tigers and
gazelles and all the other wild creatures of Bhutan.

The tallest giant wild yaks of Qinghai stand eighteen hands
(seventy-two inches), which makes them truly enormous, as tall as
the tallest of dray horses, and much, much heavier—some are
claimed to be as much as twenty hands (eighty inches) tall. Colonel
Przewalski was charged by one and managed to kill several. Today,
for fifty thousand dollars, one can get a permit from the Qinghai
Mountaineering Association to kill a single animal, but success in
the effort is hardly guaranteed.

How did man tame the great yaks if the American Indian was
never able to tame the bison? Although I am no expert, it seems possible that man has never actually tamed any animals at all, and that
friendliness to humans results from a natural proclivity. It is in this
that dogs differ from wolves; the tame yak, as big as he may be, is
simply a different breed from his wild cousin. Our sheep and cows
were perhaps just born amiable to man, as are the reindeer of Lap-
land and Siberia that are "tamed" simply by separating them from

the herds in which they live, and the elephants that Indians train for life in only two or three weeks away from the wild.

In taming the yak the Tibetans secured the services of the most versatile and useful animal in the world.

To begin with, one can ride a yak, and in many parts of Tibet a good riding yak (preferably without horns) is worth three times the price of a horse. Surefooted, able to sniff out and avoid crevasses on glaciers, immune to snow blindness, capable of bulldozing its way through snowdrifts, the yak's ponderous, heavy gait provides a remarkably smooth ride. Tibetans make yak saddles with stirrups and all, and yak races are held in many parts of the land. As a beast of burden a yak carries twice the load of a horse. Being ruminants, yaks have it all over horses in that they need not waste hours grazing. They hurriedly guzzle their daily ration of hay in the morning and then spend their time on the road chewing their cud. Among the many other benefits of the yak is its meat, delicious when fresh, dark red due to the abundance of red blood cells that catch the little oxygen available at high altitudes; and, according to many experts, healthier to eat than beef. Alas, most Tibetans eat it dried once the cold thin air has reduced it to a fiberglass-like, ropy substance. Yak wool is used by Tibetans to make their tents, their basic rope, the awnings of monasteries, bags, and the soles of boots. Not only do yak hides make shoes and other apparel, but sewn together and drawn over willow branches they make up the hulls of coracles, the only boats found in Tibet. As if this were not enough, one can drink *Dri*'s (female yak's) milk. And, of course, *Dri* butter serves as fuel to light up tents and honor the statues of holy shrines when not being eaten in a variety of ways. *Dri* cheese, so hard a hammer can't break it, is sucked and chewed upon for hours by Tibetans; a good food, it keeps for a century when dried and smoked, and is occasionally fed to horses when the grass is running out. Of all these services to man, none compares to the greatest gift the yak offers, its dung, which Tibetans burn for warmth in the extreme winter cold of the high plateau.

There are several varieties of yak in Tibet, and although they have not been rigorously studied, there are at least three major families: the square-headed yak, the long-nosed yak, and the miniature yak. I am certain closer examination will reveal many more breeds, not to mention the various hybrid yaks crossed with regular cows, animals called *Dzo* (the female is called *Dzomo*).

Like all herders, the Tibetans have hundreds of words to describe different cattle according to their markings, their horns, and their general appearance. And in Tibet, the road to heaven, or rather to fruitful reincarnations, is paved with yaks. Those yaks whose lives are offered up to the divinities cannot be butchered, and are singled out as sacred by a red woolen collar. They live in peace, unmolested until they die of old age, bringing merit on their owners.

The great central highlands of Tibet are yak country, and it is the herds of yaks that determine the seasonal migration of the nomads. Unlike other cattle but like reindeer, the yak has a singular capacity to digest mosses and lichen; it was designed with freeze-proof feet and legs, and special reduced sweat glands to further prevent freezing. The yak even has a stomach specially engineered to store fat for the long winters with little food.

In spite of the myriad benefits of the yak, Tibetan herders on the roof of the world couldn't survive on yak alone. There is little else available to them in the highlands, just a few grasses that can be made into salad, and the odd wild onion added to the more abundant stinging nettles (at a foot high, the tallest plant in the tundra), which make a delightful soup. Beyond these scant greens, there is nothing else to eat but that which the nomads can hunt, such as wild sheep and gazelles. The Tibetans never eat fowl, kiang, or horseflesh, as do their Mongol and Chinese neighbors.

Thus it is that, in order to survive, the nomad herders of Tibet depend on trading with their lowland cousins, who sell them the barley they need to balance their diet. This interdependence of nomads and barley growers is what gives Tibet its special character and what determines the nature of Tibetan politics.

"You must understand," I found myself explaining to Jacques, "Tibet is, in a way, a human zoo. Locked away from the rest of the world, protected by the high altitude, Tibetans for centuries thrived untouched and undisturbed by their lowland neighbors. Many valleys are so isolated and remote that they harbor tribes with a unique specific genetic heritage. There are Tibetan tribes with beards, Tibetans with Western features, and some with Mongol features. There are even tribes that look like American Indians—in other words, a whole variety of people yet to be fully studied and recorded."

Jacques was not impressed by Tibetans. A doctor, he was almost Victorian in his aversion to dirt, which in our low warmer lands is equated with bacteria and disease. Because Tibet is so high, both the cold and the ultraviolet rays act as a natural sterilizer, killing most bacteria. As a result the people don't have to wash to be clean, and indeed they often don't. The result is that most Tibetans are dirty, yet healthy, and therefore cleaner than they look. Of course there are exceptions. A well-scrubbed Tibetan maiden, her shiny pigtails anointed with fresh yak butter, is a true pleasure to behold, with rosy cheeks and clear white skin. The generally darker appearance of the Tibetan is, in fact, due to sunburn and plain grime: their legs and other parts of the body not exposed to sunlight are surprisingly white in contrast to the skin of most Asians. Fair ladies go to great trouble to escape being suntanned by covering their faces with a mixture of water and ground burnt goat's horn, a black paste that makes a hideous mask, to which can be glued dabs of wool. Thus one occasionally meets hairy black monsters, wholly unrecognizable as pretty ladies just taking care of their complexion.

Three men alone, bumping our way hour after hour on the road to Yushu, we inevitably gravitated to women as one of our favorite subjects. Ling, unlike my previous QMA guide, was not much of a ladies' man. That notwithstanding, when it comes to talking about women, the Chinese are very much like the French. Perhaps this is no coincidence that the Chinese and the French also share a passion for food and especially for talking about it. Sensuality in China, as in France, is as much in the realm of the mind as it is in the realm of the flesh. It was not until Rousseau, with his back-to-nature ideas (combined with puritanism), that wit was separated from love, and love was reduced all too often to just plain sex.

The Tibetans also have a humorous approach to love, in which flirtation is seen as a game of wits. As is common in several Asian cultures, girls and boys will congregate in opposing teams to exchange teases in song or verse. The boy or girl with the wittiest repartee is considered the most seductive.

"Even Great Lamas have fleas" is a popular Tibetan proverb, to which one might add that some are bitten by the bug of love. The libertine sixth Dalai Lama, for instance, is famous for his attempts to reconcile in verse his spiritual calling with his powerful attraction to young maidens:

> *If I unite with the heart of a maiden*
> *The religious merit of my life will end,*
> *If I turn to the hermit's cave*
> *I will go contrary to the maiden's heart.*

In the end, the maidens had his attentions at night, and the monastery during the day. He seems to have managed his double calling quite well until he was murdered by an invading Mongol force in 1706, leaving to history a collection of his naughty love songs.

Lamaists are extremely tolerant, and the sixth Dalai Lama is revered today as much as, if not more than, his chaste brothers in reincarnation. Of course one should know that some Tibetans actually strive to perfect the sexual orgasm, in the belief that it is the best attainable approximation to nirvana. All this, of course, is difficult to understand for those of us of the Western religions, in which sensuality has little or no role to play.

Can we truly hope to understand a world as far removed from ours as the world of Tibet? For years I believed that I understood the Tibetans, and yet on this journey I began to appreciate for the first time how little I actually knew of the manner in which they perceive us as foreigners.

Whether in the case of the American Indian of the Wild West, the inhabitants of New Guinea, or the Tibetans confronted by the Chinese, the reactions of invaded peoples seem historically to have certain basic similarities. Faced by a culture with superior technology, whose objectives (gold, land) are incomprehensible to them, the indigenous population can do nothing to avoid being overrun and destroyed.

In general, the foreigners are welcomed initially, but when their true purposes become evident, it is too late and the native high priests and aristocracy are either killed or exiled if they object. Deprived of spiritual and political leadership, demoralized at having lost their pride and identity, the victims often abandon themselves to alcohol. Thus many once-brilliant people become despondent and "ignorant fatalists, resigned to their plight," as American Indians are often described. Much of Tibet is now at the beginning of this funeral process. Their leaders in exile, forced to work for the Chinese, many central Tibetans are beginning to have the resigned and hopeless look of the downtrodden American Indian.

Such thoughts assailed my mind as we drove across seemingly endless grass-covered valleys running between low hills, occasionally cut by slightly higher snow-crested ranges. Black tents surrounded by great antlike herds of yaks were all around.

We were nearing the heart of Qinghai, the remotest portion of the Tibetan highlands, the ultimate frontier, where the confrontation I have described is still in its first stages, as the Chinese meet the last of the free men of central Asia. Planning to go beyond where the Chinese had traveled, I hoped to be able to grasp the true spirit of a people yet unspoiled.

Night was falling as we crossed the sixteen-thousand-foot Karong pass and began a slow descent toward the upper Yangtze River. We were following a shallow torrent meandering in a broad green valley hedged in by mountains. Here at dusk the previous year I had witnessed a timeless tragic scene. A yellow wolf with gleaming golden eyes was stalking a delicate Tibetan gazelle. I saw both the wolf slinking along and the gazelle, ill at ease, unsure of where exactly the danger was that it could smell but couldn't see. Predator and prey: the same drama played out today on the high plateau between Chinese and Tibetans.

I wasn't so much concerned with who was right and who was wrong, not believing in the simplistic Manichean interpretation of history, as I was curious to know if perhaps today, as we approach the end of the millennium, the nomads might once again stand a chance of being victorious over "civilization," as they always had been in the past.

I believe that the confrontation taking place on the highlands of Tibet is not just a battle between the Chinese and the Tibetans, but the last great confrontation of our planet between two totally different concepts of existence: a confrontation made all the more cruel by the fact that it is occurring at a time when many of us are questioning the ideals of modern society, and expressing serious doubts about the worth of what we call progress.

This century began with great hopes that science and technology would free man from ignorance, hunger, hard and inhuman labor, disease, and the horrors of war. But no such thing has happened, and some now, on the contrary, look to Tibet for an answer to the unkept promises of our technological society. Maybe in the ancient world of Tibet are to be found the solutions to our overworked, overpopulated, violent, and slum-riddled new world.

In setting out to find the source of the Mekong, I was treading in the footsteps of those early Victorian explorers I had once admired, men who had, in fact, been the unknowing spearheads of a destructive process. Could I escape repeating that process now?

Regardless of what happened ultimately, the irony was that I was enacting all over again the same ritual that had led to the results I deplored.

It was dark and hailing when we took the great Chinese bridge over the upper Yangtze and began our short but steep ascent toward Yushu.

At eleven o'clock, drenched to the bone, we reached the darkened hostel of the Public Security Bureau, a dismal cement building on the main thoroughfare of the sprawling Chinese garrison town.

Exhausted from the altitude, the three of us panted up two flights of stairs, hauling our bags to the cell-like rooms allotted to us. These were on either side of a smelly cement corridor lined with spittoons. We shuffled about this corridor by candlelight, the town's electric generator having been shut down. I was surprised to hear French spoken down the hallway, and found the rooms occupied by a party of French and Chinese scholars, members of the team that since 1980 has been studying the geology of Tibet and the composition of the earth's crust beneath the high plateau—a detailed, multidisciplinary research project involving experts in plate tectonics, paleomagneticisms, geo-chronology, and seismology. From the formidable work of this team, which has explored virtually all Tibet's last "empty quarters," we are beginning today to understand the mechanisms of the formation of the Tibetan highlands.

I paid a brief visit to the head of the mission, Professor Paul Tapponnier, and his American wife, Kevin Kling, the author of several beautiful picture books on Tibet. Dr. Tapponnier's present mission was to study the upper basin of the Yangtze River. He informed us that to his knowledge no such study of our destination, the upper Mekong, had ever been undertaken. He had no news or details of the Sino-Japanese expedition, our potential rivals, whose exact purpose we had still not been able to determine.

That night, once again agitated by the lack of oxygen and exhausted by the long day's drive, I went over our plans. So far, so good: our two vehicles seemed in excellent condition. Our weak points were that our provisions were both inadequate and insufficient. Our last chance to find anything like a can of pork, Chinese noodles, sugar, or rice, would be here in Yushu. I also hoped to be able to buy surplus Chinese saddles, as I still carried around last year's scars, inflicted by Tibetan saddles, which, as elegant as they are to the eye, can be far from gentle to one's seat.

Come what may, I wanted to avoid spending another night in Yushu, lest someone else reach the source of the Mekong before us.

5

THE KINGDOM OF NANGCHEN

⌘

The following morning Sebastian announced that I had snored. Jacques had a splitting headache again, and Ling thought it a good idea for us to stay in Yushu and enjoy ourselves. I drove everyone to the market to buy all we would need for the last leg before the Mekong.

Yushu is dominated by the impressive fortlike cluster of the Jeykundo monastery of the Sakya-pa sect, a sect whose monks converted the Mongols to lamaism in the early twelfth century. The Sakya-pa, although considered a "red hat" sect of the old school, is, in many ways, the most intellectual of all the sects of lamaism, each sect (and there are seventeen of them) having its own particular religious texts or commentaries. For the Sakya-pa, the text is the Sakya-kha-bum, or one hundred thousand words of Sakya.

Jeykundo (today's Yushu) has always been an important, although remote, staging point for the few travelers to northeastern Tibet. The monastery and town stand at a major crossroads. Here the trail south from Xining splits in three: One branch goes southeast across the kingdoms of Kham to Chinese Sichuan, another due south across Nangchen to Chamdo, the capital of eastern Tibet, and a third trail heads out to the gold fields of the upper Yangtze and, from there, to the main trail leading from Xining to Lhasa across western Qinghai.

It is here at Jeykundo that many a past traveler has been turned back from entering central Tibet, among them the American Rockhill in 1889, and Mrs. Alexandra David-Neel in the 1920s. To my knowledge, no foreigner has ever succeeded in reaching Lhasa by this route. In fact, as we would discover the following year, the difficult northern route to Lhasa from Jeykundo, across both the Mekong and the upper Salween, remains unexplored to this day.

The only foreigners on record as having entered northeastern Tibet by crossing Nangchen are the Russian explorer and scientist P. K. Kosloff and Sir Eric Teichman, the remarkable British consul in Chengdu who, in 1913, single-handedly traveled among the warrior tribes of Kham and successfully pacified them, at least temporarily, in what has been described as one of the most daring and remarkable diplomatic feats of recent times.

A third person, the German Albert Tafel, gave us the only account we have of the political organization of the kingdom of Nangchen in a book he wrote of his travels in 1914. He himself, however, never traveled much beyond Jeykundo.

It was a day's riding east of Jeykundo where, exactly a century before us, in June of 1894, Dutreuil de Rhins's small caravan was attacked, leaving dead the man who first claimed to have discovered the source of the Mekong. De Rhins's claim had been challenged by others, but no one had actually formally proven it right or wrong by checking it out on the spot. It was now up to us to settle the matter, as long as all went well and the Chinese authorities didn't change their minds, and someone didn't beat us to it.

⌘

As we sat down to yet another breakfast of raw dough in a little tea-house near the Yushu hostel, Ling mumbled that he had to go to the police to register us and obtain clearance for us to proceed to Zadoi, the remote garrison town set up to control the nomads of the upper Mekong basin.

The preceding year, thanks to the patronage of the Chinese Ministry of Agriculture, I had been among the very first foreigners allowed to travel to Zadoi and three other garrisons in the modern Chinese district of Yushu. My quest not only had led me to record the region's finest thoroughbred horses, but also allowed me to make my first contact, however brief, with the various tribes of Nangchen.

I had used Yushu as a base, setting out systematically to the four corners of the ancient kingdom. Founded in the eighth century A.D., Nangchen had been brutally erased from the map in 1958 before any European had had the chance to explore its immense territory, which is populated by twenty-five distinct nomadic Khamba tribes.

The events that were to lead to the destruction of the kingdom began in 1950, when news reached the king in his mountain retreat of Nangchen Gar that a new breed of Chinese was coming—an army that neither looted nor stole but had come to right the wrongs of the ruthless opium-smuggling warlords.

Qinghai was then still dominated by the fearful Muslim warlord, General Ma Pu-feng, a man with dozens of concubines, who at the time was planning his escape, hoping to take with him his wives and a fortune in gold and jewelry. The king of Nangchen thought it appropriate to give his support to the apparently honest and sincere People's Liberation Army and offered one thousand soldiers to help the Communists rid the land of the terrible General Ma.

Thus, like many other Khamba leaders, the leader of Nangchen had at first been in favor of the Communists and had hoped they would drive off the corrupt officials who had plagued the remote borderlands for dozens of years. How could a tribal king have understood the hypocrisy underlying the tactics of Mao Zedong? Mao had sworn to bring Tibet and its tribes to heel, to achieve what no other emperor—and no wall, however great—had ever achieved.

However, no sooner had General Ma's ten DC-3 planes, loaded with his women and his gold, lifted off from the grassy airstrip at Xining, ultimately headed for Cairo (where the warlord would end his days in luxury), than the People's Liberation Army turned around and trained their guns on the Khambas, whose leaders they branded as feudal tyrants. Calling for social reforms, which would have resulted in the overthrow of the local aristocracy and the destruction of Tibetan Buddhism, the fanatics of the PLA triggered a secret war to dominate Kham and unleashed the modern Chinese Army against the primitive Khamba cavalry. This six-year war, known as the War of Kanting, went largely unreported and lasted until 1959, when the Khambas, falling back on Lhasa, forced the Dalai Lama to back their struggle in a last-ditch, hopeless effort to oppose the Chinese.

To establish their control over Nangchen, the Chinese set up their headquarters in Yushu and began to fight their way west, deploying a smaller garrison in the Mekong River valley at Zadoi. The PLA pushed on, chasing the Khamba leaders before them into the deserted and uninhabitable wilds, where hundreds would die. Farther north up the Yangtze at Zaidoi (pronounced, in fact, "Driduo," and not to be confused with Zadoi), the Communists established their second fort, and then, at Nangchen Dzong, site of the winter residence of the kings of Nangchen, they built a third. I visited all three of these garrisons in 1993, but I was forbidden to proceed farther west toward the source of the Mekong. Instead, I traveled back downstream to the ruins of the summer capital of the kings of Nangchen, a vast campsite beside a monastery and the kings' former fortress. The spot is strategically set in a circle of towering mountains and is accessible only through a narrow pass, which was ideal for the traditional annual gathering of the leaders of the region's twenty-five nomadic tribes, who would set up their black tents and pay homage to the king.

In the recently rebuilt monastery, behind closed doors, I was read pages from the history of the once-glorious kingdom. I was eager to learn more, but I had at the time already set my sights on the source of the Mekong.

After breakfast, we hurriedly set about combing the bazaar in our last chance to purchase anything we might still need for the road ahead. Yushu/Jeykundo has always been more than a simple crossroads: today, it is the main market town for two hundred thousand nomads, who sell the hides and wool of their sheep and yaks there and also the meat of their herds. More important still, it is host to the greatest of the great annual fairs of Kham. Each July the finest riders of the country flock to Jeykundo with their best mounts to compete in virile or equestrian sports against the other tribes. During the three-week meet events range from straight horse racing to target shooting with guns and bows and arrows at full gallop. In the past, many of the tribes were locked in bitter blood feuds that led to murderous retaliations. No amount of money could bring to a halt the killings, as deep hatreds and quests for revenge were passed down from generation to generation. Yet, according to tradition, the great fairs of the land—Jeykundo's in particular—came under the protection of a truce, which lasted for the duration of each fair. These annual gatherings were vital to the survival of the nomads in more ways than one—as markets where they could buy the grain they needed and as occasions for them to find wives from other often-antagonistic tribes, thereby avoiding the damage of inbreeding over the years. Girls were enticed by various traditions ranging from flirtatious singing competitions to outright wild girl chases on horseback. Abduction was also not unusual.

What made the fairs in Nangchen all the more spectacular were the horse races and other demonstrations of the agility of the local riders, not to speak of the stamina of the local breeds, which were the finest in Tibet.

It was the fabled Nangchen horse that as much as the Mekong had motivated my return to this kingdom. With childish pride I showed the horses in the bazaar to Sebastian and tried hard to persuade Jacques to appreciate their beauty.

"Note the small ears and fine manes," I said, teaching my companions two of the characteristics marking horses "of blood" according to ancient Arab beliefs. Jacques seemed doubtful. More versed in human anatomy, he was, as he had admitted, a stranger to horses and basically afraid of them. On the other hand, Sebastian nodded in consent as I went over the finer points of the Nangchen horses before us. The thin legs, the hard oval feet, the delicate necks, the straight backs and, of course, the barrel chest that housed the enlarged lungs, a genetic evolution that adapted these horses to the roof of the world.

The Chinese hadn't failed to appreciate the remarkable conformation of these beasts, which they called the "Yushu horse." A year before I had read a detailed report prepared for the Ministry of Agriculture in Beijing that began enthusiastically, but then led to a rather dim conclusion. "In spite of the excellent ratio of meat to bone of the Yushu horse," it was deemed not a particularly desirable food item for modern China. Consequently, the report stated, the nomads should be encouraged to stop raising them in favor of yaks, which the Chinese considered a far more profitable beast for the motherland.

It is estimated that as many as five hundred thousand Khambas had preferred to die during the War of Kanting rather than give up their rifles and their right to carry their traditional silver-sheathed knives. It seemed to me unlikely that they would now give up their horses.

In 1993, with Caroline Puel, I had covered almost twenty-five hundred miles all over Nangchen trying to locate the best sub-breeds of the Nangchen horse. These we found to be raised in the district of Ghegi, close to the region where we were going in search of the source of the Mekong. The Ghegi *do-ta*, literally the stone horse of Ghegi, is distinguished for being markedly taller and more robust than the rest.

It was ten o'clock when we set out for Zadoi. Both jeeps were packed, the roof racks piled high with our mess and kitchen tents, pots and pans and food. Sebastian, Jacques, Ling, the driver, and I rode together in the lead vehicle; the cook and the second driver followed behind. Despite exhaustion from two rough days on the road we tried our best to face this third day in good spirits. Just outside of Yushu we reached a broad valley called *Ba thang*, or "plain of the Ba," the Tibetan tents of black yak hair. There are many *Ba thangs* in Tibet, of which one is a large town in Kham. The Tibetans are not terribly creative when it comes to names: All major rivers are called the *Tsang-po*—"the clear ones"—when not simply called *chu*, which means both "river" and "water," or *dam chu*, meaning "marshy river."

Before us lay a broad green valley hedged in by majestic mountains crested with rocky pinnacles. One could see for miles across this immense, luxurious lawn peppered with large black rectangular tents, each accompanied by a smaller white one—the private tent reserved for the one son in each family whose life had been dedicated to religion and the study of the Tibetan canon. These would-be young monks are attached to a monastery, but spend a lot of time at home with their families sleeping in their private little tents. We now began driving down into the rich valley, noting along the way that the tents were set about two miles apart. All these tents belonged to the same tribe—one of the twenty-five that make up the kingdom of Nangchen. Each tribe keeps to its own particular valleys in a well-defined territory divided roughly into winter and summer pastures. The summer pastures are generally higher up than the winter pastures, though not always. In certain places the snow melts more quickly at higher altitudes because of the strength of the sun; as a result, sometimes in winter there is grass high up where the snow and ice have melted, while down in the valley the ground remains frozen under a blanket of snow.

Depending on the lay of the land, the size of their pastures, and the abundance of grass, the nomads may have to move their tents up to ten times a year. Rarely are two tents seen side by side, and, all told, the life of the yak herder is a lonely one centered very much on the family, with little outside social interaction.

The *Ba* is no ordinary tent but rather the Tibetan counterpart to the Mongol yurt. While the yurt is a white, very warm but heavy and cumbersome felt tent that is stretched across a lattice of willow stakes, the Tibetan *Ba* is much lighter and made of twelve-inch strips of loosely woven yak hair, sewn together side by side. The tents vary in size and shape from one tribe to the next, but are generally rectangular. Here, near Jeykundo, they are large, measuring twenty-six by thirty-three feet. Only two wooden posts support the tent on the inside, while between six and twelve posts hold up the sides and corners of the tent from the outside. Ropes of braided yak hair, alternating with stronger ropes of yak sinew, are run from the tent over the top of the outside poles and then down to the ground, resulting in tents that look like gigantic black spiders.

Softening this image, many of the support ropes of the tents we saw were festooned with white prayer flags of cotton cloth, printed with mantras and holy images.

To enter a nomad tent is a privilege that can be earned only on special invitation, as each tent is guarded by at least two and as many as four ferocious mastiffs. The immense popularity in the West of Tibetan lapdogs—the Lhasa apso and shih tzu, or *kyi-tsu* (which, incidentally, just means "small dog" in Tibetan)—makes one forget that Tibet is primarily the home of large guard dogs. Some Tibetan mastiffs are truly enormous, and nearly all are trained to be vicious. Leashed to long steel chains by day, they guard their owner's tent and his cattle. Trained to attack strangers, wolves, snow leopards, and bears, many are so wild that even their owners can barely enter their tents, having to throw the rogues food to be able to slip by unmolested.

Upon entering a nomad's tent for the first time, I was surprised to discover how bright it was inside, as sunlight percolates through the loose weave of the yak-hair cloth. For some strange reason, maybe due to smoke black or capillarity, rain and snow do not come through the translucent material. In spite of their flimsy, drafty appearance, the tents are surprisingly warm, as their black color absorbs solar heat by day, and a yak dung fire lit in a clay hearth helps heat them by night. The hearth is set to the left as one enters the tent. Hearths in Tibet are considered the doors to the earth and the underworld, while the door to the sky is the chimney, or rather slit, in the tent's roof between the two inner poles. This opening can be closed when it rains or snows by letting down flaps of cloth attached to the tent.

Each tent—poles, ropes, and yak-hair strips—weighs some five hundred pounds, and it takes two yaks to carry one tent. Every year the nomads weave three new foot-wide strips of yak hair, each strip as long as the tent is wide. These three strips of cloth are then sewn onto the back edge of the tent, while three old and worn strips on the front of the tent are cut off. Thus, while it may take ten years or so for all the tent's strips to be replaced, the constant renewal assures that the tents last indefinitely, all the while remaining in good repair. It is bewildering to think that the tents one sees in Nangchen are the very same that one might have seen hundreds or even a thousand years ago.

I wanted to show Jacques one of these architectural wonders, but at my suggestion that we stop, Ling became livid and started mumbling something about not talking to the local people, adding that it was, in fact, forbidden! Instead we stopped in a barren spot to have a rather dismal lunch of cheese and bread that we had picked up in Yushu.

It took us two hours to cross the great grassy valley before we found ourselves climbing once again up a steep pass. Just as we reached the summit, marked by sticks flying red and white prayer flags stuck into a cairn of stones, the sky suddenly darkened and it began to hail. In an instant the mountains were white and it seemed that winter had surprised us, but shortly afterward the sun reappeared and everything began to melt, causing rushes of water to run down the dirt trail.

On the other side of the pass we descended into yet another broad valley hemmed in by great hills and mountains. In the middle of the valley the trail split in two, one branch turning south leading to Nangchen Dzong some 190 miles away. *Dzong* means "fort" in Tibetan and was the word used to designate a large stronghold of the kings of Nangchen. Today, Nangchen Dzong is surrounded by Chinese army barracks. Once a mere village, it has become a small town and the new capital of the region, as the old royal campsite of Nangchen Gar, the true capital, is too remote and inaccessible.

There is a certain amount of controversy as to the exact meaning of *Nangchen.* One etymology has it as "many faithful" or "land of great faith." Whatever the case, there were, at one time, seventy-two monasteries in Nangchen, which is a large number if one believes the old estimates of Nangchen's population. Today the total population is estimated by the Chinese to be 250,000, of which 200,000 are nomads. There are no precise early figures, although in the 1930s one estimate fixed the population of the nomad tribes at 12,133 families, or 71,410 souls. This figure was recorded by Ma Ho-t'ien, a Chinese who accompanied the Panchen Lama on his journey back to Tibet from China, a journey on which the Panchen Lama died. It seems Ma Ho-t'ien received his census figures from a Chinese resident of Jeykundo, whose connections to the nomad chiefs and the king of Nangchen were tenuous at best.

A few hours south of the split in the trail lies a large monastery of the Gelug-pa sect, which is today home to nearly one thousand monks, making it the most populated monastery in Tibet, the large monasteries of Lhasa having been disbanded in 1959. According to the abbot, the monastery in question had had close to three thousand monks in years past.

The monastery, like so many others in Nangchen, appears to have been air-dropped into open pastures at the edge of the foothills of the large mountains looming above it. The monks' assembly halls are the only rigid structures of the high plateau and are unexpected monuments to the faith, and to the architectural ability of the nomads, who themselves have never lived in anything but yak-hair tents. These monasteries are the only anchors of the nomadic tribes and in them one finds tangible evidence of the herders' wealth, a wealth that has increased now that the Chinese purchase much of Tibet's beef, mutton, and wool.

The present abbot of the large Gelug-pa monastery, a man in his early fifties, is a cathedral builder, a true heir to the abbots of the Middle Ages. He has entirely rebuilt his monastery, which was completely destroyed by the People's Liberation Army. Starting in 1984, the year in which Tibetan monks were once again allowed to practice their faith and build or restore their monasteries, the lama collected vast sums of money from the nomads; he then hired Chinese coolies, along with architects and engineers, and began to rebuild with an eye to the future. Some of the buildings are made of the dry earth bricks that appear all across Tibet, but others are of steel-reinforced concrete, chosen for a longer life, as they are both fireproof and earthquake safe. The reinforced-concrete beams are sculpted in true Tibetan style with flower designs intertwined with dragons that are lacquered and gilt. The lama hopes to have some fifteen hundred to two thousand monks soon.

More than anyone I met, the Gelug-pa abbot symbolized the cunning, endurance, and dynamism of Tibetans, who adapt overnight to new customs and techniques while preserving unspoiled their character and culture. It is this versatility that is the hallmark of the people of Tibet, a land where the young are admired and encouraged, and, at an early age, given both political and economic responsibility.

In this respect, Tibet is the opposite of China, where ancestor worship and reverence for the elderly has long bred a slow-moving traditionalist society. The earliest Chinese chronicles mentioning Tibet expressed shock at the Tibetans' unusual respect and admiration for the young.

In Tibet, when a young man marries he takes over outright his father's estate and his father's responsibilities. We in the West, as heirs to an agricultural tradition in which power and money rest in the hands of the old, have a lot to learn from Tibet. Ironically, we too seem to worship youth in our magazines and movies and in the world of fashion, yet most people still have to wait until they are well into middle age before they can inherit and/or play a significant role in politics or business.

The Tibetan custom of favoring youth no doubt comes from the ancient hunter-gatherer tradition. Around the world tribes that hunt for a living reward skill and speed—the virtues of youth—and consider them more useful than wisdom and experience.

As we drove on I couldn't help thinking that maybe the advent of agriculture hadn't been such a good thing for humanity, after all.

There are two ways of looking at agriculture. Some believe it was a great step forward for humanity because, with the planting of crops, one could support a larger population on a smaller territory—a dubious blessing that led to crowding, eventually overpopulation, and, in the case of a crop failure, famine.

I am among those who believe that stable agriculture brought about worse evils still, among them the universal and often ruthless exploitation of farmers worldwide by those who seized control of the farmland.

At best, farming was tedious and boring for a species that had evolved over hundreds of thousands of years as hunter-gatherers. Humans were long accustomed to roaming free and putting to use their wits and physical skill in the exciting pursuit of something to eat—in the course of which they felt challenged, and developed a genetic loathing for routines and immobility.

One doesn't need 20/20 vision to watch leeks grow, nor does it require much intelligence or wit to fatten a pig or, for that matter, to milk a *Dri.* It seems that what we call progress has been achieved by exchanging freedom for comfort, excitement for security, and intelligence for diligence.

The Tibetan nomads of Nangchen, though they are herders, still hunt for a living and need all their wits about them to survive in the high-altitude tundra. To be smart and quick, fast and keen, young and alert, rather than old and wise, are the virtues they most need to survive.

> A real man does not live in comfort.
> A goat does not dwell on level plains.

So goes a popular Tibetan saying, and anyone who has traveled in Tibet knows that comfort is unknown except, to a limited extent, in Lhasa.

> Those who love not comfort, can do a thousand deeds.
> Those who cannot love hardship, cannot do one deed.

This is another of the Tibetan proverbs collected by missionary Marion Duncan, who lived in Kham from 1921 to 1936.

Ever since I first explored remote Tibetan regions thirty-seven years ago, I have been struck by how quick and clever the people are, how keen and enthusiastic, how much smarter they seem compared to the slow and stolid farmers of central France, not to mention the affectless peasants of India. But more surprising—even a little bit aggravating—I have encountered many young Tibetans who seemed to be smarter than I. What was I to make of that? Were we in the West not an "advanced people"? Weren't primitive people supposed to be "backward"?

Many would argue that intelligence is inherited—genetically determined. Others claim that environmental factors play a role in it.

I decline to enter the fray here, but one thing I am sure of is that there has not been a major biological mutation in man for thousands of years. This means that Stone Age man was certainly every bit as intelligent as we are in the twentieth century. As to the effect of acculturation on the sharpening of our intelligence, Stone Age man, like the nomads of Nangchen, lived in a world where skill and wit were essential for survival. How much skill and wit is needed to serve hamburgers and French fries with medium Cokes? Today many of our daily work activities are pathetically simple, and if one adds to the equation an average of five hours of mediocre television, it is hardly surprising that our innate powers of reasoning should compare unfavorably with those of our oldest ancestors.

The streetwise children of our flourishing ghettoes are perhaps our last hope. Living by their wits and on their own, they have to be sharper and smarter than the office clerk or the farmhand.

But of course we aren't allowed to say such things. To be judgmental is forbidden, and it is taboo to insinuate disparities in intelligence levels among people of different races and cultures. Why? The answer, again, is found in the West, where skill and intelligence are more feared than appreciated. In an overpopulated world, discipline and homogeneity are virtues, and the innovations of the mind and the unpredictability of the independent thinker are thought to be disruptive and fearful.

In short, there is nothing organized society fears more than the intrusion of smart, carefree, gutsy, horseback-riding "barbarians" of the sort who have come down from the central Asian highlands for the last six thousand years to shake up the sedentary "civilizations" of China, India, and Europe in wave after wave of conquest. All these so-called barbarians came either from Nangchen or from similar adjacent pastoral regions of Tibet and Mongolia.

While I harangued Jacques and Sebastian with my theories on native intelligence, I was unaware of a lone handsome Khamba riding on the open plain, a gun on his shoulder, a silver knife in his belt, eyeing our vehicle with hatred and suspicion. Our four-wheel-drive jeep was a symbol of China's domination of his land, a reminder to all that his people had lost a war for the first time in their history.

Traveling with Chinese citizens in a Chinese vehicle, we ourselves became the enemy, allied with those who had killed his brothers, uncles, aunts, and children, and who had burned the libraries of his people's monasteries.

It was going to be hard to persuade him that we were friends— even if we had no sympathy for China and disapproved of the invasion, were we not ourselves the spearhead of another invasion, with its devastating effect on his way of life?

Just by being here with our clothes, our cameras, and our money, we were the vanguard of an alternate lifestyle that has swept the globe and has stamped out many of the traditional customs of the people of Asia, in particular. A self-indulgent way of life, and so easy to join, all one has to do is shave one's pigtails, buy a pair of designer blue jeans, a cheap T-shirt, black sunglasses, and racy-looking sneakers, and to start smoking cigarettes and drinking carbonated sodas. Eventually one would exchange one's freedom for a job, any job, as long as it paid.

"Do you want Tibet to become a human zoo, to refuse all progress?" Jacques asked.

Although I never dared admit it, I *had* been tempted years ago by idealistic projects such as establishing ecological reserves in Amazonia and "knitting my own windmill." In the comfort of my Paris flat, its central heating generated by nuclear power, I would often dream of the delights of going back to live in a lovely damp cave. How I wished to sleep on the skin of a bear I had killed without fear of being awakened by the telephone.

No, I was an idealist no more, and I knew that in penetrating the isolated world of the remotest inhabitants of Nangchen, even as a friend, my visit would be destructive. I knew that the Tibetans in the nineteenth century had been right to close their frontiers, for it was true that explorers, missionaries, and scholars were as much to be feared as soldiers, and all of them were emissaries of a different way of life that would make others doubt the validity of their own.

Today in Lhasa or Yushu, and even in remote places like our next stop, Zadoi, Tibetan youth in black sunglasses are wasting their time playing billiards and drinking Chinese-imported Coca-Cola. These handsome, clever boys, sent to town to join the local monasteries (the universities of Tibet), have become a major problem in Lhasa, in particular: having nothing productive to do, they form a large, uneducated, unstable population that may prove China's best ally yet in obliterating Tibetan society and culture.

As we headed to the limits of explored territory, I could not help feeling that I was approaching the last frontier of two worlds. Here was the very last place on earth where two worlds and two civilizations are face-to-face. Everywhere else, in America, the Amazon, New Guinea, Africa, and Australia, the aborigines have lost out to the modern world. But somehow, desperately, I hoped that here in Tibet the natives would win, as they had in the past, vanquishing, against all probability, the most advanced civilizations. Had not Beijing, Rome, Babylon, and Byzantium, for all their splendor, might, and sophistication, been overrun by barbarians born in tents and yurts?

Could it be that in the last years of the twentieth century the spirit of those barbarians, the only force ever to challenge on a grand scale what we call civilization, will be forever obliterated? Or will *they* win out and once again bring to our decadent societies the dynamics of their reckless innocence?

One look at men like Lama Urgyen, the cathedral builder of Nangchen, one conversation with the strong, proud, and intelligent Khambas, and it is hard to believe that they will fall for the cheap glitter or the ideals of a Western world.

As the Khamba horseman turned and proudly rode away from our jeep, I secretly looked for a sign that an ongoing fight by his brothers and cousins, the last barbarians, was about to break out, and would once again shame what we call the civilized world.

⌘

Lulled by the roar of the engine, I dozed off, dreaming of the wild barbarians of my childhood tales—the Goths and Visigoths; the Heptalites, the mysterious "white Huns" described by Procope, the fifth-century Byzantine historian, as "barbarian in their manner but with human faces"; the Francs who invaded the Celts, a tribe considered by some to have come from the East; the Vandals who ended up in (V)Andalusia; then there was Attila and, later, in the year 1000, the Magyars who invaded the French Riviera, a rather sophisticated destination for barbarians, I thought. I was awakened when the jeep suddenly swerved and skidded sideways. Mud and water were flooding the road, confined within the rocky cliffs of a high, narrow gorge.

It was only five o'clock, but dark clouds smothered the sky. I knew there was no hope of our reaching Zadoi by daylight. I was worried because I recalled that the last fifty miles of road lay on a narrow shelf overlooking the upper Mekong, a dangerous and slippery ledge. I am generally not afraid of bad roads, or even of bad drivers. Ever since I became interested in the Himalayas, bad roads have been an integral part of all my expeditions. But why risk an accident? I decided after conferring with Jacques and Sebastian that we should stop before dark. Aside from the risk factor, experience has taught me that one should always set up camp well before nightfall.

Liquid mud is no help at all in securing tent pegs, so I became hopeful when I spotted a stone shelter ahead. Leading up to it, the road continued to deteriorate, and I was hardly surprised when we came upon a road gang out to repair the track. The men, mostly Tibetans, had sought shelter from the hail in their canvas tents by the roadside.

I asked the driver to stop. Ling wanted to know why, and I explained that I wanted to ask whether the road was this bad all the way to Zadoi, and where we might find shelter. The driver stopped, but as I opened the door Ling shouted frantically, "No, no, do not go out, these people are dangerous, they are all liars! We must go on!"

We were all surprised by this outburst. I was worried because our journey was only beginning, and I wondered what Ling would think of the rough muleteers we would have to hire at the end of the road. How would he react to the truly arrogant tribesmen? Only then did it occur to me that maybe Mr. Ling had no idea what lay ahead, or worse, had no intention of allowing us to strike out into nomad territory on horseback in search of the source of the Mekong.

Slipping and sliding for a long hour, we lurched across the muddy trail, looking back to make sure the other car was following. I was amazed by the calm professional manner of our driver, a man far more self-possessed than the excitable Ling. The driver spoke a few words of Amdo Tibetan, although he did not want Ling to know it.

It was practically dark when we reached the foot of a high gray rocky mountain where a row of barracks stood, set within a walled enclosure. The hail had abated, and although the ground was still white and soaked in patches, I had the driver stop. Again Ling began to protest as I got out to talk to a small crowd of Tibetans. There were nomads in great red fleecelined *chubas* (the traditional Tibetan toga-like garment), and with them a few official-looking men with assorted Chinese Army surplus clothes. As usual, it took some time before someone realized that I was actually speaking Tibetan. Tibetans are so certain that no foreigner can speak their language and are generally so surprised at our odd appearance (long noses and yellow eyes) that they never think of paying attention to what I am saying, convinced that they will not be able to understand. I have to repeat a phrase over and over before someone exclaims, "But he's speaking Tibetan," upon which they all lend an ear.

"Is the road as bad as this all the way to Zadoi?" I asked. "Will there be snow?" The men assured me that the road actually got much better a little farther on, at the foot of the pass, but that we were still a good four or five hours from our destination.

As I spoke, Ling got out of the jeep and stood beside me, glaring and repeating angrily in his broken English, "These people cannot be trusted."

"Maybe we should try to spend the night here," I suggested, at which Ling again completely lost control of himself. "No, no," he said, "these people will steal, we must go on." I tried to reason with him about the danger of driving over the pass in the dark, along the cliffs overlooking the Mekong. Once again he argued that we were "not allowed to stop in any place not protected by the Public Security Bureau," adding that at Yushu they would have phoned (via satellite) the police of the Zadoi garrison to inform them of our imminent arrival.

When the Tibetans explained that there was no room for us to stay in the old barracks, I rather foolishly agreed to hurry on and try to cross the high pass before nightfall.

At least the Tibetans had been right: After a few miles the road improved and appeared newly repaired. We began to rise quickly, bend after bend, through the pass. Below us the scenery opened up, revealing vistas of distant great peaks in a chaos of snow-covered ranges. We were approaching the southern edge of the high flat plateau of Qinghai, where the ravined, tormented mountains that form eastern Tibet begin their thousand-mile stretch to the south. This web of ranges separates isolated valleys that go on to become the parallel, deeper valleys of the Yangtze, the Mekong, and the Salween Rivers as they make their way south across Tibet.

Our satellite map showed us clearly the high-level plateau, studded, like a glacier, with gigantic fragments of many mountains and cut by deep gorges—the inaccessible home of the Khambas.

In spite of the late hour, when the clouds cleared, it became light again, a reminder that in Tibet the sun doesn't usually set until 10 P.M. This oddity is a result not of its northern latitude but of a "democratic" decree that the whole of China should keep time by the clocks in Beijing, regardless of the fact that the country spans four time zones.

When we reached the summit of the pass, at over sixteen thousand feet, before us stretched a horizon that early explorers called "a frightful desolation." A crowd of jagged peaks hiding and peering out from behind one another packed in the full 360 degrees of the compass, a true petrified ocean out to drown us in sinister gray waves crested with white snow.

I suppose this stark scene reflected what was in my heart as much as it did a daunting landscape. On this, the eve of our third horrible day bumping across Qinghai, I felt tired and depressed. Depressed because Ling had become so unpleasant; depressed because of the menacing thought that our thrust to the Mekong might prove an absurd comedy if we were beaten to the source; depressed because now, seen from these heights, the very motivation for this journey appeared picayune. What on earth was I doing here, I who had never really been interested in the sources of rivers? I hated traveling by jeep and longed secretly for my past expeditions, when I had traveled on foot alone or in the company of a monk or with some other Tibetan with whom to share the arid beauty of the rugged land. Granted, I found Sebastian good company—an Etonian, he was cultured and pleasant and as keen as I was about Tibet. Jacques, although a bit dour, was fascinating to talk to for his detached and analytical frame of mind. Yet what was I really hoping to achieve in Tibet without the company of so much as one Tibetan?

I took pleasure in seeing myself as some sort of romantic adventurer in the tradition of Hodgson and Moorcroft. I had lived so long in the shadow of those semimythical characters, on adventures similar to theirs in remote, romantic areas of Tibet reached only by caravans. Now, I was a little bit upset at being confined to a short-wheelbase Mitsubishi Pájaro four-wheel-drive motor vehicle, in the company of four Chinese plainclothes police officers-cum-guides, an Irishman, and a doctor of medicine and cinematography. I was, to say the least, far removed from my romantic ideals.

Where was the man of thirty years before, his hair blowing in the wind (I am now balding), struggling alone behind a recalcitrant yak, and headed for the unknown on a trail so narrow as to be almost unnegotiable? Had I changed or had Tibet?

Here in the same pass the year before I had seen a wolf stalk a flock of sheep in the snow. Today the rocks were wet and deserted as they tumbled down into a stony vale, beyond which, somewhere before us, bordered by rocks, flowed the Mekong.

Slowly, as we began to sway around endless hairpin turns, darkness descended until it was practically night when we came upon the edge of the great river. Hardly visible, a black expanse in the dark night, yet moving, it flowed swiftly, mysteriously, not with a roar, but with a rustle that broke in swirling twirls upon the surface—tokens of great strength, of great depth, that spoke of urgency, as the water ran past us in the dark on its long, long road to the sea.

If there is magic in words, there is mystery in names. A name lights up with a thousand impressions. As I looked upon the dark waters, my mind was flooded with visions of war. Ever since I was young the word *Mekong* had evoked in my mind sampans bristling with guns, water clogged with dead bodies, marshes hiding snipers, and banks torn by mortar shells.

More than anything, great rivers are associated with power, and power with violence, the decline and fall of those civilizations born of the abundance of water that floods and fertilizes the fields. The ruins of Babylon and Karnak, the lands of the pharaohs and tyrants whose temples, forts, and wealth sooner or later inspired the envy and strife that would topple them. Thus, over centuries, the same waters that brought life and wealth would drown the victims of their own greed.

6

GOLDEN PRISONS

⌘

More than any other river in the world, the Mekong has a variety of cultures flourishing upon its banks. Today it crosses seven countries: Vietnam, Cambodia, Laos, Thailand, Burma, Chinese Yunnan, Tibet, and, of course, lower Qinghai—the kingdom of Nangchen.

The great delta of the Mekong in Vietnam has nine branches, the nine dragons of the river according to local tradition. Every year these branches pour hundreds of thousands of tons of alluvial sand into the sea, some of which hails from the distant plateau of Nangchen. Every year the Mekong adds between 200 and 330 feet more land to Vietnam, extending its course that much farther into the South China Sea. The great delta region is one of the most fertile in Asia, as it benefits from a tropical climate reaching south of the tenth degree of latitude—as far south as the southern tip of India or the Panama Canal.

Flowing from north to south the Mekong experiences a great variety of climatic zones, from the Arctic cold of the high Tibetan plateau where we stood, right down to the sweltering tropics of southern Vietnam.

A journey up the Mekong to Nangchen is impossible for both geographical and political reasons.

In the delta—peaceful at last after five decades of war—the nine dragons are easy to navigate, slipping by the protruding wrecks of sunken vessels, monuments to the tragic past. The nine branches unite as they enter Cambodia, some 150 miles from the sea. The Mekong then flows 220 miles through the heart of Cambodia, just now emerging from the bloody rule of Pol Pot's Khmer Rouge. In Cambodia the Mekong leads right to the capital, Phnom Penh, once the most beautiful and charming of the French colonial towns.

In 1975, refugees fleeing the Communists brought its population to a teeming two million. A few months later Pol Pot's guerrillas entered the town and the massacre began. The entire population was ordered to leave to work the land as farmers. Intellectuals and those who simply happened to own reading glasses, along with those who did not evacuate the city fast enough, were murdered on the spot. The city became a ghost town reeking of decomposed bodies. Over a sixth of the population of Cambodia died in the following years, many of their bodies swept away by the Mekong.

Phnom Penh is built where the river leading to the Tonle Sap enters the Mekong from the north. The Tonle Sap is a huge inland lake whose outlet flows south for about sixty miles before reaching the Mekong at Phnom Penh during the dry season. During the rainy season, when the Mekong is high, this river reverses its course, flowing north to fill up the lake. Few rivers I am aware of flow in two directions, and in many ways this two-way natural canal is an integral part of the Mekong River. Ankor Wat, the ancient capital of the Khmer kingdom, lies just north of the Tonle Sap. After flowing peacefully across Cambodia, the Mekong enters southern Laos at the foot of the Khone falls, the first serious obstacle for ships heading north. Thousands of tons of water roar over huge gray boulders falling down steps fifteen feet high like surf breaking upon a rocky beach.

Past this closed door the waters of the Mekong become the official border between Thailand and Laos for hundreds of miles. In this stretch of river one finds a frightening but harmless dragon, the monstrous *Pla Buk*, a giant catfish, which can grow to be fully ten feet long and weigh up to 550 pounds. Today it is the largest freshwater fish in the world, since the extinction of its cousin, the even greater European catfish, the *Silure* of the Danube.

In Laos, the Mekong flows past the land's new capital, Vientiane, where more rapids are encountered. Leaving the Thai frontier briefly, the Mekong cuts into northern Laos to flow between jungle-covered hillocks past the ancient royal capital of Louangphrabang, a sleepy town whose old Buddhist temples and stupas are located on a bluff above the great river. Farther north the Mekong again becomes the border between Thailand and Laos before forming the extreme eastern frontier of Burma, with Laos along the eastern edge of the infamous Golden Triangle. Here the Mekong is an ally to the opium trade, a witness to violence on both sides. After this the Mekong enters Yunnan, today a province of China, and the river takes on its Chinese name of Lancang.

In Yunnan the river banks are inhabited by various colorful hill tribes whose languages are related to Tibetan. It is in Yunnan that one first encounters the narrow gorge through which the Mekong has flowed for approximately six hundred miles, receiving very little water from tributaries. This canal-like deep gorge crosses the whole of eastern Tibet, spanned here and there by terrifying chain-link swing bridges. Eventually it reaches Chamdo, the second-largest town in Tibet. Once a monastic city ruled by monks, Chamdo today is but a huge, bustling, ugly, polluted Chinese garrison, the headquarters of China's eastern command and the key to the control of Tibet. At Chamdo the Mekong splits in two, the southern branch flowing past the monastery of Riwoche, and the longer, northern

branch running up into Qinghai where it turns west, flowing past
Nangchen Dzong before heading toward Zadoi.

I could not hope to fully grasp or visualize such a varied and
amazing course, measured arbitrarily at between twenty-six hundred
and three thousand miles in length. The truth of the matter is that
no one has ever been allowed to follow the river along the whole of
its course; so that meant that not only was the location of the source
undetermined but so was the river's actual length.

It is impossible to establish how many millions of people inhabit
the Mekong basin, but it is certain that no other river in the world has
such importance for so many different nations. Today the Mekong is
seen by the United Nations as an axis for the economic development
of Southeast Asia. Efforts are being made to try to regulate the construction of dams, both for hydraulic power and for irrigation, not to
mention modifications to improve navigation along this lifeline to
seven nations.

The specter of war in Cambodia, of strife between Laos and
Thailand, the ancestral antagonism between China and Vietnam,
and the political instability of Burma are all obstacles to a happy set-
tlement of differences regarding how the waters of the lower
Mekong should be used.

Night being upon us, I could find no alternative to Ling's insistence
that we proceed to Zadoi in the dark.

Thus we began to negotiate the deadly ledge above the mighty
river, but it was so dark that we could no more see the river than
guess where the dreaded void began, somewhere just beyond the
sandy yellow strip of road lit by the high beams of our vehicles.
Hugging the cliff, our wheels a few feet from disaster, we wound our
way up the Mekong's gorge. Occasionally the headlights caught the
form of a lone juniper, a reminder that just enough humidity to support trees traveled up from distant Yunnan—over six hundred miles

away. These junipers were surely the only ones to be found in the whole of southern Qinghai.

I had admired these trees with enthusiasm the year before. The sight of something tall and green, however scraggly, was extraordinary after the endless barren plateau. Even more delightful was the fact that they were junipers, sacred to Tibetans in so many ways. The oldest pre-Buddhist beliefs claim the juniper tree to be the abode and symbol of the goddess of fertility, number two after the divine goddess of fortune. Juniper twigs are the symbol of life, and to break a twig is symbolic of death; the incense of juniper is the perfume of the gods, and it is the juniper branches that are burnt as incense in all the monasteries of Tibet. In the Himalayas water mills rub juniper wood back and forth against rugged stones, resulting in a pulp that is then collected in cloth sieves and dried to form thin incense sticks that are burnt night and day in chapels all over Tibet.

When sacrificing a goat to the goddess of fortune in far western Tibet, the pagan priests hold a twig of juniper in their teeth. If the twig breaks, it is taken as the worst of omens. Juniper is all important as a symbol and as an ever-present fragrance all over Tibet, yet juniper forests are all too rare.

Ancient texts and stumps indicate that juniper forests might once have covered much of Tibet not so long ago. I have seen the reduced traces of such forests in Mustang and elsewhere—gnarled trees hundreds of years old, these "pencil cedars," as some botanists call them, are slow-growing trees. Even in Beijing they are the favored trees of the ancient courtyards in palaces and monasteries. Some of these junipers are believed to be over five hundred years old.

In western Ladakh the beams and posts of houses are occasionally of juniper, forming twisted columns that recall the baroque homes of imaginary gnomes and elves. In treeless Zanskar a log of juniper is worth a fortune.

It soon began to hail, and once again we were peering anxiously into the dark, driving at a snail's pace through slush as the hailstones hammered the roof of our vehicle. I prayed that we would not find ourselves at the bottom of the gorge before we had had a chance to make a run for the source of the river.

At eleven that evening we were all exhausted when we floundered down the muddy dark main street of what seemed like a frontier town of the American West. We had reached Zadoi, the last town on the map before the Mekong trailed off into the unknown.

There is no describing the agony of sleeping in a Chinese garrison. To begin, one drives through a portal dominated by the red star of the People's Liberation Army. Be it in Madoi or Zadoi or Zaidoi, they are always the same—row upon row of one-story barracks made up of stable-like blocks of one-window, one-door cells, the basic housing unit that serves equally ill as a home for one Chinese family, a three-bed bedroom for passing travelers, or a four-bed barrack for local occupation troops. The roofs are of machine-made dirty red tiles, the walls of whitewashed adobe, the floors of the same rough planks that make up the beds upon which one lays one's sleeping bag.

All this would not be so sinister were it not for the dirt: the dusty floors, the spit-stained walls, the broken doors that won't shut and then won't open, and last but not least, the all-pervading smell of the garrison toilet—a beast whose reputation is, thank God, too well established to need description here. As if all this weren't enough, one must add the invariably cross Chinese commissars who run these prison-like camps.

We were too exhausted by our marathon across Qinghai to bother to light the yak dung that lay waiting in a tin can stove in our room.

I awoke the next morning to note through the dirty windows that it was gray outside. Having at last reached Zadoi, the end of the road, almost, I went over our next step with Sebastian and Jacques. We would seek to encounter Tibetans, monks or laymen, in the hopes of finding one or two to accompany us. Their immediate mission would be to hire horses to carry us on up the river.

My satellite map showed the dotted line of the Mekong ending some 125 to 155 miles away. I knew, however, that we should count on a 190-mile ride, approximately, as we could not hope to follow the river through all the gorges it must take.

This meant that we were faced with between eight and ten days' riding. After yet another dismal breakfast, I mustered my optimism and decided we should set off to the local monasteries because monks, I explained, are the best guides and companions. Free of family obligations, generally erudite and moral, they had in the past proven to be reliable and pleasant company.

Finding a monk seemed easy—search for a monastery. There were two near Zadoi, and it was their presence that had determined the establishment of the Chinese garrison in the area, for before the occupation there had been neither town nor hamlet in the vicinity. We were now in the heart of the Ghegi district, the pastoral homeland of the Ghegi tribe, whose horses are the best of the Nangchen breed.

Finding horses would be less of a problem than finding monks, and, as if to confirm my suspicion, we passed dozens of horse-riding Khambas leading a short string of pack ponies—some fine animals and others less so. I was convinced all we needed was a nice honest young Tibetan to help us negotiate the hire of the animals, and soon we would be rid of the two Chinese drivers and traveling off the beaten path.

We drove off in one of our vehicles to the monastery of Dzer, belonging to the Kargyu sect. To reach it we drove along a little ledge that gave us our first daylight view of the Mekong River. It was like meeting a long-lost friend. At last, what had been but a word during the preceding year was now a reality. Although we were close to the source, the river flowed fully one hundred yards wide, the swirling waters a deep, rich, milky red. Filling the riverbed, the water was high as a result of the preceding day's rains. It was also swift but it did not break, being too deep here for waves. Looking down into the gorge we saw a long cement bridge linking both halves of Zadoi sprawled out on the banks of the river.

The road we had followed to get here was now but a very narrow track that, to our surprise, entered a short tunnel in its effort to skirt a cliff dominating the great river. From the tunnel we emerged on a grassy slope, home to the white buildings of the partially restored monastery, which surrounded a squat, dark red assembly hall. In no time we were standing in front of the buildings looking out upon the magnificent panorama of rock-crested mountains. The great river ran off to the west and out of sight between two grassy slopes.

I was elated in anticipation as a crowd of young monks came to greet us. I had some trouble making myself understood until I singled out a great, burly, handsome middle-aged monk with a shaved head who spoke a form of Tibetan I could clearly understand. His smiling round face reassured me that here at last was someone I could trust with my plans.

Would he help us find some horses? I asked. He would. Soon he was riding back to town with us. We stopped upon reaching the main street, the one and only road in Zadoi, a broad earth and gravel expanse bordered by the high walls enclosing the garrison's various barracks. Scattered before little hovelly restaurants and teahouses by the side of the road were a half-dozen billiard tables. It seems that billiards is the great gift of the Chinese to Tibet. These are not full-sized billiard tables but half-size pool tables with six pockets and the same numbered balls used in America. The tables are left outside at night, protected against hail and rain with simple, ugly, clear plastic covers weighted down with stones.

Some people criticize the Chinese for having brought idleness to Tibet's youth, but it is hard to tell whether this accusation is true. It is clear that the Tibetans have little to do when visiting these dismal garrisons other than to shop and sell their butter, wool, and dried meat. In Lhasa, on the other hand, the problem of idleness among the young is on the rise, as the Chinese give the Tibetans fewer and fewer jobs. Today the garrisons even import coolies from China to perform menial tasks. As for education, in spite of what is claimed, few Tibetans get any serious schooling.

Loaded yaks and ponies circulated between the billiard tables, pushed or pulled by their owners, who had come to town from their remote camps. These herders walked at a slow pace, their legs slightly apart, plodding along with a steady assurance. Some had rosaries in their hands, others clung to yak-cloth bags as they peered through the square opening of the stalls in which cloth and hats were stacked along with stirrups and reins, thermos bottles and batteries, matches, sweets, plastic mugs, enamel flowered wash basins, plastic shoes, and a variety of aluminum pots and pans.

Our monk talked to several of the shoppers and then encountered some colleagues before explaining to us that it might prove difficult to find the horses we needed. When I asked him again if he himself would come with us, he began to explain in a circuitous manner that he could not. I encouraged him to keep searching while I decided to try to find the local Tibetan administrator. I surmised that if there were any horses to be had (and we needed about two dozen) they might be most easily collected from the nomad camps outside Zadoi.

As one man put it, "Here we have bicycles and jeeps—the cattle are in the mountains." In vain I searched the surrounding slopes with my eyes—not a tent in sight. I was no luckier in seeking out the headman of Zadoi.

"He is absent," his wife assured me, holding on to a great mastiff that roared and barked before the walled compound of a rather large house.

As I stomped back toward the bridge, to my surprise I was accosted in English.

"Good morning, sir."

I wheeled around to face a small, shriveled Tibetan with long hair. Upon discovering that he had exhausted his English vocabulary, I carried on in Tibetan, and he understood me as perfectly as I did his replies. In a second I had established that he had fled to India and lived there for several decades, having just returned to Kham. He seemed unconcerned that the Chinese knew of his escapade, and I remembered meeting several Khamba guerrillas who had returned home in their old age. The Chinese had spread the word in India and

Nepal that all Tibetans would be welcomed back. Not many refugees returned, but more did than it is generally presumed abroad. Most of those who return were disillusioned by life in India, or afraid of the prospect of being separated forever from those who remained behind. Many just want to die in the land of their birth. Some of those who return gain positions of importance in the Chinese-run Tibetan administration.

This old man seemed reliable enough, and so I asked that he help us find the horses we needed. By then it was midday, and we made for the local Muslim restaurant, where we found a rowdy crowd of Tibetan schoolteachers from the local boarding school set up to teach nomads' children. Later we were shown the building where the boys (no girls) resided as their parents roamed the plains. This was one of the few schools of its kind I had ever seen, and I took note that it had very few students, considering the population it served.

The reason is simple, explained a Tibetan teacher from Xining: In Nangchen today, as in the past, the second sons are sent to the local monastery, while the eldest sons are kept at home to help with the cattle and learn the skills of their fathers. Thus, the idea of a lay monastery-like boarding school does not have many adherents.

In the restaurant I also met an old lady who volunteered to help us; only later when she followed us everywhere acting as a rather noisy public relations manager, keeping all informed about our actions and intentions, did I realize that she was a little crazy. We enjoyed no privacy as our little group was constantly followed by dozens of children who stared at us, amazed, as though we were the first foreigners to reach Zadoi.

7

The War of Kanting

⌘

Very few foreigners have ever been allowed into Zadoi. Apart from my own visit the preceding year, a British zoologist had come recently, and the *National Geographic* writer-photographer team of Thomas O'Neill and Mike Yamashita had arrived in late spring of 1992 on the first leg of a journey they hoped would take them down the entire course of the Mekong. They traveled through Zadoi as far up the Mekong as possible, led by a Tibetan nomad who, upon arrival at a certain snow field, told them they had reached the sacred spring, one of the sources of the Mekong. In a February 1993 article in *National Geographic*, O'Neill wrote, "We rode behind the mountain and found in a shallow draw a sheet of ice some 300 yards long—shaped like an hourglass. Crouching down on the frozen surface, I could hear below a trickle of water. It was the beginning notes of the Mekong. Mike and I were, as far as I can discover, the first Western journalists to hear them."

This rather loose claim to finding the source was tempered when their guide explained, "There are two sources. There is the mountain source high on a glacier—no one goes there—and there is a spiritual source behind a holy mountain." The journalists and their guide had reached the spiritual source. No other details were given, such as latitude or longitude, or even the name of the mountain. Prior to my own departure, I had called the National Geographic Society to obtain details of O'Neill's findings, and had been informed that his claim to the discovery of the source had not been pressed or recorded. Moreover, the photographs published with the article, which showed the Tangla range to the southwest, seem to suggest that the journalists had been misled by their guide. It was clear to me that the true source had yet to be found.

As the day slipped by I began to wonder whether we would fare any better. The old Khamba from India returned to tell us that he had been unable to find any horses, and that our only hope was to secure them directly from the nomads in the high pastures, wherever they might be. It might take several days just to locate them. This rather discouraging news was followed by a final declaration from the handsome monk that neither he nor any of his colleagues of the Kargyu monastery could accompany us. Without a local to help us gain the nomads' trust, we stood little chance of hiring any animals at all.

I decided, therefore, that we should try to meet the abbot of Zadoi's other monastery, a larger institution of the reformed yellow-hat sect of the Dalai Lama. This other monastery stood several miles away up a trail inaccessible to our vehicles, so we were directed to the abbot's town residence. Panting and out of breath (Zadoi is 15,400 feet above sea level), we entered a long, one-story mud-brick building overlooking the town. Wooden latticework windows faced a walled yard. Atop a tall pole, a white prayer flag fluttered. A young man wearing Western clothes invited us in and offered us cups of salty tea, asking us to sit down on low-lying mattresses covered with blue, orange, and white Tibetan carpets. The young man, the lama's secretary, informed us that His Holiness was away on a pilgrimage. He said he doubted that anyone could accompany us in search of the *chu-go* (which means literally "the head of the river," as opposed to the word *chu-mik*, which means "water eye, or spring").

In talking to the erudite young man, who spoke the sophisticated Tibetan of Lhasa, I began to grasp how much I had taken it for granted that everyone in Tibet would understand what I meant by the source of the Mekong. Even in Europe, there had been discussion about what could rightly be claimed as the source of any given river.

Was it the spring farthest from the sea, or the end of the branch with the greatest flow of water? Or was it simply the historical source, the source recognized by the locals? The official source of the Mississippi is neither the one farthest from the sea (that being the source of the Missouri River) nor the branch with the greatest flow. In the case of the Mississippi it is the historical, traditional source that has prevailed in atlases, as opposed to what geographers and hydrologists might have preferred.

My knowledge of Tibetan was essential in determining the historical source of the Mekong, but it would probably not help me to explain to the local people what modern geographers consider to be the true source of a river. To begin with, I would have to explain what a sea was. The only seas the Tibetans in this area know are large lakes, the only oceans, the mythical ocean that surrounds Mount Meru, the epicenter of a universe that the local lamas believe to be flat and formed in the shape of the shoulder blade of a sheep. Needless to say, nobody here knew how far the Dza-chu actually flowed or that it was called Lancang by the Chinese and Mekong by us.

All this was practically impossible to explain, and, no doubt, in the end, it would be up to us alone to travel along the Dza-chu, measuring the flow of each tributary as we went to establish which was the principal course of the river. We would carry out this quest in consultation with our satellite maps and with the help of any local nomads we were lucky enough to encounter, but we were really, in the strictest sense, on our own.

I was at a loss about hiring horses when someone told us that a track traveling south from Zadoi, up the valley of a river called the A, would lead us to a motorable trail that could, in turn, bring us over several high passes to a place called Moyun located on the upper Mekong. Further questioning and brief consultation of a Chinese map in the compound where we had slept confirmed that there had been, at one time, a track going up the A River; from there another cut back north to the Mekong and Moyun. I knew we couldn't trust these maps, and when I inquired about the road, the local Chinese official claimed it was impassable because of the recent rain. Next, our drivers made some inquiries of their own and announced that it would be madness to take this dirt track because we would only get stuck.

Since the prospect of finding horses in Zadoi seemed slight, I was keen to get out and try the trail, were it only a few miles to the first nomad camps. Being stuck in the high pastures seemed a better fate than being stranded in Zadoi, a town I had begun to see as increasingly sinister.

"But Mr. Psl, we do not have enough petrol, and the Public Security Bureau . . ." I didn't let Ling finish his sentence.

"We must get some petrol right away, and you know as well as I do that we have permission to go to the source, wherever that may be."

Ling looked desperate and went into a huddle with the drivers. He then pronounced the cars too heavily loaded, whereupon I suggested that we leave behind some of our provisions and whatever else we could part with. That done, I again insisted that we go and find petrol right away.

It proved no easy matter. First we hunted down the only man who could give us the necessary written permission to buy petrol, a rare and expensive commodity there, thousands of miles away from the nearest oil well. Letter in hand, we drove to a huge hangar where a man rummaged among heavy folded black yak-hair tents to find a funnel, through which he finally pumped petrol from a rusty barrel into our jerry cans. This accomplished, puffing away and exhausted, with Sebastian and Jacques lugging our camera equipment, we again crossed the great bridge over the Mekong in a final attempt to talk to the headman of Zadoi. We still hoped that he might find us a reliable local man to help us on our way.

The headman had not returned, but as we marched back up the main dusty road of the town, we bumped into the old "English-speaking" Khamba and then into our monk friend. It seemed we knew everybody, and it was certain that everybody in town knew about us and our search for horses. When I addressed a small crowd of Tibetans who followed me into a general store, they shot back, "How much will you pay?" I avoided a direct answer. "Who has horses here?" I asked; none did.

Sitting on the cement steps of the porch of the barracks, I again had a long argument with Ling about the necessity of our setting off as soon as possible.

I understood that Ling was too young to impose his views on our drivers, who were at least ten years older than he and who had no intention of being told by a greenhorn where they should go and what they could do. Ling was at their mercy, and the drivers were not very amiable fellows.

In China there is a golden rule that probably stems from generations of living at near-starvation level: In a world where dog eats dog, if you have any leverage on a person, you use it for all it's worth. Bullying, blackmail, and extortion are common practices in many parts of China. Even before the Communists and their rigid bureaucracy, the Chinese civil servant was a true tyrant if he had any leverage. Our drivers knew they had the upper hand with Ling—they might even have been his superiors in the complex internal hierarchy of the Qinghai Mountaineering Association.

Try as I could to convince everyone of the urgency of our mission, I couldn't help feeling a little bit foolish. What would Burton or Speeke or those other explorers think of my paltry outfit, and of my dependence on recalcitrant drivers? I liked to think that what I had acquired from a year at the Harvard Business School was a special skill at haggling, but my negotiations with these jeep drivers were a total failure.

As it happens, I hated jeeps, Land Cruisers, Range Rovers, and every other type of four-wheel-drive vehicle. I am strictly what you might call a foot and horse man. I've always ridiculed the latter-day Marlboro-man explorer, smoking cigarettes in his muddy Range Rover, roof stacked with spare tires. Since there are no roads into the unknown, such vehicles are really made for safari parks or for driving to suburban supermarkets. For my part, I wanted nothing so much as to get rid of our vehicles and their drivers in exchange for the only really effective means of off-road transport: the overhead-twin-eared, four-legged, lead-free, hay-eating *Equus caballus.* We were, after all, in the home country of the finest breed of horse in the whole of the Tibetan highlands. But where *were* the horses?

Breathing the fetid air of our compound, I was negotiating our departure for the following morning when two civilized-looking young Chinese men drove up in a jeep. They weren't policemen looking for us, as I thought they might be at first, but part of the backup team of our rivals—members of the Sino-Japanese expedition to the headwaters of the Mekong. They didn't immediately identify themselves, however, and it was only later that we discovered who they were. We learned, nevertheless, that their Japanese team was from the Department of Agriculture of the University of Tokyo and was currently ten days ahead of us, information that did little to boost our morale. Even Sebastian lost his good humor momentarily, and Jacques, always in the same state of calm, seemed for a fleeting moment positively catatonic.

It might have been advisable to rest a few days, but we couldn't afford to hang around, even though we didn't know for sure that the Japanese were also looking for the river's source.

Dutreuil de Rhins, ill-fated leader of 1894 French expedition that got the closest to the source of the Mekong. He was shot by Khamba villagers over a question of stolen horses.

The death of Dutreuil de Rhins as his servants flee. His companion Grenard tried in vain to carry him off under heavy fire. He may have been thrown alive in a nearby stream.

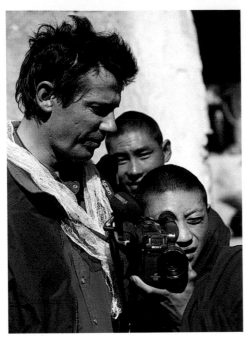

*F*ilmmaker and doctor Jacques Falck was ever busy shooting or attending potential patients.

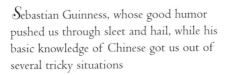

*S*ebastian Guinness, whose good humor pushed us through sleet and hail, while his basic knowledge of Chinese got us out of several tricky situations

*L*ess than 100 miles from the source of the Mekong, our camp, exposed to the wind, faces a bleak horizon, home to the proud though mostly unknown and generally invisible nomads of Ghegi. (SEBASTIAN GUINNESS)

$\mathcal{A}$ tent of prayer flags, a fluttering cathedral to the horse god of the winds, one of the few signs of life on the harsh highlands of the very top of the "roof of the world"

"Wild and accustomed to living by loot"— so the Goloks have been described by the few Europeans to survive a visit to their elusive homeland in the Amne Machin range.

Every family has at least one member who is a scholar, sent to study several months or more each year at the local monastery. Back home they teach their brothers and sometimes their sisters how to read and write. These monks have raised the intellectual standing of most Tibetan peasants high above that of their neighbors.

A fine family of nomads from Amdo. The man is wearing the same top-knot as his ancestors 2,000 years ago, a hairstyle that crowns all the soldiers of the famous army of clay of the Universal Emperor's tomb in Xian.

*C*arrying red silt, two hundred miles from its source, the Mekong is already a powerful river.

*N*angchen Gar, the capital of the vast, sprawling nomad kingdom of Nangchen, is but a campsite for the chiefs of the land's twelve tribes who come here to pay homage to their king, camping beside the monastery and giant stone pile cairn.
(SEBASTIAN GUINNESS)

*T*he monastery of Nangchen Gar, one of the seventy-two monasteries of Nangchen, a kingdom not yet fully explored

Riding out of nowhere on a small but well-formed miniature horse, this nomad from Nangchen comes to see what we are up to.

Michel Peissel straddling the infant Mekong just below the spring field, it's source, which rises behind him to the Rupsa-la pass.

Similar to the mysterious Horse No. 2 of Stone Age cave drawings, the isolated Riwoche horse, locked in by high passes, has not evolved like its brothers, the other domesticated horses of the world. The drawing here is of horses from the recently (1994) discovered Chauvet Cave in southern France.

At 9:30 A.M. the following morning we drove out of Zadoi across the mighty two-lane cement bridge over the Mekong. Our hopes renewed, we looked west up the gorge from which the river emerged, its red waters flowing swiftly, at the beginning of their twenty-seven-hundred-mile course to the South China Sea.

If rivers and their valleys form ideal routes of travel in the lowlands, they are far from that in the mountains. We could no more follow the river that slithered out of sight between two rusty cliffs of rock than we could say we knew exactly where it led.

A mile out of Zadoi we turned south and began to climb up a narrow rocky valley dwarfed by pointed gray peaks. The road was nothing more than two ruts of caked earth cutting across the grassy landscape with no trace of tires. Could it be that the road was closed, after all?

I was happy to be leaving Zadoi, and now especially so, as I saw coming toward us a large herd of yaks driven by three handsome young men on horseback, each with a rifle over his shoulder. We stopped as the burly yaks, loaded with great bales of sheep's wool, brushed past us, prodded forward by the cries and whistles of the arrogant Khamba cowboys. They were off to sell the wool in Zadoi, and the fact that they were armed surprised my companions, not used to seeing men with rifles who weren't hunters or soldiers. Mounted on the fine local horses, draped in ample sheepskin gowns with one sleeve hanging at their backs, fox-fur hats on their heads, the men with their rifles cut romantic, aggressive figures. The yaks advanced ten abreast, jostling each other in a disorderly fashion.

The men had long hair and Amerindian features, thin noses, and slightly slanted dark eyes. For once Ling was perhaps right—there was good reason to fear such men. Even if the Khambas had officially been defeated, they hadn't laid down their arms. In fact, in 1953, efforts by the Chinese to disarm the Khambas had been what triggered the War of Kanting, the secret war that pitted the Khambas of eastern Tibet against the People's Liberation Army.

From firsthand reports collected some years later in Mustang, the Khamba guerrillas' last headquarters, I had patched together the first account of that war. Now, in the heart of the remotest province of Kham, I hoped to find the sites of the unsung battles, and to meet the last survivors of the secret war that had raged for six years in the mountains.

Judging from news of the recurrent uprisings and the arrogance of many of the men we had met, the Khambas of Nangchen have not, it seems, entirely given up their struggle.

If the men of Kham proved to be excellent warriors, the reason wasn't the quality of their arms—in 1953, most of them had only archaic muzzle-loading matchlocks—nor were their successes due to discipline and training.

Looking at the self-assured, handsome men brushing past our vehicles with their rifles, I felt that the secret to their endurance might be found in the very nature of their life on the high plateau.

The nomads' survival depends on their herds, whose size depends, in turn, on the amount of territory they control. To have and keep a definite territory, one must be able to defend it. Whole books have been written about the "territorial imperative," yet little attention has been paid to the difference between a herder's notion of territory and that of agricultural societies.

The earliest written Tibetan documents tell us that the nomadic tribes were arrogant and proud, yet dedicated to their leaders, who were rarely questioned. Loyalty to them was instilled and maintained by pledges of allegiance that were the very basis of the tribes' military strength. This social system stands in contrast to that of agricultural communities of the same period, whose leaders' power was derived from their ownership of land and of serfs, not from the trust of their kinsmen. The nomads ruled over kinsmen as relatives; the agriculturalists ruled over farmers as subjects. Therein lies one of the capital advantages of nomadic warrior societies over feudal agricultural states run by landed princes. Machiavelli, no doubt the best analyst of what constituted the power of princes, clearly appreciated that their vulnerability lay in the fact that any loss of their land meant the loss of their subjects. Farmers changed their allegiances as fast as their fields changed hands. Not so with the nomads, for their land belonged not to the prince but to the tribe. Traditionally the leaders of each Tibetan nomad tribe owned 10 percent of all the animals belonging to the tribe, and the tribesmen were to care for these animals as their own. To guarantee that there was no favoritism, the chief could choose any animals he wished (presumably the best). This was an accepted custom, and in return the chief was responsible for the tribe's defense, and for the observation of tribal laws.

Rifles were the private property of the nomads, necessary to protect their cattle from wolves, snow leopards, bears, and rustlers from neighboring tribes. Needless to say, it was now advisable for us to be on the good side of these armed men before us. (A lesson poor Dutreuil de Rhins learned the hard way just before he died.) I tried to feel at ease, protected, I hoped, by the fact that I spoke Tibetan.

Having passed the first group of Khambas, we ran into another herd of yaks blocking our way, nomads on their way back from Zadoi, their animals laden with brown and white goat's-wool bags of barley. It was useless to try to overtake them because the road ran between a cliff and the raging waters of the A River. I decided, instead, to get out of the jeep and walk along with them. They were happy to chat with me and asked the usual questions: Had I met the Dalai Lama? Where had I learned Tibetan? Where was I from? And, of course, what were we doing here? When I said that I had taken my first Tibetan lesson from the elder brother of the Dalai Lama, Tagster Rimpoche himself, I was looked upon with open admiration, and that was heightened when I explained I had also met the Dalai Lama.

The encounter, which occurred by accident and was anything but glamorous, was at the Harvard Center for World Religions in 1980. Over the years I had never sought to meet His Holiness, mostly to avoid being noticed by the various intelligence services that spied on his activities in India. I knew the Dalai Lama must have been aware of my book on the Khambas, a book in which I had perhaps been a little bit too critical in condemning the lenient attitude of his entourage toward the Chinese between 1950 and 1959, not to speak of his own.

When we were introduced, His Holiness jumped in surprise, but then he and his assistants and I had an animated conversation. I asked for his forgiveness for having been a little bit harsh in an article published that very same day in the *Boston Globe,* in which I wrote that "the Dalai Lama must be reminded that it is his duty to instigate political action for the liberation of Tibet during this visit to the United States." The Carter administration had demanded that he not make any political statements during his visit, and he had agreed not to, which I and others had considered unacceptable, given that he was the political leader of Tibet.

The Dalai Lama's reluctance to oppose the Chinese has caused much ill will in Tibet and elsewhere, especially between his entourage and the Khambas, who had to fight the People's Liberation Army alone between 1950 and 1959, while the Dalai Lama and his entourage, ministers, abbots, and the aristocrats of Lhasa, collaborated with the Chinese in order to hold onto their privileges.

The rift between Khambas and Lhasans was an old one, stemming from the Khambas' longtime refusal to recognize the Dalai Lama as their political leader. The rift was deepened after October 6, 1950, the date the Chinese invaded Tibet by attacking Denko, a garrison on the border of Kham, and Amdo, ninety-five miles southeast of Jeykundo. Under the leadership of the local Khamba military chief, Muha, the Tibetans counterattacked and momentarily stalled the Chinese.

In the meantime, the Dalai Lama sent a minister by the name of Nawang Nagbo to Chamdo, the Khamba capital of eastern Tibet. Nagbo the traitor, as he is now generally known, was a firm believer that Tibet should cooperate with the Communists. When news reached him that Chinese troops had overrun Denko and were head-

ing for Chamdo, Nagbo refused to open the city's arsenal and arm
the local Khambas in their own defense. Instead, he blew up the arsenal and fled the town. Later he gave himself up to Chinese troops
without a struggle—to troops that had entered Tibet unopposed.
Seven months later in Beijing he signed the infamous seventeen-
point agreement, a sellout allowing the Chinese to enter Lhasa and
the Lhasans to keep their privileges under Chinese rule, but at the
cost of their independence.

Then sixteen years old, the Dalai Lama had been unable to
muster the support he needed to oppose his minister or, for that
matter, to expose the Chinese, who falsified the Tibetan seal that was
stamped on the seventeen-point agreement.

When, by 1953, the Chinese had consolidated their foothold in
Tibet by building strategic roads, they believed that the time had
come for the application of Communist style reforms in the territo
ries no longer under the Dalai Lama's control. The reforms in question called for the destitution of the traditional tribal leaders of
Kham and Amdo, who were declared to be "corrupt enemies of the
people." Then came the attacks on monks and monasteries, those
peddlers of religion, the "opiate of the masses."

The Khambas, as we have seen, were quick to rise up against such
"reforms" and back their tribal leaders. The day the War of Kanting
broke out, appeals were sent to the Dalai Lama and to his government for support. The answer was more than disappointing: Lhasa
advised the Khambas to lay down their arms and try to get along
with the enemy.

I have recorded elsewhere the atrocities the Khambas had to suffer, and the long and bitter efforts they made to get the Dalai Lama
to back their struggle.

Having seen their country invaded and their monasteries
destroyed, the Khamba guerrilla fighters took refuge in the mountains and great plains, from which they continued to harass the Chinese. Outnumbered, outgunned, and forever chased farther into the
barren wilds, the Khambas were constantly on the run as the Chinese

slowly extended their network of roads, forts, and garrisons, flooding the countryside with three hundred thousand troops.

By early 1959 the Khamba soldiers, along with thousands of civilians, were forced to seek refuge in the Dalai Lama's "Tibetan Autonomous Region," which had remained neutral. Lhasa, the holy city, was by then full of angry, frustrated, and armed Khamba freedom fighters—men hoping that the Lhasans would at long last join them in their desperate struggle against the Chinese.

In February, the hopes of the Khambas were relayed to the Dalai Lama himself by the much-esteemed young lama of Jeykundo, Chime Yudong, who had reached Lhasa after fighting his way across Nangchen. His escort of one thousand Khambas had been machine-gunned from the air by Chinese planes and repeatedly ambushed, and over half his men had been killed. As spokesman for all the Khambas, Chime Yudong asked to be received by the Dalai Lama to make the ultimate plea for assistance.

Their meeting on February 16, 1959, as recorded by the British journalist-author Noel Barber in his book, *The Land of Lost Content*, was one of the most dramatic and perhaps tragic events in Tibet's recent history. Here were two young men, both from Amdo, both reincarnated monks, who could not have been more different. One of them, Lama Chime, had for six years opposed the Chinese and had seen them bomb and destroy monasteries from the air, killing thousands more in murderous raids in the mountains, while women and children were imprisoned or deported to China. The other, the Dalai Lama, was a pious and relatively shy young man of twenty-five who was torn between his religious duty to oppose all violence and his moral obligation to save his countrymen from Chinese aggression. Since 1950 the Dalai Lama had lived a sheltered yet difficult life. Courted by the Chinese, he had involuntarily been drawn into tacit collaboration with their plan to seize the whole of Tibet.

The young Dalai Lama had, to a certain extent, been brainwashed by the Chinese. While in Beijing in 1954, he was induced to write an ode to the glory of Mao in which he compared the Communist leader, murderer of so many Tibetans, to "a person like the sun that enlightens the world, born of an infinite number of good deeds."

In the desperate interview the young lama of Jeykundo went over the long list of horrors of the War of Kanting, and then begged the Dalai Lama to send troops, at long last, to help defend the people of Kham. Noel Barber reports that the Dalai Lama refused categorically.

Upset and angry, the lama of Jeykundo dared say that "he did not believe the ministers of His Holiness's cabinet understood what exactly the Chinese were doing to the people of Amdo and Kham." In fact, as the Dalai Lama's own memoirs confirm, he and his ministers were quite aware of the situation. The Dalai Lama was torn, as he declared himself, between his desire to do something and his aversion for violence. In the end, he offered no help whatsoever.

Deeply upset and disappointed, the lama of Jeykundo complained that after six years of fighting alone to preserve their religion and customs, his people believed the Tibetan government didn't give a damn about them. The courageous young Khamba made a last desperate appeal, stating that he couldn't just stay there and watch as his people were being murdered. To this the Dalai Lama replied:

"I can do nothing. Your people [meaning the Khambas] should show more tolerance and try and observe the seventeen-point agreement. I admire the courage of the Khambas but their deeds cause great harm to those of us who are seeking to coexist with the Chinese."

The Khambas now realized that they had no alternative but to force the Dalai Lama and his government to oppose China. Thus the stage was set for the rebellion of Lhasa—a Khamba-led rebellion of the people of Lhasa against both the Dalai Lama's cabinet and the Chinese invaders.

The event that triggered the rebellion occurred just two weeks after the disappointing interview: the Dalai Lama was invited by the Chinese to attend a play inside their headquarters in Lhasa. When, on the first of March, two Chinese soldiers asked the Dalai Lama to fix a date for his attendance, rumors spread that the Chinese were planning to kidnap him. On the ninth of March, a day before the show was to take place, the Khambas, followed by crowds of Lhasans, surrounded the summer residence of the Dalai Lama to prevent the god-king from going. Their fear was further justified when the Chinese, at the last minute, requested that the Dalai Lama attend without his usual bodyguards.

The Khambas' anger was directed particularly at the Dalai Lama's ministers, among whom Nagbo the traitor—infamous for blowing up the Chamdo arsenal nine years before—was still prominent. Sensing the Khambas' hostility, Nagbo slipped out of the summer palace where the ministers resided and sought asylum with the Chinese. Another minister, Samdrup Photrang, also known for his pro-Chinese leanings, had his jeep overturned as he drove to the summer palace and barely escaped with his life. A third Chinese sympathizer called Phakpa was not as fortunate. He was killed, stabbed to death by a Khamba, and his body was paraded in the streets of Lhasa.

The rebels held the Dalai Lama's government hostage in his summer palace and proclaimed themselves a Liberation Committee for Tibet. They declared the seventeen-point agreement void and dissolved the Dalai Lama's cabinet, placing four of his ministers under house arrest. Desperate, the Dalai Lama wrote the first of three letters to General Tang, the Chinese military chief, in which he expressed his regret and condemnation of the actions of the Khambas. In the letters he assured the Chinese that he was trying to calm the evil reactionaries and would take refuge in the Chinese compound as soon as he could elude the rebels.

These letters were later the source of much controversy, in that they confirmed that the Dalai Lama was held by the Khambas against his will, as the Chinese claimed, and it exposed for all the world the deep rift between the Dalai Lama's entourage and the people of Tibet.

The Dalai Lama was without a doubt a hostage of the Khambas in his own palace, and his captors smuggled him out of Lhasa to make certain that he couldn't strike another agreement with the Chinese. They took him (he didn't flee) to southern Tibet, where, at Lhünze Dzong, they persuaded him at long last to declare Tibet at war with China. The newly unified Tibet included Kham and Amdo, alongside central Tibet, as it had in the past.

Only after the formal declaration of war, followed by the appropriate dances and protocol, was it decided that the Dalai Lama should leave Lhünze Dzong for India.

The revolution was short-lived. In less than two years the Chinese succeeded in chasing the Khamba guerrillas out of central Tibet. Their ally Nagbo was placed at the head of a committee for the newly designated Autonomous Region of Tibet, a puppet of the Chinese government, of which the Panchen Lama was later made titular head. Tibet had lost its independence. The Khamba guerrillas who had survived regrouped in the little Tibetan principality of Mustang in northwest Nepal, from where, with aid and advisers from the CIA, they harassed Chinese convoys just over the border until 1972. That year Nixon met with Mao Zedong, and the CIA abandoned the Khambas, many of whom were killed in a joint Sino-Nepalese military operation to clear them out of Nepal. Some of the survivors joined the Indian frontier forces, but others committed suicide when the exiled Dalai Lama asked them once again to lay down their arms.

Such was the desperate twenty-year struggle of the Khambas to uphold their faith and pride. Yet as I had observed in several journeys to Kham, the spirit that had animated their fathers was still very much alive. Now, however, as we neared what had been one of the most advanced strategic roads built to wipe out all Khamba resistance, I wondered whether the Chinese had finally won the war.

I walked for a long time in the company of the second caravan we encountered, talking to the men and joking with the young women. With rifles and fine horses and grazing grounds that extended for thousands of miles, they were, I realized, barring their complete extinction, still free of most of the constraints of modern civilization.

We bumped on along the trail, overtaking at last the caravan loaded with barley—enough grain for several families for a year. Three hours out of Zadoi, we were advancing only as fast as a horse's plodding gait. We had begun to rise up a very narrow ledge, the left wheels of our vehicle just inches from a terrible drop, when suddenly the motor coughed and stalled.

It refused to start up again. In minutes both drivers were under the hood talking excitedly. I was seriously worried. All along I had wondered what we would do if we had a breakdown. The simple answer was to keep going in one jeep, but I knew the drivers wouldn't agree to that. The other solution was to wait for help, which might never come. The best solution would be for a few of us to find some horses to carry on, but I knew Ling well enough to appreciate that he would oppose our going on ahead without the others. Since we left Jeykundo, his reluctant manner had clearly showed that he wasn't interested in what we were trying to do.

While the drivers played with the motor, I went off some distance to take a reading of the GPS. We were at 15,600 feet and surrounded by pointed, rock-crested peaks, one of which was so conical as to seem volcanic. We were heading for a pass, but without a map showing the trail it was difficult to figure out where we were exactly. Only by transferring the GPS reading onto our map drawn from satellite photographs could we determine our location. The wind made it almost impossible to perform such an operation, however, and all I could do was huddle at the front of the jeep and proffer some lame advice about the motor.

Fortunately, the engine started again. Apparently a condenser had blown, but Sebastian, not being fluent in Chinese mechanical terms, was unable to offer details. The breakdown had been a sobering experience, which we prayed wouldn't further undermine the morale of our recalcitrant crew. One driver reiterated that it was late in the season to be on this road and that, were it to snow, our vehicles might not be able to get out for a full year—a prospect that made Ling turn white, but which I thought an exaggeration. It was, after all, only the beginning of September, and the Indian summer would soon be on us. In fact, to our knowledge, there were no weather charts for this remote region. I had tried in vain to secure anything like an indication of rainfall and temperatures for southern Qinghai. We were soon to find out that the higher portion of the great plateau has a very strange climate all its own, one that, at this time of year, is characterized by hail and thunderstorms whose true level of violence we had yet to experience.

Soon after our breakdown we reached the summit of a pass and began a descent beneath great cliffs, one of which harbored a huge cave halfway up its face. We were slowly descending toward a barren valley, fenced in on all sides by staggering red and garnet mountains coated in patches of pale green grass, a color combination so startling as to form one of the most pleasing and grandiose landscapes I had ever seen. The color of the earth reminded me of heather, and the combinations of the deep pinky-red with the green grass evoked, albeit on a far more dramatic scale, the mountainous moors of Scotland.

Descending from the pass we looked back and saw another mountain, crested with towering bastions of rock, which we recognized from a photograph taken by Yamashita for the *National Geographic* article in which it was claimed, erroneously as it turned out, that he and O'Neill had found the source of the Mekong in 1992.

As we reached the valley floor we sighted a blue fox. It wasn't frightened in the least by our noisy arrival, and we were able to get out and film it as it trotted off on its errands, letting out a yelp before disappearing into a burrow. I had always believed the term *blue* to be an exaggeration, but there was no denying that that was the color of its tail. Was it a seasonal hue? Did it disappear on the pelts of dead animals? Whatever the case, I had never seen a fur hat made of blue fox on the heads of the Khambas or a blue fur stole around the neck of a Western lady.

We next found ourselves driving up a broad valley bordered by the incredible red mountains with contrasting green cloaks of grass.

Suddenly I spotted a herd of horses in the distance, a romantic sight in the majestic surroundings. A few miles on I glimpsed another herd of nearly thirty horses galloping up a steep grassy slope on the other side of the river. They were close enough for me to establish that they were of the typical fine Nangchen conformation: elegant animals with slim limbs, straight backs, long flowing manes and tails and, of course, with the characteristic barrel chest and huge lungs that gave them a body all too comically proportioned in relation to their limbs.

Until roughly a hundred years ago in Europe and America, what constituted a good horse was a subject that was as important as, let's say, the relative worth of various jet fighters today. The horse was for so many centuries not only the backbone of all armies—a strategic instrument—but also the essential mode of transport of everything from humans to building materials. The improvement of horse stock and horse blood was at the heart of the subject of countless treaties, studies, and experiments, with the result that in Europe and America there are literally hundreds of different breeds of horses. Some are natural breeds that have developed on their own in isolation in remote areas, but most often they have been created by man with a specific objective in mind: ponies to work underground in mines; horses to wage war, bred for a behavioral gene that makes them freeze instead of bolt when they hear an explosion; horses raised for speed or jumping, to pull heavy loads, or for endurance over long distances. They vary from the tall Clydesdale dray horse bred in Scotland to eighteen hands (six feet)—"to meet the demands of the Industrial Revolution," as one author put it—to the miniature horses bred in Argentina, which, at about six hands (2 feet), are too small to ride.

In the age of genetic engineering, we tend to forget that horse breeders were way ahead of us in the art of manipulating DNA. Over the centuries, close observation had allowed European and Arab breeders to determine the characteristics that made a horse fast, among them a slim, long neck, large nostrils, high withers, long cannons, and oval hooves. Speed became a primary factor at the beginning of the last century when the European thoroughbred, or racehorse, was developed by crossing Arab thoroughbreds with horses from Russian Turkestan, Galway pony racers, and other assorted British and French horses.

What is certain is that the best horses, be they Arabian or Turkomene, come from areas with little grass, where men were forced to feed and take care of them, and eventually to stable them, making it easier to select individual mares and stallions to be bred. This interference, or assistance, of man in the selection of stallions and mares is the cornerstone of fine breeding, and was unknown in the grasslands of Mongolia, for instance, where the horses ran free and bred according to their fancy. As a result, the Mongolian pony is a rather crude animal compared to the Arabian, or to the Caspian miniature thoroughbred, which was discovered in 1960 and which, it is believed, was developed by the Persians to pull their war chariots.

What is interesting about the Nangchen horse is that, like the Arabian, it is a selected horse, because on the highest Tibetan plateau, there is not much grass and so many wolves and snow leopards that it could not have survived without the constant intervention of man. As it is, the nomads of Nangchen make coats for the young foals and feed their horses cheese, and occasionally meat, even when they themselves have little to eat. Most important, they choose the mares and stallions they wish to see reproduce, to meet their needs as yak herders and as mounted warriors who like nothing better than a good race.

The end result is that the Nangchen horse is one of the few thoroughbred horses of the Far East, and possibly the finest.

It is a horse with a long and very interesting history. As we drove, we admired what looked to us like wild horses galloping on the mountainsides. It was hard to believe that fourteen centuries ago, when Europe was in the darkest of the Dark Ages, the nomad inhabitants of this very region were already busy selecting and raising horses. More amazing still, they were writing about them—a fact that came to light in 1907, when Sir Aurel Stein made what must be considered one of the most remarkable archaeological finds of the century. In the deserts of Xinjiang he discovered four tons of ancient documents hidden in a walled-off section of a cave in the ancient cliff-face monastery of Tun-huang. There were manuscripts and painted scrolls that had been sealed up since the tenth century. The cave had just been opened by a Taoist monk, who, after much negotiation, agreed to sell some of the priceless manuscripts to Stein. A large portion of the rest was later purchased by the French linguist Paul Pelliot, leaving a remainder to be split up, sold piecemeal, pilfered, and lost.

This extraordinary treasure of ancient documents included texts in three forgotten languages and even a book dating from 868, which is believed to be the oldest printed book in existence. Most of the manuscripts were in Tibetan and Chinese because the caves of Tun-huang were a part of what had been Tibet in the ninth century. Tun-huang is located on the famous Horse Road, which links China to Turkestan—Turkestan being, with Arabia, home to the finest horses of the Middle East.

Among the documents discovered in Tun-huang were several thousand-year-old treatises relating to horse care and horse breeding in Tibet. Many of these documents were classified, translated, and analyzed by Anne Marie Blondeau, with whom I had attended the lectures of Professor Rolf Stein (no relation to Aurel), the eminent French Tibetan scholar and linguist.

Needless to say, I was fascinated by Dr. Blondeau's thesis on horse breeding and care in ancient Tibet. In the Tun-huang documents, it was clearly established that the Tibetans had been keen horse breeders, and that for ten centuries or more the blood stock of the Tibetan horses was very different from that of the horses of the Asa, an ancient Turkic people inhabiting the Silk (or Horse) Road. In other words, the blood stock of Tibet's horses was not Turkic or Arabic, but indigenous.

When I first read Blondeau's translations in 1992 and began my own field research into Tibetan breeds, it was still generally assumed by equine zoologists worldwide that the only horses of Tibet were the crude ponies of the Himalayas—ponies accurately described as "rough, hardy, rustic small creatures." No one had bothered to search beyond the mixed-blood mountain ponies for the finer breeds that Tibet had to offer, horses whose reputations had once spread far and wide, east to China and west to distant Pakistan.

In 1983 I visited the northern Pakistan province of Baltistan (the ancient Tibetan province of Bolor), where the Muslim population still speaks an archaic strain of Tibetan. Locals there told me that the best horses came not from nearby Chinese Turkestan or Samarkand but from Siling—"Siling" being the ancient way of pronouncing "Xining."

Which horse was this? I wondered. Had it survived in Tibet for thirteen hundred years since it was introduced in the seventh century into northern Pakistan, or was it simply a horse from Xining, the capital of Qinghai—in other words, just a horse from the Horse Road, one with Turkish, Arabian, or Mongolian blood? The only other possibility I could think of was that it was a specifically Tibetan thoroughbred that had been lost to history, that came not from Xining but from Amdo (the term *Sining,* or *Siling,* often being used to describe the whole region).

It had taken me three journeys traveling all over Tibet to answer this question. One by one I had eliminated the various sub-breeds of horses found in the border regions, horses whose bloodlines were mixed with those of India, Bhutan, China, Mongolia, or Turkestan. This left six specifically Tibetan breeds, and even some of those might have had Mongol blood in them, introduced by the many Mongol incursions into Tibet starting in the sixteenth century.

Only in 1993 did it become clear to me that the Nangchen horse was the finest and the most unusual Tibetan horse, the "Siling" horse mentioned to me in Pakistan.

It was the finest because its conformation matched what Europeans and Arabs alike have come to agree constitutes an excellent horse—the thin neck, essential for speed; the large nostrils; the fine-haired forelock and long mane and tail; the flat back and straight hocks. It was the finest also for its spirit and stamina, to which I could attest after a five-day, 250-mile ride I had made the preceding year over three passes above sixteen thousand feet. With seven horses selected near Nangchen Dzong, I had ridden up and out of the middle valley of the upper Mekong to visit Nangchen Gar, the virtually impregnable ancient camp of the kings of Nangchen. I had traveled up and over the sixteen-thousand-foot rim of the circus of mountains that hem in the royal campsite. The horses actually galloped to the summit, fighting to be the first, a remarkable—not to say staggering—feat at an altitude where most beasts would be utterly out of breath.

Now, as I looked at the horses before us, I dreamt of introducing them to Europe. At the Animal Health Trust in Newmarket, England, and at the INRA, the French agronomical research institute, I had spent many hours describing the Nangchen horse, trying to establish with scholars what other research should be carried out by specialists in the field to further pinpoint the breed. They wanted to know its heart size, its volume of blood, its cardiac rhythms and regulation rates, and a hundred other details.

The Chinese had made it impossible for my team to carry out DNA studies by forbidding us to take and export blood samples. I had then run into financial problems as promised funds had not been forthcoming. To lead an expedition to the remote parts of Tibet is an expensive proposition indeed, which explained why I had been forced to return without the veterinary surgeon we needed. We would have to put off a larger scientific expedition for another year.

It was for lack of greater resources on this return journey to the heartland of Nangchen that I had decided to concentrate primarily on geography and finding the source of the Mekong, limiting our research on the horses to testing their stamina and trying to establish their distribution and regional variations inside Nangchen. We had hoped Jacques could double as a vet, a hope shattered when he was unable to locate the horse's heart behind its forelegs.

Not very far from Nangchen to the east lies the land of Ling, the home of Kesar, or Cesar, of Ling, the most popular legendary hero of Tibet. There are thousands of verses about him recited by Tibetan bards, and his life story, in a dozen versions, is printed in large books that tell of his adventures. Most scholars agree that he might have existed, and some have suggested that he was in fact the well-known minister Gar, who served the great king Song-tsen Gampo.

What is certain is that Ling exists as a district and that, like the district of Gar, it is named for a man (real or imagined) who rose to power because of his skill as a horseman and his winning record in horse races. Today, horse racing is still the favorite pastime of the nomads of Nangchen, who practice all year round and then select their fastest horses to take to the annual fairs like those at Zadoi or Jeykundo.

The moment the herd of fine horses disappeared over the ridge, we drove on, up the broad grassy valley that slowly led us to another pass. On the way we encountered yet another caravan of nomads, but this time they were neither taking their wool to market nor returning with barley—they were simply on the move in search of better grazing. Two yaks were loaded with a heavy tent whose post scraped the ground. Most of the other yaks carried nothing but their empty wooden pack saddles. I admired the elegance of the horses and the ease with which the nomads, including the women, handled them. Along with the herd of yaks, the nomads were accompanied by a large flock of Tibetan sheep with long flat horns twisted like a corkscrew, famed for their wool because it is their fine undercoat that produces cashmere.

No sooner had the caravan passed than a wolf strutted across the trail so slowly and unconcerned that it was almost an insult. It did not so much as give us a second look or accelerate, but just loped on its way, stopping twenty yards to our left to examine calmly the kind of motor-yak we were riding.

As we rose ever higher, the landscape began to open up, the peaks to sink below the horizon, the red earth momentarily giving way to gray soil with patches of short grass intertwined with edelweiss and moss. The wolf, coming just after the fox, was the first clear signal that we were entering a land more familiar to wild animals than to man. Now and again, looking across the flat expanse of the plain, we could see peaks so distant, they seemed miniature mountains. We were soon back upon the flats of the world's highest plateau. Not a bush or tree or plant in sight—even eagles had to light on the ground for lack of anything like a perch.

We were nearing yet one more pass, or, more precisely, one more watershed, when we came upon a little stream. We stopped and our drivers committed the terrible crime of catching the little fish that swarmed in the pools beside the stream (the worst sin for Buddhists because fish cannot cry to defend themselves). Fish living at close to 16,500 feet above sea level seemed something like a record. I duly photographed them, praying for forgiveness, thinking how strange that the adepts of the Buddhist religion should be so kind toward all living creatures, yet consider human life of little worth, as a mere "illusion of the senses." But then of course I have been so corrupted by materialism that I had trouble understanding that respect should in no way be proportionate to worth. The most humble creature is just as worthy of respect as the most formidable of beings.

As we looked at the fish, a huge eagle owl started up from a rock outcropping, its six-foot wingspan casting a devilish shadow over the hundreds of burrows of glacier rats that dotted the landscape.

A few hours later we found ourselves once again surrounded by red earth and two shades of green grass, then all of a sudden the track was gone and we were riding up a giant bright red dune—a sand dune. As we reached the summit of a pass we realized we were lost.

A freezing wind was blowing from the west. Holding onto my hat I peered out to the horizon; contemplating the seemingly endless expanse of the great plain, I felt as if we had entered a new world, one disconnected from any I had known.

8

BUBBLES ON WATER

⌘

I have always had a linear concept of my existence, the idea that wherever I stood I was connected by a path to my past, and that in relation to this trail of events, things lay to the left or right, north or south, backward or forward. Looking onto the horizon now, I had a feeling that this notion was dissolving around me, that the immensity of this great plateau was endless, shapeless, and all-encompassing.

In their concept of the creation of the world, the Tibetans tell how demigods were born on earth, but linked to the higher gods in heaven or to the summits of mountains by a sacred thread or ladder called a *mu*. As the world evolved the *mu* was broken, the thread cut (at first by accident), and so man was born, severed from the gods.

I suppose we all have some sort of *mu*, a mysterious thread that links us to nobler ideals and to our past. Here I felt totally disconnected and quite alone. We were in a land without towns or villages, a land whose population was elusive, ever-moving and changing camp, a world without signposts or fixed references, in which we had no place—we, who were out looking for a concept, something that did not exist, a nonplace, the point of extinction of the Mekong. We were in truth searching for an absence.

Once again I asked myself why. Why bother, why come out here so far, for what purpose? I had no valid answers. At first I had seen our venture as something akin to sport, something to be racked up as "an achievement." Then I had seen it as a way of indulging my pride, a frivolous vanity. Now I saw our enterprise as utterly meaningless or, at best, as an alibi to roam where few ever had the chance to, with the added hope of discovering a little more about ourselves.

I am not a mystic—not anymore, anyway. Having been raised a Catholic, I used to believe with all my might in the teachings of the church. As a child I had learned not to let reason tamper with my faith. To believe, to have faith, is to stop the process of logic and analytical thinking. Faith is an act of will, a will to adhere to a belief regardless of everything. As a result I had been induced into a world of magic and miracles, of supernatural beings, of angels and saints; I never allowed my reason to interfere.

My faith was lost to me when I grew to appreciate tolerance in the company of Tibetans. My eyes opened and I saw how intolerance was all too often the result of blind faith.

Thus was my *mu* cut, my link with heaven severed as I realized that I was but a mortal and very much alone.

In a nihilist vein of Buddhism, the great Tibetan mystic and poet Mila Repa proclaimed that "one was born alone, one lived alone, and one died alone." I had never liked that view of existence, and I certainly hadn't agreed with it, but up here it did have the sinister ring of truth.

Since leaving Xining I had felt that even the bonds of friendship that had united us—Sebastian, Jacques, and I—had vanished.

Was it plain fatigue, or was it the uncomfortable proximity of being packed in and shaken together for hours on end in the backseat of a lurching jeep? We were no longer just friends on a journey together—our vehicle had reduced us to passengers, an abstraction, human objects living in that indefinite no-man's-land between two destinations. Cooped up in a narrow metallic box on wheels, we couldn't exist as normal individuals as we bounced past a vast, ever-changing, odorless, windless scenery, a world looked upon from a glass cage. Was it Matisse who commented, deploringly, that driving at speeds in excess of five miles per hour, one could no longer see "the leaves moving in the wind?"

With no trees in sight, it was truly a dead landscape that we contemplated. On getting out of the jeep, I was struck by the wind, a wind from far, far away, the main denizen of these immense, desolate wastes.

I remembered how thirty years before, on my way to Mustang, my companion, Tashi Karmay, had exclaimed on reaching a pass overlooking the arid kingdom, "Mustang appears as barren as a dead deer."

"The road is very bad, I do not think we should drive on!" Once again I felt that Ling was wavering in his resolve, influenced by the drivers, who both seemed even more worried than he was.

I paid no attention to Ling's remark. Plodding on, I beckoned the jeeps to follow me slowly as I searched for the trail that had vanished under the red sand. To my left I saw a ravine that fell away from the pass along the tilted flank of a dune. With unfounded assurance I signaled that the vehicles should drive on down, aware that any hesitation or discussion as to the state of the road could prove disastrous.

Axle-deep in sand and tilting heavily, the first jeep slithered down the gully. Then came the second. As I chased after them, I remembered thinking it was easier going down than up; what if I had made a mistake? Was this the point of no return?

At the bottom of the gully we had no choice but to drive in the water down a little stream. The road had vanished, so for about a mile we cautiously splashed our way between two near-vertical red cliffs. Rounding a bend we found ourselves confronted by two fine horses, which galloped off at our approach.

Half an hour later, to our relief, we spotted a tracklike rut on the bank of the stream. Leaving the gully, we entered a broad plain of churned-up swamp grass. Turning north, we left the stream and began to rise toward yet another pass. It was getting late when at last we sighted a great black tent close to the road, the first we had seen since leaving Zadoi.

I was quite excited, and thought we should stop and camp nearby, as I was keen to talk with at least one of the nomads of this godforsaken region. Immediately Mr. Ling objected, explaining once again, like a broken record, that "these people are dangerous liars." Paying no attention, I addressed a handsome Khamba who had come forward, his braided hair hanging loosely down his neck.

The man made no attempt to hold back his ferocious barking mastiff or understand what I was saying. He simply pointed down the track, repeating, "Go, go away." Finally, when he realized I spoke Tibetan and wanted to pitch our tents close to his, he exclaimed aggressively, "Your tent, no, not here. Not here, just go away, pitch it somewhere else . . . go. Go away." I was a little bit upset. Maybe Ling was right. Were not all Tibetans my friends? Why, then, such hostility?

"The people here are very bad," chirped Ling, victorious. Furious as I was, I had no way to argue with him.

Three miles farther on, we encountered a bridge built by the PLA spanning the crystal-blue waters of a broad river that, upon consulting our GPS, we found to be the main course of the River A, which our maps had misled us into believing we had followed earlier on.

Just beyond the ridge, a flat ledge seemed an ideal place to camp—beneath great romantic red and green mountains. Ling disagreed, stating we should drive in the dark if necessary to reach a Chinese checkpoint. I refused, knowing that doing so was sure to get us lost, and anyway, by my reckoning, we were still two days' drive from the outpost of Moyun.

Thank God the exhausted drivers agreed with me. Soon we were all fumbling together with poles in our first attempt to raise our mess tent.

"Good practice," I ventured. Jacques didn't seem amused and looked tired, while Sebastian, on the other hand, was full of energy. He had bought the tent in New York and was eager to see what it would look like.

I have always been a mess-tent man myself. I knew that a large tent was essential on any expedition, a shelter in which one can stand and sit all together. Although we had individual tents in which to sleep, the mess tent would shelter the crew: first of all the cook and drivers and later the muleteers. The trouble is that any tent large enough for ten to twenty people is usually very, very heavy, but Sebastian had found one that was extraordinarily light.

One by one we assembled strange-looking U-shaped steel poles. After much trouble we finally had a rather elegant nylon cottage with screened windows. It looked a little bit too good to be true.

Pale green and white nylon, it lacked guide ropes, and it seemed far too flimsy to stand the raging winds we were sure to encounter; furthermore, without a fly sheet (a double roof), I expected it to get drenched too easily. All that said, the tent was large and amazingly comfortable, with its vast screened windows, ground sheet, and an inner partition that turned it into a miniature suite. We found that we had no kitchen tent to go with it, however. The cook, Wang, thinking that he could operate in our large mess tent, had left it behind. He didn't know that a big warning label sewn into the side of it made clear that any form of fire in the tent would be lethal. As a result, Wang battled for hours out in the wind beside a plastic sheet trying to light our primus stove.

At dusk we hastily set up our small individual sleeping tents. As we huddled around our lanterns in the mess tent and ate a spartan meal of cold biscuits and slices of bright orange Chinese sausage, Ling's censorious boyish face lit up with a smile for the first time. He was, he explained, "proud of our setup."

Later on, listening to the sinister call of a wolf, I rustled around in my small sleeping tent, wondering again what on earth I was doing out here. My Victorian ardor for exploration had somewhat paled. On top of everything else I hate sleeping bags, which inevitably corkscrew every time one turns around at night, ending up in a sort of body-length straitjacket. They are always either too hot or too cold and never seem long enough to cover one's shoulders. Then there is the matter of dirty boots: Should they remain inside the tent and stink, or outside, at the mercy of the elements and blue foxes? I remember having had to wear frozen boots every day on a fateful journey to Mount Minyag Konka, the highest peak in eastern Kham. For hours every morning my feet were frozen, and when the ice thawed, my feet were wet for the rest of the day. I was finally relieved of the torture by breaking first one leg and then, seven days later, the other in an earthquake; my only consolation was that I no longer needed frozen boots.

Such are some of the true delights of expeditions. There are also lice and fleas, which one can't help catching (to paraphrase Ling) "on fraternizing with the enemy." The transfer of fleas is greatly facilitated by the lamaist religion—believers aren't supposed to kill them, but instead just pick them off their bodies and deposit them on the ground, usually within easy jumping distance of where I happen to be sitting. Prior to each year's journey to Tibet, I go through my "big, big dog" routine. I visit pet shops in Paris and explain that my dog is nearly man-sized and needs the strongest flea powder available.

The crime of killing fleas is, of course, committed secretly by many Tibetans. An old proverb says, "To bite a flea feeds not the stomach, but what delight for the soul."

As I pondered why I was doing all this, going over the masochistic routines of eating and sleeping poorly, I envied all those born in the days of elegant travel. Cheap air fares and the infamous forty-four-pound baggage allowance are responsible for eliminating luxurious camping.

There are, in certain museums around the world, samples of the campaign kits of yesteryear, when kings and generals, administrators and judges, spent much of their life on the move. The kits included everything from boule cognac crystal decanter boxes to elegant velvet folding chairs and tents strung up with silk held by gold passe-menterie tassels. Those were the good old days when cases of claret were carried right over the Himalayas so that gentlemen need not suffer any more beastly discomfort than necessary. Alas, travel, even Himalayan travel, is a sport for gentlemen no more, but a pastime for the masses. Just as plastic miniature sailing boats have replaced the luxurious teak yachts of bygone eras, Pepsi has replaced claret in our spartan world of cut-rate hedonism. Living was an art then. Today it's not even a hobby. People don't hesitate to spend thousands of dollars on airfares but they skimp on service, bedding, and other basic comforts. It all comes from that distorted form of democracy whose object it is to convince the rich and the cultured that they are better off living like middle-class athletes. At high altitudes I admit I'm an elitist, and I yearn for the days when just being white was enough to save one a bad conscience as one sat in a sedan chair and complained about the tubercular cough of the coolies ("If only they would just shut up!"). Imperialism is so sweet—as long as you hold the right end of the stick—while democracy is tepidly tasteless, the middle road, dear to Buddhists who pray every day to be spared the excesses of too little or too much. Frankly, we live in a time of too little. I suddenly missed being called "Burrah Sahib" and having my porters fight to tie my shoelaces.

I should have had the courage to demand service, even at the risk of reaffirming in Ling his belief that Communism was a necessary evil invented to sweep away decadent capitalists, like me.

I knew, above all, that comfort was essential if we were to push on and have enough energy to spare at the end of our journey to carry out a meaningful investigation and mapping of the high plateau.

The morning was cold. One by one we abandoned our tents, slowly stretching out to our original shapes and sizes. I felt wretched after a night of battling the discomfort of sleeping on a plastic mattress a half-inch thick in a narrow bag, not to mention the back-breaking gymnastics of fumbling everywhere for the flashlight, shoes, zipper, and then the tent flap just to crawl out bent in two to relieve myself in the cold of night. The only compensation was the immense Himalayan sky, its stars dazzlingly bright, the Milky Way afire, while I felt infinitely small as I went through the humiliating routine of having to answer the call of nature. Yes, man is a fallen angel and the *mu* that linked us to the heavens has long been cut.

Were it not for the rays of the sun that dispelled the cold and gloom of the night, we wouldn't have had the will to continue. Why bother, anyway? The source of the Mekong had gotten along perfectly well unknown to all, misplaced on maps; why spoil everything now? Curiosity is too likely to backfire; ever since the Industrial Revolution, man has been putting his nose into nature to find out how this and that worked and how it could be modified, enlarged, or destroyed.

Over the years, the Chinese have been wiser in their approach to technology: from festive fireworks we made the cannons, from mustard we made the deadly gas bombs; from the poppy we made opium and sold it back to them. From the tiniest sweet particle of all, we made the atom bomb. Technology has, of course, given us many benefits, particularly in the medical field—but also longer lives to further expose us to crowding and pollution. "You realize, Jacques," I would say to provoke him, "medicine is the work of the devil; excellent health, eternal youth, and a long, long life are its goals, when we are here for the opposite reason, to learn how to die."

How I wished there were some sort of genetic engineering that would allow us to transcend our mortal bodies and do away with the illusion of the senses. Maybe the Buddhists are right, and our life is not so much of this world as beyond the speck of dust the world illuminates. Nirvana is the world snuffed out and fused with the absolute.

Everything packed up, we collected our Mars bar wrappers and stray dirty Kleenexes, the yellow film boxes, the plastic bags, the corrugated cardboard crate, the empty pork tins, the cocoa wrappers, the plastic Pepsi bottles, the glass beer bottles, the bits of string and ribbon, the label offering a guarantee for the tent, and the silver plastic pill holder: the habitual droppings of a brief overnight stop in the wild, reminders of a society in which nothing ever comes from the spot where it is destined to be consumed, but must be wrapped, bottled, boxed, packaged, labeled, and protected so it can travel, and, most important, so it can sell. Some say we live in a consumer society, but actually we live in a society of profit, in which the sale of goods and services is the ultimate goal. Whether or not the goods and services are ever consumed is a matter of secondary consideration. Much is thrown away, but what counts is not that, it is that everything has been sold in the first place.

As we drove off I couldn't help pondering the finality of any society. What did the nomad expect of life? Did he dream of enormous herds, of becoming rich? Did he look forward to retirement? Was he obsessed with youth or age? Or were his obsessions linked to religion, and to fulfilling his karma and achieving fruitful reincarnations, in much the same way I longed for bliss ever after in the next life?

"Lives of all beings are like bubbles on water," according to the Tibetan proverb. Yet Tibetans are basically optimistic.

> Of Happiness and Sorrow it is man who decides.
> Only good fortune and the length of life we cannot control.

This proverb from Kham is an apt illustration of the positive, realistic approach of most Tibetans. Another saying goes:

> Eaters and drinkers win.
> Weepers lose.

The mystery surrounding Tibet, its remoteness and inaccessibility, has brought many Europeans to imagine that there are monks and wise men there who hold the key to the problems of the world. The letters of Tibetan sages (since proven to be fakes) were the pillars of Gurdjieff's teachings. The Theosophical Society also used Tibetans as an alibi. Today, in New York, Colorado, Scotland, France, and many other places, there are hundreds of simulated Tibetan monasteries to which thousands flock each year in search of answers to the problems of existence.

I myself have searched Tibet for some lost, secret, complex recipe for happiness, only to discover that real happiness is as simple as the Khamba proverb says it is: It's a choice, it's what you make out of what you have.

By contrast, Sakyamuni, that sophisticated prince born in the stifling Terrai jungles of Nepal, the living Buddha, observed that life was pain. His was a rather pessimistic approach. He believed that the only way to conquer pain was to control desire, along the famed eight-fold path, the middle road of right desires and aspirations. In the end, Lord Buddha concluded that life was hardly worth living, and that the best we could hope for was to live out as quickly as possible our present and future lives until we reached nirvana—the snuffing-out of existence.

Weepers lose, say the Tibetans, and I, for one, agree. I prefer to join the eaters and drinkers. As another Khamba saying would have it:

If one is without soup on earth
What use is having a ladle in heaven?

Bumping along, still in the same horrible steel box on wheels, I was far from the exhilarating nirvana I yearned for, yet I was fascinated with the world we moved in now. The red and green mountains had vanished, the ground was covered with a short, dark, bristly moss, with the earth lumped as if raked and broken into uneven sod. The very top of the roof of our planet is a place where water and earth haven't yet decided to separate. Here and there appeared tranquil pools reflecting an immense sky supported on the distant waves of snow-covered peaks. We finally reached a barren flat land that I recognized to be some sort of aquatic no-man's-land between two watersheds. We were entering the upper valley of the Dam Chu.

Dutreuil de Rhins and his companion Grenard are the only foreigners I know of who ever traveled across the upper Dam Chu, although there remains a chance that this was also the route taken by the ill-fated and dazed Susie Carson Rijnhart after she had lost her firstborn child, barely one year old, to the cold of the tundra, and after her husband had disappeared, swept away by a torrent or possibly murdered by brigands.

The American wife of a Dutch missionary, she suffered an ordeal that is one of the most harrowing in the annals of Tibetan exploration. Determined to preach the gospel in the holy city of Lhasa, the Rijnharts set out from China with the intention of crossing the whole of eastern Qinghai and most of Tibet. They soon ran into trouble, however, when their guides abandoned them, taking many of their supplies. Next, their infant son, born en route, fell ill and died, and they were refused entry to Tibet and forced to retreat eastward, across Qinghai, possibly up the Dam Chu. Their new guides also ran away and they were attacked by bandits who stole their horses. Faced with a long and hopeless odyssey on foot, Mr. Rijnhart finally left his wife and attempted to swim across a swift, freezing torrent to seek help from the nomads. Susie Carson Rijnhart never saw her husband again. Alone she eventually made it to Sichuan.

Westward as far as the eye could see, there stretched a seemingly endless plain dotted with lakes and ponds through which meandered "the marshy river," the Dam Chu. Grenard wrote in 1894 that this "must be the longest arm of the Yangtze River, up which should be found the source of this river and not to the West as believed."

At the time I had not yet read Grenard's account, nor was I aware that a Chinese professor, Mr. How Man Wong, of the China Exploration and Research Society in Hong Kong, had set out recently—that very year, in fact—to travel up the Yangtze looking for its source. He found it in "a little pond" at the head of the Dam Chu on the very plateau upon which we had just emerged.

Based on our own reckoning, Jacques, Sebastian, and I searched the terrain around us, convinced that the source of the Dam Chu must be close to where we had entered its broad valley.

The GPS gave us an altitude reading of 16,568 feet. Looking at the patches of sky mirrored in the pools reminded me of those cloudscapes one sees flying at high altitudes as night approaches. What stretched before us was a union of elements in which clouds and mountains, sky and water, were essentially indistinguishable.

On close examination it was evident that in the long months of winter the entire valley must be frozen under ice and a thin film of slowly moving snow, but that in spring and early summer it was transformed into one huge marsh, or *dam*. The Yangtze is the fifth-longest river in the world, and the longest in Asia. Twenty miles across near Shanghai and the sea, its vast basin is populated by three hundred million souls—one-third of the population of China.

According to yet another of their many proverbs, these three hundred million Chinese ought to think three times or more each day about the place where we now stood: "When you drink water, think about the source."

After the Amazon, the Niger, and just behind the Rio de la Plata, the Yangtze is one of the rivers of the world with the greatest flow of water: almost twenty-nine thousand cubic yards per second on average, with a high of fifty thousand tons of water per second. With this water bound for the sea comes five hundred thousand tons of sand and earth per year.

Today, even the simplest fields of learning have been elevated to the status of science, and hydrology and its various forms of hydrometry are vastly expanding disciplines. I knew perfectly well that there were people in those fields far more competent than Jacques or Sebastian or I—people better suited to meet the challenge we had set for ourselves, including all those experts who had pondered for years the intricacies of river flow, flood control, still waters, storage basins, and subterranean reserves and levels. They were all people who should have been here long before us but had never made it.

This, of course, raises a few questions about experts in the modern world. In Tibet an expert is a man of wisdom. "Wisdom is like having a thousand eyes," goes a Tibetan proverb, by which estimate we were, in matters of hydrology, practically blind. I had taken a brief crash course that taught me just enough to know how little I knew, and to appreciate how hard it was not only to determine the source, or sources, of a river, but to make all the detailed calculations required for measuring the flow of the tributaries.

The trouble about men of wisdom today is that they have all become professional many people who are used to being paid for their knowledge. In Tibet the idea that one should pay a person to acquire his advice, counsel, or scholarship is truly shocking. It would be like paying people to tell the truth or refusing to help those in danger.

Wise men are much respected in Tibet, and in exchange for this esteem they give out their knowledge for free, in keeping with the proverb "The wise are the servants of all." This applies to doctors, veterinarians, and scholars in every field, none of whom ever charge for their services or advice. They are treated with great consideration and given the best food; horses are sent to fetch them, and they have access to every privilege. In Zanskar I met a doctor (the *lumbo* of Karsha) who, because he was so successful, was obliged to give up medicine, in that it left him no time to care for his fields and feed his family.

In the West the wise are nobody's servants. On the contrary, they tend to be masters of the masses who are *their* servants, if not their slaves. We pay for their slightest word or deed: for a rubber stamp, a prescription, three words of advice or a recommendation. Knowledge in the West is a commodity bought and sold, patented and licensed. It is no longer a matter of intelligence, enthusiasm, and a sharp brain, so much as a matter of money. The poor can't buy knowledge, and those who aren't any good at selling what knowledge they have are also losers in a society in which we have abolished the privileges of rank, only to raise the privileges of those who know something. Trade unions, syndicates, and professional associations have grown up to protect the monopolies of knowledge. Laws are passed making the services of the wise compulsory. One has to have an architect to build, a doctor to heal, and, as we discovered all too soon, many would feel that we should have had a professional hydrologist along, were we to dare seek the source of the Mekong.

This didn't bother us, for it begged the question: Why had no hydrologist found the source before we came along? Many specialists are mountain-shy. What with the popularity of ecologists and all the polluted water in the West, several international organizations of highly paid "experts" have looked to Tibet and Qinghai *on maps* and pronounced this highland region the "water tower of Asia." In several recent articles concern has been voiced about the "management" of this great water reserve, and Western experts who have never seen the region have tried to figure out how many millions of tons of water are stored in the marshes and lakes of the great northern plains of Tibet, the Changthang, and its extension in Qinghai.

Beyond any doubt there is a large reserve of water on the high plateau, but the groundwater is insignificant compared to the amount of annual rainfall. We tend to forget that all water on earth comes from the sea. Where our water supply is concerned, rainfall is what counts, and surprisingly, only a small portion of what falls as rain actually flows back down rivers.

Here again, hydrologists have been at work calculating how much of the water that falls on a given river basin ever reaches the sea. The waters of the Colorado River, for example, represent only 11 percent of the annual rainfall on the river's basin; the rest evaporates, is used in irrigation, or is simply drunk by humans and animals. Some rivers in northern Qinghai and most of those in adjoining Xinjiang (Chinese Turkestan) never reach the sea at all, in that 100 percent of their flow evaporates or disappears into desert sands or flows into lakes without exits.

There are many oddities about the flow of a river. Some rivers have more water in winter than in summer, others have the same flow all year round, and still others flow only during certain hours of the day, drying up when snow water freezes on the high summits. The Mekong's flow varies considerably between winter and summer. In summer it rises with the added monsoon rains in Southeast Asia and the snowmelt from the Tibetan highlands.

The great rivers that flow off the Tibetan highlands are unique in that many of them possibly existed before the Himalayan chain rose up to block their passage. Such rivers as the Arun and the Kali Gandaki actually managed to cut their way straight through the Himalayas. To do this they had to carve some of the deepest gorges in the world. On the other hand, both the Brahmaputra and the Indus had to make great detours in opposite directions around the Himalayas before being able to cut through the mountains at either end of the great chain.

Ever since 1959, when I had walked along the banks of the bubbling Dhud Khosi (Milk River) that flows down from Everest, I have been fascinated by Himalayan rivers. At first I was surprised by the speed of their flow, then by the depth of some of their gorges. The Kali Gandaki flows 19,600 feet beneath the summits of the nearby Annapurna range on one side and the Dhaulaghiri range on the other. This is one of the world's deepest clefts, and one I followed in 1964 on my way up to Mustang. Later, in 1986, I tried to travel down the great gorge of the Brahmaputra, another contender for the world's deepest canyon, lying between Mount Gyala Pheri and the 25,446-foot-high Namche Barwa. Here the Brahmaputra flows nearly three miles below the peaks, whose summits are only seven and a half miles apart on either side of the river. This gorge is so steep that neither George Bailey in 1912 nor the famed botanist Kingdom Ward in 1935 was able to follow its course. Neither was I in 1986.

Many other gorges have remained a mystery to this day. In fact, the longest unexplored gorge is possibly that of the Mekong itself. To my knowledge no one has yet been able to follow the river all the way up or down through its gorge across Tibet. I well understood why when in 1995 I drove a short way up this gorge to Chamdo, just south of where the Mekong leaves Nangchen to enter Tibet, and found myself suspended on a ledge three thousand feet above the river as it flowed down into a huge rocky gorge so steep as to seem man-made.

Although we constantly see photographs of cars overturned and houses destroyed by floods, most of us are unaware of the true force of rivers. Water weighs a ton per 1.3 cubic yards; the Seine in Paris averages four hundred tons a second, one hundred times less than the Congo, yet that represents the compacted mass of five jumbo jets per second. Virtually nothing can obstruct the force of a river, and huge mountains are continuously eroded and ground away by them at great speed. Every year where the Himalayan streams open out onto the Indian plains in the foothills of Nepal and Bhutan, dozens of villages are literally swept away when the current changes direction, as it frequently does at random and without warning.

There was no fear of any such calamity where we now stood, for the plain was so flat that the Dam Chu meandered slowly among the maze of pools. As we drove on, intermittently losing the track we were trying to follow, and frequently getting bogged down in pools that cut across our route, we began to see ahead of us in the distance the familiar beetle-like outline of black tents. The upper basin of the Dam Chu in summer provides excellent grass so that here, at altitudes close to 16,500 feet, thrives a large community of nomads from the Ghegi tribe of Nangchen.

As we approached, a man riding a fine white mare galloped up toward us. We stopped, and he dismounted, revealing an elegant silver saddle inlaid with gold. His horse, moreover, was adorned from nose to tail. A red rectangular prayer flag fell over its forehead from a silver-threaded leather bridle with bright red tassels of yak wool. The saddle rested upon an ornate orange, white, and blue saddle blanket embroidered with dragons. The high pommel and the raised rear rim of the saddle were embossed with religious designs—the endless knot, the parasol, the wheel of life—of gold plating. An elaborate crupper of braided strands of different-colored leather was hitched under the horse's tail, while the tail itself ended in seven or eight braids intertwined with colored ribbons fastened to each other so as to present a flat matlike surface.

"Gold and silver are cheap in Tibet," remarked Father Huc in 1866, who was shocked, on the other hand, by the cost of simple manufactured objects such as silver-sheathed wooden bowls.

The saddle of the young Khamba before us, along with its carpets, was obviously worth a small fortune, as was the silver and gold straight sword in his red belt. The sword was similar to those of the ancient Gauls of France, and to the swords of the Scythians, as described by Herodotus.

I asked the young man how far we were from Moyun, our destination. He was vague, saying it was very far but that we were not far from Dayun, another place where, we gathered, there was a sort of government farm. Seeing our driver smoking, the young man asked for a cigarette, and then jumped into his saddle and sped off, seemingly heading for nowhere.

Bumping along again over the hardened tufts of marsh grass, we eventually reached a lone tent guarded by four aggressive Tibetan mastiffs. Two children ran out to see us. From the elder I learned the name of the valley and the tribe grazing its yaks there—Dam Chu Ka Se. The road now turned, heading north toward a line of distant crests.

Here we encountered a lone broken-down truck, and then, right afterward, we saw a masonry wall in the distance: Dayun, the so-called government farm. Drawing up to the gate we realized that it was, in fact, an abandoned military station with a walled-in barracks set beside a large broken satellite dish.

There were no Chinese in residence. I confirmed with the locals that we could not make Moyun before nightfall. Taking in the little outpost, I began to grasp the pains the Chinese had gone to in order to subjugate Nangchen. Outposts like this one, at 15,750 feet, are among the world's highest settlements.

The struggle for Kham had been to the bitter end. By the end of the war, in 1959, the only population to remain behind and fall into the hands of the Chinese were the old, the sick, the young, and mothers with small children. All others, including many young women, had taken to the hills to fight, until they were gradually forced to retreat farther into the uninhabited plateau and eventually into Tibet.

I had heard many accounts of this struggle, but perhaps one of the most tragic was the fate of a group of nomads who had decided to flee before the Chinese advance. Misdirected, they had traveled not south toward Lhasa or east, but north. Without enough food, they had veered into the heart of the Changthang, the great open void of the northern plains, where their bones still litter the tundra today, a monument to the unhappy disarray that assailed these remote communities when suddenly confronted with the Chinese "invasion of locusts."

The tragic end of those nomads who died for having fled down a road to nowhere was actually a repetition of another terrible saga that occurred in Tibet in 1910.

That year the Chinese, under General Chung Ying, invaded Lhasa and southeastern Tibet. The general and his army were ruthless, killing all those they encountered. Panic spread among the simple folk of southern Kham, who, as one would expect, began to abandon their villages and flee before the enemy. Thousands of refugees took to the road, many of them pious believers in the teachings of the lamas and in the holy texts that spoke of the valleys of Pemakoe as a sacred paradise on earth, a holy land suddenly seen in those times of hardship as a land of asylum and plenty. Thus, thousands fled for the great gorge of the Brahmaputra leading to tropical Tibet, a poor region of monkey-eating aboriginal tribes that few Westerners have any knowledge of at all. The climate there is hot, damp, and humid, and is unsuitable to most Tibetans.

Two years later, in 1912, George Bailey sneaked across the border from Assam into tropical Tibet, uninvited and without a passport. On his daring expedition to explore the gorge of the Brahmaputra, he found on his way, lying on the roadside or huddled in caves, the skeletons of the thousands who had died in flight of hunger and exhaustion in Pemakoe. As in the case of the nomads who years later wandered about until they dropped in the frozen wilds of the great Changthang, the refugees had encountered nothing but isolation and death.

Slowly we rose above the valley floor while dark black clouds formed a somber lid closing over the great plains, whose silvery pools were now brighter than the sky. Here and there diagonal rays of golden sunlight burst through the obstructed heavens to spotlight patches of rusty grassland. On the slopes the marsh grass gave way to a more sliken herb, as we neared a pass that would lead us at last into the watershed of the Mekong.

"Look, a kiang," Sebastian said. As keen as a fox, he had spotted most of the wild animals we had seen so far. Indeed, there was before us a small herd of kiang, grazing peacefully. No sooner had we spotted them than a wolf crossed our trail and a herd of gazelles scattered over a nearby ridge like raindrops on a windscreen.

Then the magic began: The whole of the rolling grasslands that rose to the rocky fringe of the nearby mountains was crawling with animals. Kiang right and left, their long wintery coats aglitter with the crude light that always precedes the inevitable hailstorm; wolves, foxes, wild goats, and more. Tibetan gazelles like quicksilver rushing here and there, stopping in little clusters to eat nervously. Hundreds of animals all visible in a landscape that offered no shelter, no place to hide, no bushes or tall grass, nothing but a painted décor over which the animals roamed or darted, eyeing each other, living in a cautious fragile harmony. I felt as if thrown back to the birth of time, and that I was but an animal among animals, part of a fantastic community of the children of Mother Nature.

I had had this feeling only once before, in the Terrai jungles of Nepal. It was at dawn, and I was strolling alone in the dry, boulder-ridden bed of a great river that cut through the forest of sal trees. A dense jungle surrounded me, and there among the boulders, out in the open, were dozens of deer, a jackal, a lone wild bull, all come to drink, some walking peacefully home, others simply enjoying the morning sun as I was. A vast congregation of those other beings for which each morning the sun rises, the dew falls, and the day unfolds.

I had never been to the Serengeti, but now I had no need to go there, as the landscape here was no more or less than an immense garden made to support life.

The moment was one of great intensity, and even Ling and the drivers were overcome by the magic of the place. We were embarrassed when the rude roar of the motors started again and we continued our way up along the approximation of a trail, hoping we were on the right track. Suddenly, we were at the top of the pass. I stepped out to take an altitude reading (16,535 feet) just as the first gritty grains of hail whipped my face. We baptized the place Kiang pass, but we soon recognized it to be the "Dzana-Loung-Mouk-La" that Dutreuil de Rhins had traveled through one hundred years before us.

On April 8, 1894, approaching from the south as we had, after having crossed the Dam Chu and crunched over the frozen marshes, Dutreuil de Rhins and Francis Grenard, along with their Russian mercenaries, their Muslim servants, and several local horsemen, climbed up this same pass in a small caravan of weary ponies.

> We had the satisfaction on crossing the Dzana-Loung-Mouk-La of reaching one of the goals we had set out to attain. From this pass 5250 meters high flows the Loung-Mouk-Tchou, the most occidental of the origins of the Mekong. The joy of such a discovery, which is enough to make any good explorer forget the hardships of travel, was

increased in our case by the knowledge that the humble thread of water, now immobile under ice, was soon to break its bonds and run across mountains and plains towards French territory, establishing between us and our homeland from which we had not heard for so many months, a link both imaginary and real.

Grenard, who wrote these lines when back in France after the death of his companion, went on to add, "Once we had well established the sources of the Mekong, Dutreuil de Rhins intended to join the north road to Si-ning [Xining]."

How well, or indeed *whether*, they had "established" the sources of the Mekong remains somewhat of a mystery. Abandoned by their guides in the very pass on which we now stood, the explorers carried on in the company of three pilgrim monks they had encountered by chance. The maps Grenard published showed that they didn't spend so much as a day in the region, but on April 8 marched on halfway down the Lungmo River. (Grenard referred to it as the Loung-Mouk; the proper Tibetan spelling is Lung-sMog.)

The geographers were quite naturally exhausted and worried. They had been on the road for an amazing three years. They were running out of money, and their horses and yaks were unfit to continue. According to Grenard's testimony, the ground was partially covered with snow.

It was freezing cold as we crossed the pass, and night was about to descend on us. We had to find a place to camp and find it quickly.

As we drove down the other side of the pass, we came upon the nascent Lungmo Chu, a trickle that drained the rolling grass-covered mountains where, as on the south face, gazelles and kiang grazed in great number.

Of course I mustn't mix here the chronology of events of 1894 with the knowledge and hindsight that subsequent history has afforded me. For me, the pass was still nameless, and so was the river. It was getting dark, and we had to stop very soon.

It was then that I sighted a black tent on a ledge above the river. Driving on a few hundred yards we found an ideal campsite overlooking the torrent. I called for the driver to stop.

We hurriedly pitched the mess tent, panting from the altitude and looking apprehensively at the dark sky. Hail had not yet fallen and the ground was dry.

In minutes our large mess tent was up, and the small ones were pitched in its shadow. The drivers parked the jeeps side by side, and the nearby nomads came over to see us. They were a little man with a thin, weather-beaten face, accompanied by his daughter and son, both short with broad friendly features. Their eyes were aglow with amazement as they stared at our vehicles and came forward to touch the magical cloth of our tents, that silklike nylon so different from the homespun wool they wore.

"Chu di la ming kare re?"

What is the name of the river? Thus I found out that we were beside the Lungmo Chu, and later had it spelled out for me as Lung sMok-chu—the river claimed by Grenard to be the westernmost branch of the Mekong.

Had he and de Rhins been right?

Excitedly, I sprang the question, the one I had been formulating in my mind for months, the big question that maybe this man could actually answer.

"Dza-chu chu-go kare re?" Where is the head of the Dza River? Where is the source of the Mekong? Such a banal question, yet one unanswered for a century.

Would the man point up to where we had come from, at the foot of the pass to the source of the Lungmo Chu?

"Ya la . . ." the man pointed northwest over the darkened ridge on the other side of the river beside which we were camped. *"Ya la, ta rempo mindu . . ."* Over there, not very far.

"Nyma katseu dro gogiduk?" How many days? I asked.

The man hesitated. He was not sure, but he repeated, "*Ta rempo minduk...*" Not far . . .

We were nearing our goal.

That night our spirits were high. Tomorrow, if all went well, we would at long last reach the end of the road. From there we would follow the river on foot and horseback to its bitter end.

For a long time we sat talking about the animals we had seen, the vision of paradise lost still vivid in our minds.

Before going to sleep I walked to the edge of the cliff above the roaring stream. The sky, as if by magic, was now limpid and the stars were unbearably bright and near. Once more I found myself in harmony with nature, bemused by my own insignificance and marveling at the grandeur of the universe, at the metronome of time, and the creation of the stars and planets and all those autonomous creatures great and small that lived under the same immense dark canopy.

I thought of the animals shivering like us, like us shrouded in darkness. Did they all live in fear as the wolves strode about and the foxes and jackals prowled?

I slept well, able at last to put aside the constant irritation of all the anxieties that had been attendant to the venture from the start. Now, maybe naïvely and a little prematurely, I believed that all would be well. I had even momentarily forgotten that out there somewhere was a crew of Japanese scientists seeking perhaps the same objectives as we were.

9

MOYUN

⌘

The following morning, September 13, we broke camp under the curious gaze of a small crowd of nomads and began the steep descent to the valley floor.

We trailed the Lungmo stream, as it got bigger, to a ledge; off to our left we could see a vast gray stony riverbed two hundred yards wide—the Dza Nak, or the Black Mekong, in which meandered a broad torrent flowing out of the west.

There was no need to be a great geographer or even to ask the local nomads to understand that the Lungmo Chu was but a minor affluent on the south bank of the main branch of the Mekong, whose stony bed ran on for miles out of sight toward the west.

How de Rhins and Grenard missed this, I cannot say, except to speculate that the whole upper valley in which we now stood was no doubt covered in snow when they arrived in April 1894. The Lungmo

River, being, at this place, steeper and faster than the main branch of the Mekong, must still have been visible, while the Mekong was ice-bound, its course not discernible in the snow fields. And indeed, on the fifteenth of April, Grenard wrote that the ice of the Mekong had broken up and that the river was carrying ice floes. If this was the case, why had Grenard not defended their discovery when it was later challenged?

I was puzzled but also very relieved, for we now were certain that the source of the Mekong lay to the west of the Lungmo River as the nomads had indicated.

On reaching the banks of the Mekong, the trail turned down-stream heading for Moyun, our long-awaited destination. We drove for about an hour along the grassy banks before reaching a small cement bridge, a striking reminder of civilization, and obviously the very first bridge to cross over the Mekong on its long road to the sea. There the river was a familiar red, the same color it had been at Zadoi some sixty miles to the west.

It was two o'clock when we came in sight of Moyun.

Set back a mile from the river, lying on a green grassy ledge and backed up against rounded red hillocks, Moyun seemed like Fort Apache or some other prop from a movie of the American West. It was enclosed by a simple twelve-foot-high defensive wall of packed red earth, three feet thick. A solitary opening perforated the struc-ture, and there was no door or gate. The garrison was abandoned. Inside, set before a small grassy parade ground, were two rows of typical barracks and an eight-foot, broken-down satellite dish, once the indispensable link with distant military headquarters. Our two vehicles came to a stop. We were at road's end. It had taken us three days to cover a mere ninety miles. If all went well, we would now begin our final thrust up river on foot and horseback.

I was elated. Since leaving Xining I had been anxious to get out of our jeeps. Encapsulated in a suffocating metal cage, between driver and door, cooped up with Sebastian, Jacques, and Ling, I found that our very proximity had caused us to ignore each other as we gaped through the square glass windows like a bunch of television addicts. From here on things were to be for real, three-dimensional with wind and cold thrown in.

As I got out and stretched I heard the unmistakable voice of a drunkard and saw coming toward me three men wearing unbuttoned dirty Chinese military jackets. The oldest of the three was talking loudly and slurring his words.

Only two of the thirty cells in the run-down barracks were inhabited. It seemed the garrison had been abandoned a long time ago, yet here were these Tibetan administrators of sorts, and their wives and several children. One little girl, about three years old, perhaps, had the matted hair of a veteran Rastafarian and a smile worthy of Leonardo da Vinci.

I approached the three men with caution, but the drunk seemed relatively amiable after his initial surprise at my speaking Tibetan.

"Would we be able to find horses?" I asked. I then explained we were out to find the *"Dza-nak chu-go,"* the source of the Dza Nak. I received a vague affirmative grunt, upon which Ling came up and, in his rasping high-pitched voice, delivered what I imagined to be the very same request in Chinese.

Then I asked the question that had been on my mind ever since Xining. Had they heard of or seen the Sino-Japanese team? They had. In fact, the men had passed through less than eight days ago, but the party had not gone up the Dza Nak but out to the Dza-Kar, the northern and shorter branch of the two prongs of the upper Mekong, according to our satellite map.

I immediately relayed the good news to Sebastian and Jacques. I was thrilled to the point of being light-headed—it seemed that now nothing could stop us from being the first to make it to the source.

My joy was short-lived, however. What if the Dza-Kar, the white Mekong, was in fact the longest branch? Or what if the Japanese group had switched from one to the other, cutting across the ridges that separated the two branches of the upper Mekong?

For the moment I had other matters to attend to. One look at the damp, rundown barracks made me decide to pitch our tents inside the walled compound. Our drivers and cook, however, set about establishing themselves in one of the dismal cells.

We set up camp and moved our gear from the jeeps into the mess tent. We were totally exhausted, which came as no surprise since the GPS showed we were at 15,243 feet. We had been banged around on the road for six full days, and I for one think it less taxing to spend twelve hours in the saddle than to sit in a car all day.

Inside the clean and elegant, pale green, bright and roomy mess tent, all I could think of was stretching out and falling asleep, or at least sitting and examining our maps and having a quiet talk with Jacques and Sebastian without the ever-present and inquisitive Mr. Ling.

This was not to be. In no time the entrance to our tent was occupied by a small exotic crowd. Among those who stood staring at us were two women, their striking hair—or I should say, headdress—worthy of close examination. They were the wives of the two men living in the deserted garrison, and their hair shone with *Dri* butter and was braided into 108 long thin strands, that being a sacred number to Buddhists. The braids were tied together at their ends to form a stringy veil. More amazing still, the strands of hair at the women's foreheads had been cut short and tied one by one to form what looked like the bill of a cap. The end of each hair being woven into the arc of a thin frontal braid, this peak served the purpose of filtering out the blistering sunlight, not much different from the screens of loosely woven yak hair that Tibetans make to act as sun goggles against snow blindness.

To enhance the women's amazing hairstyle, their braids were crowned with a transversal red leather band crossed by another running down the central part of their heads. These bands were studded with two-inch, oval yellow-orange amber beads with pink coral knobs in their centers. Turquoises an inch wide framed by smaller coral beads ran down the central band to the middle of the women's backs. These adornments, which must have weighed several pounds and cost a dozen yaks, were only a part of the women's jewelry. More beads dangled from their necks, encumbered their wrists, and fell from their waists on bejeweled pouches and purses of various sizes. As a result, when I finally chased them away, they tinkled and rattled like a mule train.

The women of Tibet must surely be among the most adorned ladies of the world. This is hardly surprising as they wear their entire dowry on their heads, a habit, it would seem, born of their lifestyle, which seldom affords them a safe place to lock up their treasures. Yet the true reason may stem from the longstanding instability of feudal Tibet, when raids between tribes were numerous and women had to be ready at all times to run and hide themselves, jewels and all, from marauding parties of brigands. The most adorned of all women in Tibet are the nomads, no doubt because of their wealth, which is directly proportionate to the size of their herds. Here, in the high remote Ghegi region of Nangchen, the nomads were not very rich, unlike their cousins living on the rich grassy fringes of Lake Koko Nor. The tribal women near the lake have so many gold and silver ornaments that they wear them down their backs right to the ground. Dozens of silver and gold studs the size of oranges adorn their hair bands, each with huge knobs of coral, turquoise, and amber.

I had long been puzzled about where the coral and amber came from, as only turquoise is indigenous to Tibet. In Amdo I was told the amber came from the British, who brought it to Tibet in 1878 all the way from the Baltic Sea. Marco Polo, always keen to sniff out good business prospects, noted that the inhabitants of the region liked coral. Some of the coral is actually coralline, however, or fossilized coral, which is in fact indigenous to Tibet, coming as it does from the bed of the Thetys Sea.

Alongside the women stood an old man with an elegant white sheepskin cap and a dark blue silk robe. Through his belt loop was thrust a traditional Khamba sword. Had he never seen a European before? As he looked on, the aides to the drunk official entered our tent, and I set about questioning them about what lay ahead.

Now our research and exploration would begin in earnest. Ever since I had had the privilege to uncover lost temples in the coastal jungles of Yucatán, I had made it my duty to record in detail everything I encountered in unexplored regions.

It was now important that I find out all I could about this area, the names of the local districts and tribes, and the various tributaries of the Mekong, along with the Tibetan names of the wild animals. And then, of course, there was the matter of locating the principal source of the Mekong.

It is important to mention that I was well aware of the delicate nature of trying to determine "the source" of a river.

Whether there actually exists any such thing as a single source to a river is an interesting question. Rivers are, by definition, the sum total of their components—little streams, themselves composed of smaller rivulets. There are of course a few exceptions: rivers that spring up ready made from a huge underground source, or those that emerge as powerful torrents at the foot of glaciers, such as the Ganges. Short of such exceptions, however, most rivers start as a web of fine rivulets or a cluster of small tributaries. Can one therefore speak of a single source?

Did the Mekong come from a glacier or from some spectacular spring? If it did, would that spring or glacier be the true source, the one farthest from the sea, or the tip of the branch with the greatest flow? And which was the historical source, the one considered the source by the locals?

On this subject I avidly cross-examined the two Tibetan administrators in our tent. It soon became evident that they didn't know the river well at all, that they were not from here but had been sent here by the Chinese in Zadoi. We would have to ask the local nomads. Where are the locals? I asked. The men explained that they lived in tents everywhere and nowhere. A lot of good this was, and so I changed the subject and inquired after the wild animals of the region and their Tibetan names, and also the names of the various local districts.

I then broached the crucial subject of horses. Where could we find them? Could we hire a guide to take us upriver?

The men seemed hesitant at first but then asked how many horses?

I had made only a rough estimate. "Fifteen or twenty," I ventured. They seemed perplexed.

"The Japanese have hired many already. We will have to send out to collect them." At this they beckoned me to follow them outside.

Hard on their heels, I crossed the grassy parade ground. I noticed a gallows-like broken-down basketball hoop next to the gap in the garrison wall. We then walked around the stockade to a large solitary black yak-hair tent.

A fierce burly mastiff growled at our approach, then a young child popped out and grabbed it by the collar, while an old man stuck his face out, smiled, and waved us inside.

Bending down under the raised flap, I found myself in the vast tent surprised again at how light such tents were inside as the sun shone through the material. A pretty girl standing by the hearth stuck out what seemed a very large tongue at me in polite Tibetan greeting. The two officials addressed the old man and explained what I was looking for. He took off his sheepskin cap and scratched his head. A young man with his braids shoved into an oversized Chinese peaked cap came forward to say he would go out and find horses but that it would take at least a day or two as the other *drok-pa* (nomads) were far away and their animals would have to be rounded up.

Although frustrated by the delay, I was happy that our request had not been turned down. Hiring horses is always a tricky business in that, in general, nobody likes to lease horses that belong to them unless they are lame and useless. On nearly all my journeys the only horses I had been able to hire were made available to me through coercion. On my journey across Bhutan in 1968, for instance, a royal proclamation had allowed me to employ the hated Ulag, a tax that required peasants to supply horses or mules on the spot to carry officials and their baggage. Ulag was a Tibetan custom, and it was because of the absence of an official permit to obtain horses that most foreigners had been stopped from reaching Lhasa.

Today, however, in occupied Tibet, the Chinese have arrogated to themselves the same privileges as the princes, kings, and high lamas of old; with Ling among us, we were under the patronage of the Qinghai Mountaineering Association, an official Chinese entity, which, no doubt, would give us the right to secure horses.

For the first time I began to discuss seriously the location of the source of the Mekong. The young Tibetan who had volunteered to round up horses explained that there were two "water heads" of the Dza Nak. One he called the *"Drug-di chu-go,"* the other the *"Sag-ri chu-go."* Although I couldn't be certain of it, the young man seemed to know the way.

I thought I had been ready for everything, but not for the notion of two sources. Which was the correct one? Were we even talking about the same thing? What did the young man understand by *chu-go*?

I was looking for the geographical source, the one the farthest from the sea, and—considering the lay of the land—the one farthest west from where we were. Yet how could I explain what we in the West understand by the geographical source of a river?

I took out my satellite map, hoping that would help—the extraordinary TPC G-8D, scale 1:500,000, published by the Defense Mapping Agency Aerospace Center, St. Louis, Missouri, November 1989. As I opened its various folds the young man recoiled as if it might bite him, then very cautiously peered at what must have seemed pure mumbo jumbo and shook his head. It took me some time to figure out where we were exactly, by tracing the latitude and longitude reading I had taken a few hours before. Only by this cross-reference could I situate us on a map with practically no names on it. So far so good: my reading placed us on the right side of the little blue line that was the upper Mekong, a line that broke up into a fan of little streams marked as dotted lines less than approximately ninety miles to the west.

However vague, from now on, this satellite map would be just what we needed to help us to plot our route. That said, I soon put it away, not wishing to frighten the nomads or overimpress the officials.

Sitting down to a cup of salty tea, I tried to tease the polite young lady who had stuck out her tongue. She was every bit as innocent and as shy as she had seemed at first. How many people had she met in her short, isolated life? I wondered.

In our promiscuous modern world we have trouble calling to mind the days when young women blushed naturally and cast down their eyes modestly when speaking to men. Similarly, proper men used to hesitate out of courtesy before staring into the face of a young woman.

Such customs as these, now considered so old-fashioned in the West, are still upheld in Tibet, where both purity and modesty are seen as virtues and not as conditions imposed by male chauvinism. Girls still blush when spoken to and complimented. *Candor*, in the old sense of the word (meaning "brightness"), is the attribute of not just women—young men are, in their own way, also shy. The greatest decorum is generally attendant upon conversations between boys and girls. I was, of course, considered either too old or too important a person to be engaged in the guarded humor of flirtation, and so I made little headway with the young woman. The old man, on the other hand, answered all my inquiries in a seemingly straightforward manner.

Just how straightforward he was, however, I couldn't be certain. After all, the men who had brought me to this tent were officials of the Chinese administration.

Back in camp we had nothing to do but wait. It was now nearing six o'clock, Beijing Standard Time, and the sun, when it shone through the clouds, was still high.

I went for a long walk around the garrison with Sebastian, keeping an eye on the fast-darkening sky, which warned of yet another sudden hailstorm.

Sebastian is the age of my eldest son; as a result, I found it both strange and pleasant to have him along as a companion. This is not to say that I ever believed that I was so much as a year older than he. The way I see it, age is an abstraction, relative and ill defined. The only bitter truth is appearance, and I have always looked or tried to look older than my age. Only recently had it occurred to me that I was old enough now, perhaps, to try to look younger than I am.

The man I saw in the mirror with gray hair, a bulging stomach, and the demeanor of some decrepit member of a common cricket club was not really me. I felt better here in Tibet, away from mirrors, with a broad-brimmed hat, ankle-high boots, and a windbreaker.

Sebastian looked much more the part. Handsome, although maybe a little bit too short to be a prototypical cowboy, he sported an eagle feather in his tall hat and wore a jaunty leather waistcoat. At least his allure in our slides and film would help counterbalance my belly and the lurid stonewashed jeans and baseball cap of Mr. Ling.

Under the guise of a happy-go-lucky, self-deprecating young man, there hid in Sebastian a very sagacious, unassuming personality. Eton was obviously the best school at which to prepare for Himalayan exploration. Had not Mallory been there when its Victorian ethics matched those of my nanny, whose reverence of gratuitous glory against all reason had served as my own inspiration?

Everything interested Sebastian, from butterflies to plants, to horses and yaks, and his curiosity was a pleasure to behold as we entered this strange land where literally everything deserved special attention. We were in a region possibly never before seen by Europeans or, for that matter, anyone from the so-called First World, other than the Japanese who had preceded us by a few days.

"Maybe they're not interested in the source of the river at all," Sebastian ventured hopefully. I hoped that he was right and that the Japanese were interested only in beetles or flowers.

For his age Sebastian had already lived a momentous life. He had forfeited Oxford to study Chinese in Beijing in 1982, when China was still very much a land of dark blue proletarian jackets and baggy pants—a costume, it was said, that was borrowed from the French factory workers near Paris with whom Zhou Enlai and others worked and from whom they were said to have learned the tenets of Communism. But this is almost surely myth, if one considers that Zhou Enlai was a mandarin, a member of China's highly educated elite. In fact, Mao was one of the few of the ascendant Communists who was not of a cultured mandarin heritage.

Sebastian had studied in Beijing for a short while only, leaving to go to Geneva, and then to Frankfurt, where he set up an art gallery. This apparent non sequitur had caused him to become a bit of a globe-trotter, and to travel to Tibet and to the rather more delightful backwaters of Bali in search of art.

By contrast, Victorian explorers had no personal lives, being, in that respect, rather like the dead. As to their having feelings, that— well, that was nobody's business. A schoolboy's jocular humor was meant to brush away whatever sentiment or anguish he might feel. Fortunately, Sebastian had a warm Gaelic (or was it Latin?) stamp and we were able to share much that is lacking in Victorian Himalayan literature: our opinions on women, love, and life in general—a nexus of subjects that we dared not broach with Jacques, as it was hard to imagine that he had ever given it much thought. We did know that he was married and expecting a second son, hopefully in the week of our return. Jacques was unquestionably more of a Victorian than either Sebastian or I.

Much of the world today is in crisis in terms of its values. Few people in the twentieth century have been spared seeing the certitudes, traditions, principles, customs, and institutions that were attendant upon their childhood all blown away. This applies equally to the mandarin who exchanged his embroidered silk and gold brocades for the blue cotton of French factory workers, and to the Etonian who traded in his tails for blue jeans once out of school. As for matrimonial institutions, how many Muslims have had to give up their many wives, and how many wives have let go their monogamous husbands in the frenzy of newborn social values?

Even here, in the remotest corner of our planet the tide had turned. We had blithely arrived, by motor vehicle, in a place that for centuries was traversed only on foot or on horseback.

Having been on the run ever since we landed in Beijing, we found it extremely painful to have to sit around for a full day waiting for horses to materialize from the broad empty plateau that surrounded the little garrison of Moyun.

We had no trouble imagining how the Chinese soldiers must have felt cooped up behind the earthen bastion of this little outpost, surrounded by elusive "wild men," barbarian nomads whom they had been taught to fear since childhood. Their fear was akin to that which the half-naked American Indians inspired in the early colonists of America. The top-hatted immigrants to the New World, moving west to start a new life, were a people who plainly understood that their fortunes depended on ridding the land of such people. To rob the Indians and remain at peace with their consciences, they had no choice but to proclaim them evil.

While Spanish priests had sought, often forcibly, to "convert" the Indians of Mexico, the Protestants of North America were less concerned with the souls of the natives or maybe just less hypocritical. Like the Chinese, the New World Protestants were firmly persuaded that their people and their culture could never mix with the natives' way of life.

The history of the confrontation in North America is well known, and the Indians have for the most part been exterminated, their remaining number relegated to reservations whose boundaries were respected, to begin with, only as long as their inhabitants didn't interfere with the interests or greed of the white man.

In China and Tibet, no such racial cleavage exists. Instead the line is drawn between barbarian and Chinese, and it must be said, to their credit, that many young Chinese truly believe their mission in Tibet (and in other provinces with large minority populations) to be a civilizing one. It is, however, the same civilizing mission the British and French colonialists laid claim to one hundred years ago as they subdued the world by the sword for its own good.

It is quite easy to establish how sincere the Chinese in Tibet really are. Forty-five years after having come to tame the land and liberate it from itself, the Chinese have seen their Tibetan subjects become poorer and less educated than they once were. The greater part of their monuments, libraries, institutions of learning, monasteries, and shrines have been destroyed. Famine, once unknown, is now frequent, and disillusionment is widespread. Every year since 1950 has been marked by outbreaks of violence as the Tibetans have again and again cried out for freedom.

Why, then, was the fort at Moyun abandoned? The answer lay with the Chinese themselves. In 1982, Beijing began to see that the cost of turning the Tibetans into docile Communists was as prohibitive as the outcome was doubtful.

Tibetans are a very polite people, and the tolerance they preach may give an illusion that they are submissive. In reality, the Tibetans simply ignored the Chinese and continued to live and pray the way they always had. The Chinese, Tibetans knew, were arrogant, obstinate, and narrow-minded, yet also corruptible and weak. No one in Tibet has ever taken the Chinese very seriously, considering them as a whole a nation of merchants concerned only with making money.

Both sides continue to stick to their guns, to the point that the Tibetan deadlock will be broken only by mass invasion and colonization. On the "roof of the world," the Tibetans clearly have the upper hand. Today, the China of big business has goals other than to seek military control over the remotest parts of Tibet. They seem to have figured out that business is better conducted with a willing population. The Tibetans have greeted warmly offers by the new Chinese entrepreneurs to buy Tibetan wool, meat, and hides, and to exploit the mineral wealth of their land.

In addition to its mineral and oil resources, Tibet's many highly valued medicinal products are of interest to the Chinese, whose pharmacopeia is one of the most complex in the world. Even if we in the West are skeptical about rhino horns being an aphrodisiac, millions of Chinese are willing to pay so much for them that rhinos around the world are being exterminated.

The highlands of Tibet harbor hundreds of medicinal plants, animals, and insects. Of the animals, the fluff from the antlers of Himalayan deer is sought after as another general aphrodisiac. Far more unusual and amazing is that very mysterious creature, half-animal, half-vegetable or, more precisely, half-insect, half-mushroom, which, in Chinese medicine, is said to cure every type of ailment including impotence.

The Tibetans call it the "grass bug" because it's a caterpillar in winter and a grass in summer. Anyone in his right mind would dismiss such a creature as an error of primitive science, which is what I did, saying it was all nonsense, until someone thrust one of the little horrors into my hand. There in my palm was a yellow caterpillar, legs and eyes and all; yet coming out of its head was a green blade of grass.

Cordycet finensis was the expert finding when I returned and displayed my naïve ignorance to a European scholar. It is a special parasitic fungus that grows on the head of several types of caterpillars. In the end, the fungus kills the unfortunate host and lives on by itself as a kind of grass.

That such a thing exists does make one marvel. At one yuan apiece, the Chinese chemists have sent thousands of Tibetans into the mountains looking for the strange insect-fungus. It is found generally at very high altitudes among the short grass to which it bears a resemblance. Western biologists have found that the strange "creature" is very rich in vitamin C.

There are no solid statistics, yet the export of such remedies is projected to be a multimillion-dollar business for the Chinese, while providing an alternate source of income to impoverished Tibetans.

The business boom that exploded in China in the early 1990s has in some ways extended to Tibet, yet not enriched the Tibetans. In Lhasa dozens of Chinese "business restaurants" entertain the new Chinese millionaires—for the most part, wool, leather, and medicinal herb merchants—whose expensive cars are parked outside.

Having nothing to do in Moyun, we began to consolidate our baggage for our thrust up the river. We all felt relief at the news that the Japanese scholars were far away, investigating what satellite maps show as the shorter of the two branches of the upper Mekong, yet we were nevertheless anxious to push ahead ourselves. When, by ten the following morning, there were no horses in sight, I became seriously worried. Should we plan to strike out on foot? To do so we would need porters, and even had there been able-bodied men available, I knew that Tibetans are loathe to carry other people's bags.

I was really getting desperate when I heard the jingle of bells, and a small herd of horses came into view. It was an odd bunch, some small, some tall, and only a few were fine specimens of the Ghegi *dota*, the local variety of the excellent Nangchen breed.

Needless to say, there was a bit of competition among us for the best mount. The horses came with their saddles—not the fine silver variety we had seen but the killer types made out of rough wood, with wicked protuberances and jagged edges that would soon make us suffer.

When I asked if there were any saddle carpets to reduce the damage to our anatomy, the answer was no.

Very quickly we discovered that the local Tibetans had learned a lot from the Chinese in matters of business. In rapid succession I was presented with a dirty old coat, a bed cover, and a rotting piece of felt at prices that would have made a Hermès salesman wince. What to do? The problem was only partially solved by using our foam mattresses over the wooden frames in a rather clumsy combination that did little to reassure Jacques, who could only barely make out the head from the tail of his shaggy pony.

It was well past noon when, at long last, feeling like Alexander the Great riding Bucephalus out to conquer Asia, I jumped on my pony and led our caravan through the breach in the wall of the little fortress. Where exactly were we going? How long would the rest of our journey take? It was anybody's guess.

Slowly our seventeen ponies, prodded on by three hired muleteers, made their way south to the nearby Mekong.

I took a deep breath. This was what I had come for, the pleasure of riding out onto the vast open plains. The wait had been long, too long perhaps, but now we were off, heading out ever deeper into the no-man's-land of that last large blank space on the map of Tibet.

10

CRY WOLF

⌘

The first miles turned out to be something of a rodeo, as one of the ponies took fright at the drumlike banging of the two steel cases it was carrying. Bolting, it charged across the steppe throwing one case and dragging the other for yards until it too came untied. No sooner had this pony been caught and reloaded in a lengthy process than another one lost all its bags as its girth slipped. We congratulated ourselves for our foresight, as we now replaced here and there weak old yak-hair ropes with nylon webbing Sebastian had brought from New York.

With only three men to care for seventeen horses, we were badly understaffed. Custom dictates one muleteer for each three to four pack animals. (I use the word *muleteer* here for lack of a better word in the English language.) In our day of air travel we tend to forget that horse and mule trains were once the principal means of transport for traveling off the beaten path, and a mule train must have muleteers, whose job it is to shout and throw stones to keep the pack animals moving. They must also constantly load, unload, and secure ever-shifting baggage, shoe the beasts (the nomads of Nangchen shoe only the forelegs), and act as a veterinarian if necessary. Moreover, they feed the horses grain and set them out to graze, and, last but not least, chase all over the countryside to round up in the morning those that have strayed overnight.

How, I wondered, would our three men cope? They were under the direction of Topgyal, the young man I had met in the black tent beside the fort at Moyun. Topgyal was probably twenty or so, but he was unable to say exactly how old he was. I am always surprised that so many Tibetans, like some Mexican Indians, have trouble telling you their own ages or even the number of children they have. This is not linked to ignorance, a bad memory, or anything like that, for they know exactly how many children they have, just as they know every one of their yaks by sight and name. It is just that numbers, large numbers especially, are meaningless to them for being very rarely used.

Just as we would rather count our sheep than name them, they prefer to name rather than number. Tibetans are in so many ways our opposites, yet once upon a time in Paris, London, and New York, one's telephone had named, not numbered coordinates, as did houses and rooms. All this is now over: cars have numbers; houses, flats, and rooms have numbers; children have numbers, as do, in certain lands, streets and provinces. Westerners take it for granted that 544 East Eighty-sixth Street #14W, New York, New York 10028, is the description of exactly where someone lives. But we like to forget that at death, aside from our passport and our Social Security numbers, a series of dates on our graves (yet more numbers) may be our only epitaph.

We had hardly left Moyun when we found ourselves wading across the bright red waters of the Dza Nak, a truly exhilarating experience.

Beneath us was the grandest river of Southeast Asia, the river whose name had echoed for so long in our minds and conversations as to have taken on the identity of an old acquaintance. I prodded my horse through the water, a little black bristly animal called *Numbo,* which means "blue." Splashing ahead we crossed the Rubicon; on the other side of the river we would enter a new world.

Gone was the road and its rail-like, compulsory itinerary. We were now blazing our own trail to follow the river itself. How many had set out like us in pilgrimage up the Mekong? Would we join the hundreds of millions who had walked its banks without ever seeing its source?

Here, the Mekong was running through low-lying red mounds where it had cut its bed. Looking west we could see where these became hills and parted as the river reached the flat vast plateau just a few miles upstream. Now we trotted and galloped on the grassy banks until I slowed the pace for Jacques. In the rear, he caught up and explained that he had already fallen off his horse twice. I admired his courage—as in everything else, he was discreet and never made any fuss. As briefly as possible I tried to give him a few hints about how to stay in the saddle, aware that only practice could teach him what to do. After about an hour my lower anatomy was already protesting the lack of adequate cushioning, but I had only myself to blame, and all I could do was shift positions or stand in my stirrups to make up for the discomfort.

The sun beat down mercilessly on our broad hats. Its deadly ultraviolet rays, unfiltered in the thin air, could, in less than an hour, strip one's flesh raw.

Only those who have known the confinement of middle-class virtues, middle-class houses, and middle-class horizons can fully appreciate the nobility of the great open spaces of our planet. There is nothing I loathe more than mediocrity, the hallmark of our Western civilization, which long ago lost the dynamic enthusiasm of our ancestors the Greeks. I am, among so many others, a product of a dying way of life, and, however much I have clung to the Concorde, to the twin towers of the World Trade Center, and to nuclear submarines and lunar probes as desperate proofs of the worth of our civilization, I can't help feeling that all these achievements are barely any better than cacophonous rock music, which is an excellent example of what's wrong with us, reeking as it does of secondhand mediocrity blown up in the name of commerce, and wildly publicized to mask the dismal reality of a culture that, in the final analysis, has little else to do but build museums and turn a blind eye to its ghettoes. If our society is so middle-class and second-rate, it is because we have lost faith in those ideals that greeted the twentieth century as the age of enlightenment.

At the beginning of this century the development of science and technology presaged a world of plenty from which want and disease would be banished forever. Now that the century is all but over, we see that we have used machines, instead, to build atomic bombs and spread war—and, more insidiously, to spread the exploitation of man *by* man, by paving roads deep into the farthest regions to sell merchandise, the destructive forerunner of the low-grade hedonism that can rapidly destroy traditions and cultures.

Over the years, I had felt compelled to seek here, at the ends of the earth, a vision of that paradise destroyed by our own brainless technologies. Yet was I not a party to the very evil I was trying to get away from? If truth be told, the original sin is travel, and my greatest transgression thirty-eight years of travel to Tibet.

As the great thirteenth Dalai Lama said, first comes the merchant, then the missionary, and lastly the soldiers. New goods, new ideals, and finally, the destruction of what was.

I certainly understood that all that I liked in my surroundings—ideas, customs, people—had been the product of hundred of years of incubation. The most interesting attribute of a people, and of a nation on the whole, is its uniqueness, which is of necessity born of isolation and which originates in even the smallest features of a culture. Thus, it is not only food but also pots and pans, language, art, and science that distinguish one group of people from another. The sale of one aluminum pot across a cultural boundary is, therefore, just as bad as the borrowing of a foreign word, in that tools and technology are as important in determining the cultural identity of a people as are rituals and customs. Imagine an Eskimo in a centrally heated home fetching his TV dinner from the freezer as he performs the walrus dance on his wall-to-wall nylon shag carpet in basketball shoes!

I have concluded that the ultimate enemy is the traveler, the tradesman of trinkets, the seeker of photographs—all those who, with their deadly small contributions, in the end destroy magical worlds it took centuries to create. If there is a central source of such pollution today, it must be the sale of airline tickets. Just as the consumption of ice cream by Eskimos—real ice cream, not made with whale oil—must signal the end of their culture, a continued shrinking of the world through air travel will guarantee a similar fate for other such isolated peoples.

I rode on, and my bitter thoughts were soon accompanied by a pernicious stitch in my side. I dismissed the pain, blaming it on the saddle and on the violently jarring trot of Numbo, with whose stamina and bad character I was just beginning to be acquainted.

Clouds had once again slowly invaded the horizon, turning day into near-night. Yet another storm was brewing, but now we no longer had the refuge of our tin box on wheels, and we would really feel the elements.

Time had come to make camp. Hastily, with a look toward the sky, we dismounted—no need to search for a campsite here, as the whole tundra was one great place on which to pitch one's tent.

I was loosening the girth of my saddle when, like an electric shock, I felt a deep pain down my side. There was no escaping it; bent in two, I could hardly straighten up. I gasped for breath, and instinctively I knew what was the matter. I cursed my fate and was suddenly terribly depressed. I had a kidney stone and with it, the pain that some compare to childbirth. I had to lie down.

By now, rushing over the shallow hills, carrying with it the momentum of miles of running and jumping ever faster, a gale-force wind struck as I collapsed to the ground.

There was nothing to break the full fury of the gale, as the others struggled to put up the vast mess tent. With whiplash reports, the tent material flogged about like a jib gone mad. I raised myself to join in the fight, and, though we managed to hoist the frames, it seemed clear that the entire contraption would soon be torn down or blown away as the wind howled ever faster and ice-sharp pellets of hail came at us horizontally, stinging our hands and faces.

The three muleteers, Ling, the cook, Sebastian, Jacques, and I managed to enter the tent, holding it down with our weight while leaning against the windblown bulging walls. I was afraid that the thin material might, at any moment, burst under the strain.

Even so, we couldn't help laughing as we battled against the unruly green material, our gasps mixing with the howling wind. Momentarily, I had overlooked the pain, but then it struck again so violently that I retched in agony.

Deep inside me I felt a flutter of panic. At 15,500 feet, exhausted, cut off from all possible hasty retreat, I knew I could die of exhaustion or heart failure, were the pain to last two or three days, as is often the case. Suddenly everything was transparently clear. To be running around at such an altitude at my age was to court disaster, and I had gotten what was coming to me. Again and again I had been warned of the risks, advised of the dangers. Again and again I had flaunted my arrogant disbelief that anything bad could happen to me.

Why? Why now? Was it the water I had drunk, and the jogging in the saddle that had loosened the stone in my kidney? The needle-sharp jabs that doubled me over were so strong that again I retched from sheer inability to stand the pain any longer. The wind was howling, and I, embarrassed, had to lie down at the feet of others, their backs to the walls, grabbing on as best they could to our tent, lest the wind blow it clear over the horizon.

"*Colique néphrétique,*" I muttered to Jacques, my only hope. What a good idea to have a doctor along. We had a full medical kit, but I knew that even the strongest pain relievers weren't always effective for my condition. Nothing could be done, in any case, until the storm had passed. It was dark outside, and all we could hear was the roar of the wind, the hissing of the hail, and the crash of thunder.

Calm to the point of annoyance, cool, and collected, Jacques had sounded quite unreasonable when he told us about his fear of lightning. I hadn't paid much attention to him, but, of course, as always, he was right. The tallest plant around was the tiny ten-inch stinging nettle, making anything that stuck out above that a perfect target. To make matters worse, some claimed that we were at the "electric pole" of our planet and that here, over the high plateau, the buildup of electricity in the air was phenomenal. Rumor or fact, all we knew was that every day we had witnessed one or more flash hail- and thunderstorms.

To our amazement, when this one had passed, the tent was still standing and only I was down, lying in a heap on the tent floor. Jacques gave me various painkillers and some other medicine, explaining that because of the altitude and the risk of pulmonary edema, he had to be careful with what he administered. I was too weak to comment. I decided to sleep where I was and I asked for my sleeping bag. I ate little and drank from the flask of murky water we had boiled and stored the previous day.

As I fell asleep I prayed for deliverance. Needless to say, I slept badly, woke, and slept again, and went out more than once to answer the call of nature, stepping over the sleeping bodies of the muleteers in the front chamber of the large tent. The sky was clear, and though I don't recall seeing a moon, the distant hills were aglow, covered with snow or hail, forming a bone-white frosted border holding up a sky alight from the brightness of a million stars. Staked to the ground our horses grazed or slept all around me.

Several times in the night, in the semidaze of the painkillers, I imagined I heard voices and shouts, and then all was quiet.

With the first glow of dawn filtering through the pale green nylon of our tent I was wide awake, feeling my stomach. I realized, in disbelief, that the pain had practically vanished. Was I cured?

I was the first outside to watch the sun slowly invade the limitless horizon and then, in a silver flash, catch the snowcapped mountains. The snow entirely changed my vision of the plateau—what had seemed to be hills were now clearly mountains. To the south rose a low range that cut us off from the Dam Chu valley, the very range whose summit had been the paradise of my wildest fantasies, with wolves and gazelles, kiang and coyotes all prowling around within eyesight of each other.

We were camped a few yards from the now-widening gravel bed of the upper Dza Chu at the confluence with the Donak, a tributary from the south. Looking west up the gray gravel causeway cut by the meandering red waters of the Mekong, I could see a fair distance to where the plain opened up to fill the horizon.

I was contemplating the landscape when a new attack struck and laid me low again. At that very moment the muleteers emerged from the tent talking excitedly. The way Ling followed them out, I sensed there was trouble. Coming to where I was, everyone began to talk at once. It took me some time to unravel what all the excitement was about.

In the middle of the night wolves had attacked our foal, and one of our mares had ripped up the peg to which she was attached. In the chaos that followed, as the mare battled the wolves, two other horses had broken loose and all three horses and the foal had vanished.

So I *had* heard voices in my doped-up sleep. Sebastian and Jacques also recalled a hubbub but had not imagined anything so dramatic as this. Had the foal been killed, I wondered, and what about the other three horses?

In Zanskar I once saw the mutilated foal of a mare belonging to the old *gyalpo*, or king of Zangla. The poor little creature had had a huge hunk of its backside ripped out. I doubt it survived. The mare had fought valiantly and had at last chased away the wolf in that case.

Now, our eldest muleteer, a man whose name I had not even had time to recall, saddled a horse and informed me he was setting out in search of the breakaways. The folds of his traditional *chuba* beating in the wind, he rode off across the grassy plateau at a gallop. That was the last we saw of him, and we never found out what became of him or the foal and three horses.

With three fewer pack horses and one muleteer gone, we were now in a bit of a fix. The only good news was that I felt a lot better, thanks to Jacques, and yet I was utterly exhausted, and we had a long day ahead of us.

Slowly, working as a pair, Topgyal, the head muleteer from Moyun, and his diminutive misfit partner, the third muleteer, began to overload our remaining horses. To saddle fourteen animals and attach packs to ten of them is a lengthy operation, which I had seen repeated a thousand times. First one must go out and catch the grazing pony, then put a saddle carpet on its back, usually a wool or straw-stuffed mattress-like affair, hinged down the middle. When this is in place it is covered by another carpet, usually of wool and formed of two identical flaps with matching designs and hinged at the weft. The panels are curved tulip fashion so that the front of the panel is longer than the rear.

On this carpet (called a *den*) the *ga*, or saddle, is placed, attached by a single *lo*, or girth, unlike the Mongol saddles, which are fastened by two girths. Finally, yet another blanket is placed in the saddle to make the mount more comfortable; here, however, this element was sadly absent and replaced by my down parka and bedroll.

The art of saddlery and riding tack is specific to each country and even each region. In Paris I had met an expert by the name of Dr. Langlois who was studying the migrations of peoples in Asia through the variations and similarities in their riding tack.

It has yet to be determined exactly who invented the first saddles, stirrups, and bits. Some claim the Chinese were the first, but this has recently been contradicted—the Chinese took to chariots and riding late, six centuries after the Assyrians, and then only reluctantly, it seems, in order to defend themselves against horse-riding invaders from the west.

The Tibetan tradition is itself hard to trace much earlier than the sixth century A.D. Baltistan and Ladakh, both integral parts of Tibet as far back as the sixth and seventh centuries, were sometimes called the land of the Asphasians by the early Greeks and Indians (*Asp* or *Aps* being the ancient Indo-European word for "horse").

What is interesting is that the Tibetan equestrian tradition, and particularly Tibetan saddlery, is quite different from that of the Mongols, just as the Tibetan breeds, such as the Nangchen horse, are very different from Mongolian horses, in spite of what many writers have said.

All this leads to one very interesting question: Who were the very first men to ride horses, and which horses did they ride?

In the prehistoric cave paintings of France and Spain—notably in the caves of Lascaux, Niort, and the recently discovered caves of Chauvet (1994)—depictions of horses are numerous. These paintings have been dated as going back between seventeen thousand and thirty-four thousand years. In those days all horses were wild, or at least, no one rode them, which is not exactly the same thing.

What kinds of horses roamed Europe in those days? Examination of the cave paintings shows that there were two types: the Przewalski horse, frequently represented and easily recognizable because of its white, donkey-like nose, its big jaw, short bristly mane, its arched neck, and short ears. Then there is another horse depicted in these caves, the mysterious horse number two. It is an animal with a triangular face, a flat forehead, and a straight nose without the white donkey muzzle, but with flat, elongated duck-bill nostrils, narrow slanted eyes, a weak jawbone, and very light hindquarters. What breed did this strange horse belong to?

The first known tame horses, whose skeletons were found in a tomb by the Black Sea, were smaller than the wild Przewalski horse, but otherwise unidentifiable. Some experts believe that our domesticated horses actually came from two separate breeds, one rustic breed and one refined, taller horse, possibly akin to an Arab. Yet others believe that they all developed from crossbreeds of the wild Przewalski horse and other types. The problem remained unresolved in 1994, as we rode toward the source of the Mekong. Maybe it would never be solved. In practice, it was easier to follow the skeletal evolution of horses over millions of years from fossils around the globe than to determine the skin color and shape of a specific breed from a mere five thousand years ago.

Sebastian and I would have been thoroughly surprised had we been told that in less than twelve months' time, barely 200 miles from where we now stood, we were going to shed new light on the unsolved mystery of which horses were the first to be tamed by man.

By the time the horses were saddled at last, the sun was up and the snow on the hills around us was melting fast. In no time our pack animals were stretched out in disarray along the flat grassy south bank of the Dza Nak.

Now my primary concern was to map the tributaries of the upper Mekong, which involved trying to learn their names and then recording the exact position of their confluence with the main river. Last, but certainly not least, we had to make sure that we were following the principal course of the Mekong. So far this had proved easy, as the gravel bed of the main river was very wide—between 200 and 650 feet wide and getting wider as we progressed west, passing the Donak and the Lungmo tributaries on the right bank while on the other side, passing between the two, were the Tranak oma, then the Tranak coma (upper and lower black cliff rivers). I gathered these names by questioning our horsemen and various nomads we encountered along the way.

I presumed that the vast riverbed we were following must be filled with water only a few days, maybe a few weeks, a year when the spring brings on the thaw.

I once witnessed the thaw in early June in western Tibet, and though it seemed a little foolish to draw too quick a comparison, there must be some analogy. The hot spring air reaches a critical point, and the frozen earth, pools, streams, rivers, and marshes all start to exude water, running at once, as if the whole landscape had been sprayed by torrential rains. In no time vast dry stony beds are filled to become huge moving lakes rushing away on this unexpected flood.

Unlike the upper Dam Chu or the upper course of the Yellow River, the high plateau on either side of the upper Mekong was not dotted with lakes. After the famed junction with the Lungmo chu (mistaken by Dutreuil de Rhins for the main river), the right bank began to rise sharply, forcing us to cross to the other side. Hail began to fall, mixed, yet again, with rain driven by a sharp wind. I stopped to put on a rain poncho, and the rustling of its material in the wind frightened my already frisky pony, which started off at a gallop as I hung on, the poncho flapping more than ever, and driving poor Numbo on.

When I managed at last to slow the pony down, the hail and rain had stopped, and although wet and miserable, I took solace that I could contemplate the vast horizons around me in air that was newly clear and washed.

Off to the west, the direction in which we were heading, lay two ranges of low hills, white with hail, now clearly visible on either side of the river flowing past us. To the left (on the south bank) was the Drug-di range, to the right, the Sag-ri range; these two names were soon to become a part of our daily conversations, but from where we now stood we couldn't see if the two ranges eventually merged, closing the gap that separated them on the horizon.

Various nomads offered me what they believed were the origins of these ranges' name. *Druk* means "dragon," and so it seemed that the hills to our left might be the "dragon hills." The other's meaning was less clear: *Sag* means "pile"; could it be the "rock pile range"? This seemed possible, since the highest point we could see on our right was rocky, as opposed to the rounded summits of the Dragon Hills on our left.

Once again we were told by our muleteer that there were two sources, two heads of the Mekong, one in each range. What could that mean? Which one of the two should we choose to head for?

We stopped for a brief lunch. As our cook had nothing to offer but his infamous plastic pink-red sausage, the time had come to tap our precious stores brought all the way from France. Food was not just a necessity but an obsession. Even the frugal Jacques could not help but talk about it all the time. We would list aloud how many chocolate bars we had, the types of sweets, the varieties of French *saucisson* and the cheese. Where were they packed? How many could each of us have? How delicious they would be! We recounted gastronomic orgies from our previous lives in what seemed like a very remote land of plenty where people ate with knives and forks instead of sticks. My kidneys were forgotten for now—it seemed that I had survived, and I was now just ravenous, if bone-tired.

Looking at Sebastian I felt somewhat reassured that I wasn't the only one who was drained of energy. Jacques, too, seemed washed out, but I couldn't help admiring his determination, for as we literally flopped to the ground after dismounting and lay there waiting to eat, he somehow found the energy to shoot film of our horses and our makeshift camp. Having eaten, I immediately fell asleep on my back in the sun, protected by a thick coat of white zinc oxide that made me look like a scarecrow.

Getting up half an hour later, we started to follow the river along its north (left) bank, which began to rise slowly, giving us a good view of the broad flat plain on the other side of the Mekong—a plain covered with short, dry golden grass. Far in the distance I could make out the familiar black dome of a solitary tent.

It is hard to describe a full day's riding, for there is both an element of sameness and a constant stream of novelty about it. Unlike journeys by plane, train, or even car, it is hard when riding or walking to ignore one's surroundings. When traveling at high speeds one must be constantly alert, with an eye on the road ahead. One is apt to forget what has just passed. On the other hand, from atop a horse, minutes slowly turn into hours, the sun becomes important—the way it moves through the sky—and the heavens themselves make a difference, not just the clouds but the birds. The call of the great black common Tibetan crow is one of the strangest sounds in the feathered kingdom: a deep honk, a sort of hoarse foghorn alternating with a metallic sound, like a low-key tuning fork. These birds are the size of chickens, and, in spite of their blackness, are not sinister, just strange, an odd and always surprising sort of company in the most desolate areas of the highest passes of the remotest regions.

More than ever we began to understand that here on the highest tundra, life for the wolf and the gazelle, the great Tibetan vultures, and the smallest of sparrows was carried out in the open with nowhere at all to hide. Only the lowly fox, the large marmots, the little glacier rats, and the giant-eared Tibetan hares had burrows as a refuge.

The fact that there were no woods, bushes, or even solitary rocks behind which to hide had a strange effect on us. I felt vulnerable, totally exposed. Looking around I knew I could see and be seen a hundred miles away.

No need for smoke signals here to announce the approach of intruders—I knew from experience that one could often watch a caravan coming for two full days before finally meeting it!

Looking east back down the broad bed of the Mekong, I could see the crystal-clear outlines of great snowy peaks and rock-crested mountains whose bases were below the horizon.

Overloaded, our horses were constantly stumbling and losing their packs, and yet Ling, who had been up to now habitually somber, seemed pleased with himself as he rode the finest of our horses—a gray gelding with large flared nostrils, protuberant eyes, and very fine limbs.

Blowing in from the west, a new bank of dark clouds soon invaded the horizon, and once again it began to hail. The marble-sized stones stung our faces like gravel, forcing us to close our eyes, leaving our horses to figure out where to go. We were lucky that it was not yet one of those storms whose stones can kill yaks, for here in the open, in a storm of that kind, with no available refuge, we might well have become casualties ourselves. Lightning scratched the sky, making us shudder as we recalled Jacques's sinister warnings. We felt terribly vulnerable sitting erect on our horses, vertical marks in a horizontal landscape.

Buffeted by the wind, we advanced, outlined against a backdrop of mountains and surrounded by endless vistas of inescapable nothingness. I now began to question not just the reasons for my being in this desolate place but the very essence of it all. For years I had been striving for a life that could match my dreams. I had dreamt of lost horizons, beyond which I imagined a utopia that would satisfy my cravings for the absolute. And now, here I was, as close to reaching the ends of the earth as was possible, and what was there for me?

Where was El Dorado, Shangri-La, my paradise lost? So far there was nothing—nothing but the ever-increasing certitude that all I might encounter was what I had carried inside myself all along.

Had I reached the mythical end of all exploration, in the words of T. S. Eliot? Had I come full circle from my dreams back into reality, back to where I had started, in a world where dreams and reality are one and the same?

I *had* come full circle, but unlike Eliot, I recognized the place where I stood. Since childhood I had visualized this place just as it now appeared around me, immense, empty, forbidding. With this, my whole plan of finding the source of the Mekong lost the little significance it might once have had.

I had thought of rivers only as roads of a sort, not as symbols. I had used rivers for transport, rowing up the Dvina and down the Dnieper on a wild journey across Russia in the footsteps of the Varangians, with Jacques, an eccentric Irish camel breeder, a dozen Russians, assorted hippies, philosophers, and even a physicist from Soviet Georgia.

I had nearly drowned in a Himalayan river, the Arun, when my hovercraft overturned in an ambitious attempt to conquer white water with a new technology. After nearly ten years of playing around with nuts and bolts, trying to invent a means of sailing over unnavigable waters, wishing to transform all rivers into highways, I had eventually given up on hovercraft, but not before I succeeded in roaring through the great Himalayan breach between Annapurna and Dhaulaghiri in 1972.

I had dreamed that coming to the heart of the Tibetan highlands, to the source of the Mekong, I would somehow learn the secret of the nomads, the key to their insurmountable strength. I had hoped to meet a sort of superman whose words would suddenly put into perspective the chaos of our modern world, would give me the answer to all the queries raised by a century of wars and bombs, of fast planes and cars whizzing around in a cloud of polluting smoke. From their vantage point, I thought, surely I would see the smoke rise. The nomads surely could answer the unsolved problems of our world.

So far the only sounds I had heard were the whistle of muleteers and the clatter of hooves. It was really all slightly ridiculous, even the little stream that we Westerners call the Mekong. Why carry on, why bother, was it not all as Buddha had said, an illusion of the senses, a sort of terribly bad joke?

The fall of one of our overloaded horses made me realize that it was getting late. With the arrogance of the white man I decided unilaterally that we should stop and make camp immediately. The spot seemed perfect against the sheltering face of the steep north bank of the river. Here there would be little chance of our tent being blown away.

The young head muleteer disagreed. I tried to explain in my best Tibetan that we needed the shelter from the wind, but still he insisted that we cross the river to camp on the other side, out in the open. We continued to argue until, exasperated, I grabbed the young man by the arm roughly, perhaps too roughly; he was frightened and turned to me saying he was going to head back.

My heart sank. I felt guilty. I knew that on more than one occasion, I have been accused of insensitivity; had I hurt the young man's feelings? But why was he so obstinate? What about the wind? What if our tent disintegrated? Anyway, couldn't he lead his horses to graze on the other side? Or was it that there was something I didn't understand, such as a matter of grazing rights? Communication is difficult at times even when two people are presumably speaking the same language.

There are so many things I have failed to understand in other people. I apologized, excused myself, and reluctantly agreed to ford the Mekong yet again. By now the river and the banks had lost their red color, and the water ran a silty gray among the gray pebbles.

The reluctant muleteer selected a stony site just on the edge of the river to unload our beasts of burden. With a mechanical rigidity that betrayed the punishment his seat had suffered, Jacques dismounted, falling to the ground with his boot caught in the stirrup. I too felt the rigors of the ride as I stood tottering on firm ground to help him up. Sebastian jumped out of the saddle of his tall mare. The three of us cut a bizarre, yet not unfamiliar image, with our broad-brimmed felt hats, our chaps and boots, holding the reins of our weary horses. It was an image that for many centuries has been commonplace all over the world among the descendants of those barbarians whose ranks we had joined: the civilization of *Equus caballus.*

How much man owes the horse we will never be able to say exactly. Both as a weapon and as the spearhead of civilization as we know it, horses have, throughout history, been magical and powerful creatures.

The horses of both Alexander and Cortez were legendary and were actually venerated and adored by the tribesmen of India and Aztec warriors they helped to vanquish. *Equus caballus,* that elegant extension of man's arrogance, was a noble conquest that bred chivalry in our societies, yet at the same time carried man farther from home than he should have ever ventured. If the alliance between man and dog has proven a sad one for wild game, the alliance of man and horse has proven devastating for millions of humans.

Our tents pitched, the horses out to graze, I reconciled myself
with our young muleteer by giving him one of those gadgets that,
like the green glass beads Cortez used as bribes, were so avidly
sought by the natives. How I despised myself for that easy way of
dazzling a fellow human. My only excuse for such behavior was that
the same gadget, a little solar flashlight, also fascinated me. That
man could capture the sun in daylight and return the light by night
was, without any question, indeed a marvel that bordered on the
supernatural.

Although possessed of perfectly adequate intelligence for most
things, I still don't fully understand the miracle of technology that
allows an impurity implanted in a silicon chip, when excited by a
photon, to release electrons nonstop without wear or tear. The muleteer had more reasons than he knew to be amazed, and we were now
friends again.

As the natural light slowly faded, leaving us alone in the dark to
listen to the gurgle of the waters of the Mekong, we all gathered in
our mess tent around a candle that caused the walls to dance with
giant black shadows. Now we felt united in our common cause. Rid
of the two drivers, who were perhaps too streetwise for their own
good, our young cook and Ling had suddenly become much more
personable.

The cook busied himself lighting a fire in the open and we were
soon drinking that noble American drink: chocolate. It was the
Olmecs, once the greatest horticulturalists on our planet, who first
made a sweet hybrid of the bitter wild bean they called cacao, just as
they took a tiny common grass and by some miracle of genetic engineering blew up its seeds to make the great grains of corn upon
which so much of the globe relies for survival today. The Olmecs
also conceived of zero before the Arabs had heard of Allah, devised
a sophisticated calendar, and—we now know—invented the earliest
form of Mayan writing, those strange symbols that scholars have
struggled so long to decipher.

What had the nomads of Nangchen invented? Had they learned how to capture the sun in a small black box? Had they discovered how to transform grass into grain? While the answer is no, they invented and discovered nothing, what they have accomplished is a way of life so successful that their numbers inevitably increased to the point that they had to send their sons north, south, east, and west at full gallop to conquer new horizons.

The tundra, the world's highest, most unpleasant place, had produced those "real men" who, as the Tibetan saying goes, "do not live in comfort, just like goats do not live on level plains." According to history as written by the "civilized" world, the barbarians who issued forth from the same nameless steppes that now surrounded us have done pretty well for themselves, flashlight or no, and their lives and values are a challenge to the rest of us. Are we in the West real men no more? Has a life of comfort overtaken all else as the byword of our hedonistic consumer culture?

For years I had wondered what we were made for. Were we made for comfort or discomfort, for hardship or for pleasure? The prominent anthropologist Marshall Salins claims that Stone Age men worked less than four hours a day in order to eat, that they lived a life devoid of undue strain or worry, not even bothering to store meat or fruit, even when they could. They lived day to day without much concern for tomorrow. This image of Stone Age man is very different from that of the inhabitants of the heart of Tibet—nomads who brave hail daily in summer and steel themselves against bitter cold and snow in winter.

Could it be that just as each of us has in our character a lazy side and a hardy side, man is made for both the good life and the hard life? Or, could it be, just as races arose from adaptations to the environment—some humans evolving with brown skin and others with white or yellow—that maybe there are people who are given to comfort and other people who are hardy and despise it? Are the Khamba, who call themselves a race of kings, not just a group of the latter?

Known to the Chinese as wild barbarians, they are driven by an ardor and strength that for centuries bowled over their neighbors, the comfort-loving societies of the lowlands.

Many have claimed that the two-pronged revolution of the late Stone Age was comprised of nomadism and agriculture, producing Abel, the honest, nomadic pastoralist, and Cain, the greedy landowner and jealous farmer.

I, for one, am a strong believer that man, just like his brothers in the animal kingdom, has both a built-in genetic expectation of life and many genetically determined patterns of behavior. It is clear to me, for instance, that man hates boredom. Moreover, according to Carlton Coon, the grandfather of modern anthropology, hunter-gatherers have no hobbies—because they are never bored.

For my part, I love the adventure of the hunt because of the sheer pleasure it produces. There is no outdoor exercise quite as exciting as stalking and then riding after an animal. I was twenty-three when I realized that, as I galloped full tilt after a wild boar, I had suddenly gone wild myself, struck by something that I could define only as "basic instinct," something akin to discovering that without a teacher one knows how to make love. Tracking game is utter delight, and something I believe we were made for.

So what of the nomad and his dull routine of watching cattle ruminate?

I put myself to sleep, ironically, bored of counting sheep, and I dreamt instead of things more exciting, like galloping at full speed on the plains behind a herd of fleeing gazelles or, better still, chasing on horseback after a beautiful Amazon—the ultimate of all chases and the authentic pursuit of true happiness.

Once a year the nomads of Nangchen live out this amazing chase. The prettiest marriageable girls are decked out in all their finery, covered in turquoise and coral, silver and amber, their braids shiny from butter, their finest silk blouses tucked over their breasts, the belts of their *chubas* loosened to allow them to sit astride their ponies.

Young men and boys of another valley or tribe look over these beauties, often the daughters of their traditional rivals, even their enemies. Then, suddenly, the game begins, the chase is on. The rules are as simple as they are shocking to our modern Western ideals. The boys choose their lucky victims, and on their side the girls appraise their suitors and make choices of their own. The girls gallop off, with the boys in hot pursuit. Men and women are on equal ground, their success depending often on the swiftness of their horses and their agility as riders.

To pursue and be pursued—the ultimate game of tag, the most popular game on every playground around the world, and in every bedroom.

The instinct for the chase is a basic instinct without which mankind could not have survived as long as it has. Today, now that man can feed himself without it, he is naturally bored. In the slums of our cities, boredom leads to crime and to another form of the chase, in which both predator and prey are humans, and the battle is not for procreation, like the chase on the fairgrounds of the upper Dza, but for life itself.

1 1

WHERE BEGINNING ENDS

⌘

In a tent there is no escaping dawn, no need for a clock. When I emerged into the wind, the clear sky announced a glorious day. It was September 17.

As I looked to the south I saw a lone rider in the distance. Ten minutes later I could say for sure he was coming our way. In this great void his slow approach was a little unnerving. By the time we had eaten our breakfast of chocolate and biscuits, with a little cheese brought from France, the rider was at last upon us.

He slowed the pace of his gray horse and cautiously moved around our camp examining our tents and kit bags. He smiled and then addressed our chief muleteer. I could not understand what they said to each other, but the muleteer translated, saying that he had not seen or heard of our runaway horses, which had been frightened off by the wolf. I gathered that the man's tent was somewhere out there behind a hill.

The man didn't dismount, but, shifting a cap on his head, he smiled again, took one last amused look at us, and was off, disappearing from sight just as he had come.

Perhaps more than anyone we had encountered he symbolized for me the fugitive aspect of life on the open plain—a world of isolation in which families must live apart because of the territorial imperatives of their herds. He was of a people whose solitary existence, in which families see little of anyone but themselves, was nevertheless constantly tempered by the awareness of others nearby and by their prerogatives and limitations. Whereas those of us who live in crowds are certainly familiar with urban solitude and loneliness, bred of our reluctance to talk to strangers, here all encounters are seen as a happy event.

Slowly we broke camp and set off on our long march west. Our chief muleteer explained that in two days' time we could reach the source of the Drug-di chu-go, one of the two local springs that we believed might be the source of the Mekong. It lay, he said, in the shadow of Dragon Mountain.

The day began well under a radiant sun. Crossing the gravel bed of the Mekong once again, we followed the northern bank and came upon a tributary that I believed might be the Mekong's longest northern branch, one that probably took its source in the Sag-ri Mountains, the "rock pile" hills.

I wanted to ascertain the volume of its flow. This was made easier by the fact that the tributary joined the main river in the center of the vast gravel bed. Both waterways ran down the same slope and, therefore, had approximately the same speed and flow.

First I measured the breadth and depth of the tributary where it encountered the main stream of the Dza Nak, coming from the east. It was a little less than one-third the width of the main river and shallower by a foot. There was no mistaking that the main river still lay to the west.

I was taking readings of our position from the satellites (a frequent ritual that bordered on modern magic) when from out of nowhere appeared a monk dressed in a flowing gown with a bright yellow elongated cotton hat.

What a monk was doing on the edge of the northern tributary of the Dza Nak that morning nobody knows. He seemed to be connected to the herd of sheep that grazed nearby on the bristly short marsh grass of what was now a dry swamp, a vast bumpy expanse of churned-up hardened sod.

I asked the monk the name of the tributary ("Jalgo chu") and bade him write it down (*rGyal-rgo*). Was it up this tributary that lay the Sag-ri source? He said no, further confirming that the sources lay farther up the main river to the west.

Progress in the sun was difficult, and we tried to shorten our way by roughing it over the turned-up surface of the dry marsh.

Lack of oxygen is known to cause certain people to hallucinate—they see and hear things that don't exist. Worse still, high altitude, in depriving the brain of oxygen, has a whole series of odd side effects, among them the erosion of willpower. Suddenly, everything appears futile, useless, and trivial. Why, after all, climb to the summit? Many mountaineers have turned back without being able to explain themselves—for no other reason perhaps than that they suddenly saw their entire endeavor as childish, ridiculous, not worth the trouble.

Such were the thoughts that now overwhelmed me. Why go any farther? The Japanese expedition had no doubt found the source ahead of us, so why bother? Did anyone really care? Jacques had tried to explain to me what mysterious chemical reactions went on in the brain and the body as a result of the change of atmospheric pressure. He told me about the terrible disasters that might disrupt the delicate equilibrium of fluids behind the membranes that controlled cells and hormonal distribution (whatever that meant). These were weird chemical reactions on the molecular level that could have such devastating effects as making one blind, momentarily deaf, or, worse still, could trigger a heart attack or pulmonary edema, causing the lungs to fill with that deadly foam about which Jacques had spoken with such apprehension.

Altered perception being a natural corollary of high altitude, I advanced like an automaton, with my mind racing around the inner globe of my head, conjuring up odd images of Mexico and its blissful climate, a swimming pool under palm trees, and hibiscus blossoms floating on the water.

Mine were dreams of comfort in an uncomfortable world—a world that had driven the nomads to praise discomfort, great effort, perseverance, struggle, and combat, just like the Victorian public school principals who produced Younghusband and all those other nomadic, masochistic colonial civil servants and explorers who were really happy only when it hailed pigeon eggs, when their ponies died under them and their supplies fell over cliffs and the flood washed them all away. How I loved the hardship of expeditions, that self-inflicted torture that gave me a good conscience, allowed me to overeat in Paris, frolic in London, and drink too much in New York, while enjoying the holier-than-thou feeling of those who know what it is to pay the toll. I considered hardship noble, necessary, and virtuous, as all through my childhood and school days it had been drummed into my mind that all things pleasurable were evil—sex, wines, sweets, pretty pictures, lovely dresses, sports cars, luxury limousines, gold plate, late-night parties, dancing, and most music. In the end, all those things would, like masturbation, make you mad or blind. Yes, pleasure was like drugs: addictive and destructive, leading to crime and then death. These were the thoughts and mores of my nanny, my puritan housemasters, and those noble explorers on whom I had modeled my childhood dreams—to whom I owed being where I now stood, buffeted by the wind, scorched by the sun, my seat blue from abrasion, my face cracked from sunburn. I would be lying if I didn't say that I was happy—happy like those Muslim saints who sang songs of joy as the Crusaders cut them to pieces, in the kind of slow martyrdom they had always wished for themselves.

Looking ahead I saw yet another of our horses trip and fall. Weighed down by our baggage, it lay there exhausted, unable to get up, no doubt ill-fed and in poor condition when hired. Pressing on, I galloped up to the young man in charge.

After a brief discussion, I was given to understand that if we set up camp now and left our baggage behind, we could gallop ahead and reach the Dragon water head, one of the so-called sources.

I was a little bit skeptical, as the young man had so far proven slightly devious. Was he shy or just playing stupid? I couldn't tell. Since leaving Moyum I had had my doubts. First there had been no saddle carpets, then the attack by wolves, and the too-hasty departure and nonreturn of the senior of the three muleteers. Could all of it have been a ploy? None of us clearly remembered hearing a wolf, but then I suppose wolves don't bark or howl when attacking.

Seeing the condition of the horses and considering that the grass was greener where we were than along much of our stony marshy trail, I thought it could do no harm to give the horses a half day's rest. We had been under way for nearly four hours, and from what I gathered we could return from the Drug-di spring that very night. The following day, with rested horses, we could carry on with our bags to seek out the other source, the Sag-ri chu-go. Beyond any doubt, without baggage we could travel faster.

I discussed the plan with Sebastian, Jacques, and Ling. I had learned from bitter experience that it is never good to be separated from one's baggage or to split forces, but, with the sun shining and not a cloud in sight, why not push on ahead? We decided to leave the cook behind with the second muleteer. Hastily, together we erected the mess tent in a sheltered hollow, had a fast nonlunch, and jumped into the saddle. I felt pleased, in good shape for a change, with no pain anywhere except for my saddle sores.

Jacques looked tired. If only we had had six weeks to acclimatize. To my doubtful queries about making it to the source and back, Sebastian, cheerful as usual, just smiled, and mumbled "piece of cake," his pet Cockney expression, and one that we had adopted to ease whatever formidable obstacle we encountered.

It was close to one o'clock when we set off. Our urge to gallop was soon dampened by the built-in spitefulness of our saddles.

The unadulterated blueness of the sky accentuated the immensity of the plateau stretching out on three horizons; the fourth, our western vista, was partly obscured by the rounded yellow mass of the Drug-di and Sag-ri ranges. The gap between the two seemed to be bridged by a low ridge we imagined to be a pass. As we advanced I became more and more convinced that, indeed, there must be two sources, one in the left range and one in the right. We would have to determine which of the two was the true source of the Mekong. If all went well, I thought, tonight we would get to the Drug-di source.

My hopes were brought up short, however, when our lead muleteer, who had until now professed a knowledge of the land and even a familiarity with the source, suddenly admitted that he needed help, in that he didn't know the way. Having confessed as much, he galloped off toward a distant tent we had just sighted.

I was a little bit rattled. Had I given our muleteer the benefit of the doubt too often? Was he just a crook, lying to us about his knowledge of the land, lying to us about the three horses escaping and the third man not returning? What did it all mean? Were we about to join the ranks of Dutreuil de Rhins and others who had been murdered by sly Khambas along the isolated trails of eastern Tibet?

I have often been called naïve, and my passion for Tibet has undoubtedly often obstructed my good judgment. We might just have hit upon a bad egg. Was our man a collaborator of the Chinese? His family's tent had, after all, been pitched beside the abandoned garrison, where the drunken administrator also resided. Had we fallen in with a local mafia, and were we now at their mercy miles from nowhere?

Bandits are somewhat like saints—one can know their real identity only when it is already too late. Could our young guide be a bandit? He seemed so physically weak, and, anyway, we outnumbered him—indeed, it was unlikely, unless of course he could find reinforcements or a third man lay in ambush somewhere.

I dispelled these thoughts when the young man returned at a gallop. Now he seemed rather more ridiculous than ferocious, not the least because he had attached the solar-powered flashlight to the already-strange cap he wore atop his braids.

We took to riding in the very bed of the upper Mekong. In spite of the fact that rounded pebbles are not the best support for horses' hooves, our animals seemed to manage all right. The Nangchen breed is so surefooted, I had never known any to falter or trip. This surefootedness, so useful along the edges of rocky vertical mountain trails, might seem wasted on a flat high plateau, but, in fact, the flat plains of the high plateau are one vast death trap for conventional horses, filled as they are with minute hoof-sized burrows of glacier rats, millions of them everywhere, three feet or less apart, making the entire tundra a sponge of these deadly holes. The horse that didn't have total control over where it placed its four hooves would in an instant break a leg and die or have to be shot. That our horses could trot and gallop on this terrain required of them at all times an amazing mastery of their gait. They advanced as if dancing to avoid the deadly burrows.

In comparison, the gravel bed of the river was easy going. Once our guide had made his inquiries, we raced up to where the river split in two at the foot of a steep and rocky moundlike hill.

To the left a small clear stream joined the large muddy waters of the main river at the contour of the hill. Our guide explained that the Drug-di chu-go, the headwater or spring he had referred to, was up this small clear tributary. He said that the spring was a holy place whose waters were beneficent. We needed little more to understand what we had suspected all along—that what our guide and everyone else had mentioned as one of the sources of the Dza Nak, the black Mekong, was in fact a bubbling source of water known to be a holy place. It is common in Tibet to consider as holy and auspicious, and worthy of being turned into a shrine, practically every unusual work of nature. From springs to cliffs to caves and stalactites and stalagmites, everything is considered miraculous and a work of the gods.

Believing us to be pilgrims rather than geographers, Tibetans quite naturally would wish to show us the "sights" and here in the Drug-di range was one such spot, a clear, deep, gurgling spring.

No need to follow the stream up to the spring, in that it was obvious that the main course of the Mekong lay beyond this little tributary and flowed from the west between the two ranges. After consultation with my companions, we decided to carry on up the main stream.

Since the river made a large arc behind the hillock, to save time we decided to ride up on the northern bank and cut across dry land. This route led us toward what we had mistaken as a pass linking the two mountain ranges. We now realized that the saddle-like pass was just a buttress of the Sag-ri range that eventually fell to the Mekong.

After a grueling ride to the top of the ridge, we saw in the distance the black outline of yet another tent. From this ridge, I believed for sure we would be able to see the land in all its expanse and have an idea as to how much farther the river flowed to the west. Only then would I decide what to do: turn back to rejoin our camp or carry on.

The sun continued to beat down on us relentlessly, and the sky remained so clear that I was not overly concerned with the fact that we were getting even farther from our base.

As we rose we had an increasingly precise view of how the main bed of the Mekong cut an arc into the northern flank of the Dragon range.

We were now well up the flank of the buttress of one of the tallest summits of the Sag-ri range, crossing a great spill of loess and gravel that issued from what seemed like a valley but turned out to be no more than a gully of dry rocks.

It was four o'clock when, after having scanned what seemed like an ever-receding horizon, we came within earshot of two furious dogs guarding a solitary tent.

Dismounting and waiting for someone to come out and hold the brutes, I turned my head to the east and caught sight of one of the most majestic landscapes I had ever seen, although "landscape" is perhaps too narrow a word to encompass the true immensity of the view. As I had in Mustang thirty years before, once again I understood why Tibet is called the roof of the world, for truly from here one looked down on the world, down over the horizons onto high mountains as the earth curved and dropped away.

A handsome man in his early forties with a scruffy braid at his back, a green waistcoat, and a broad friendly smile came out of the tent. Having quelled the mastiffs, he asked our guide who we were and what we were up to. A young boy of about fifteen came and joined the jovial man while three tiny children in homespun woolen miniature Tibetan gowns crawled out of the tent and then sat on a bale of wool and stared at us, amazed, with immense eyes.

The tent was not quite upon the summit of the ridge, so we could not yet see the Mekong on the other side. Ling asked the man a question or two and explained to me that the Sino-Japanese party had been seen to pass by behind us. The Tibetan confirmed the news: He had seen that party cross over the Dza-chu going in the direction of the holy Drug-di spring, from which we had turned away to carry on up the main river.

This was tremendous news. Now we knew that our would-be rivals had not traveled to the source, which, we were now convinced, must lie somewhere to the west up the main branch. If all went well, we might yet win the race.

Above all else, I was ecstatically happy to have found a local man living so close to the source and able to give us the names of the various tributaries. After all, the mapping of the source or sources required not just latitudes and longitudes, but names.

I obtained the names of the two tributaries we could see running off the Sag-ri range. Moving over to the ridge behind the tent, I then got the names of three small rivulets that flowed into the main Dza-chu where it made a large arc along the contour of the foot of the ridge upon which we were standing.

Pressing on with questions, I heard mentioned for the first time the name Rupsa. Was it a river? No, it was the name of a pass. The Rupsa-la. This pass, I was led to understand, was possibly the watershed, beyond which lay the basin of the upper Dri chu, or the Yangtze River.

Where exactly was the Rupsa-la? The man pointed to a hill to the west. The pass lay beyond that, out of sight, he said. I speculated that this pass was no doubt set upon the ridge that linked the two ranges. The source should lie somewhere near there, unless, of course, there was another surprise in store for us.

There was only one way to know, and that was to keep going. It was now four-thirty, and we risked being caught out with no food or shelter in the dark. Should we go back to our camp and move forward the next day?

In my head I was coming to another conclusion altogether. Why go to the source anyway, now that we were practically certain where it lay? Why bother? Why not just turn back and go home, or rather carry on with our initial project and go back down the Mekong to Nangchen Dzong and then to Nangchen Gar, the fascinating capital of the nomad kingdom?

I was tired and must have spoken aloud. Sebastian looked at me in shock. "Go back now?" He thought either I had gone mad or, as a result of altitude and fatigue, I had lost all determination.

I called our guide. "Listen," I heard myself say, "we go on, with or without you, right up to the very end of the river. We must hurry."

Sebastian looked relieved. "I thought you were crazy wanting to turn back now." He had been right: I had lost my reason for a moment. Or had I?

There were in fact good reasons (as we were about to discover) to have been a little more cautious. I knew, of course, that there was little chance we would be able to go to the source and come back to our camp in daylight. Yet the horizon was cloudless, the night would be clear, and finding our camp should prove easy. How could we get lost when all we had to do was follow our steps back down the river itself?

My reasoning was a little bit simplistic. *"On y va!"* I exclaimed to Jacques, and we all mounted and rode up and over the ridge down to the river.

We had won the first race, against the Japanese who were, no doubt, now on their way home, out of sight behind us. Now began another race, the race against the setting sun.

I kept on telling myself we had plenty of time, yet how far we had to go nobody knew. Not even the nomad knew for sure.

It all depended now on the river and its tributaries, on our determining which was the largest and the longest. We would now have to measure the relative flow of each tributary carefully, and as it had not hailed or rained or snowed, this was an ideal day to make such measurements. The water level in each of the rivers and streams we would encounter could be considered representative of its normal mean relative flow. In simpler terms, the water in the rivers would not be freak high water due to rains or storms. By following the widest stream we would be sure to follow the principal fork of the longest branch of the Mekong River.

Below the nomad's camp we reached the Mekong just where it received the waters of a large torrent coming down steeply from the Sag-ri range. The torrent was half the size of the main river, whose bed here was very much wider than that of this affluent. Looking up we could see the craggy rock heaps that had given the Sag-ri its name. No doubt up there lay the second, "sacred" source, but not the geographical source we were seeking. We carried on up the main river bed, now about thirty yards wide.

Two hours later we passed a clear mountain torrent perhaps ten feet wide, and we saw then that the main river's width had diminished. Here and there more small yet not insignificant lateral streams rushed down from the mountains that slowly had begun to close in on us.

With a feeling of great anticipation mingled with urgency, we pressed on, now and then breaking into a little canter in spite of the pain to our rear ends.

I would be embarrassed to describe these last moments of our quest in those moving terms that made the readers of Victorian tales shudder. There were no heroics, and there was no danger. For the moment the sun shone golden upon the mountains, which were now so close that we could actually see the water of the streams tumbling down toward us.

The Mekong, although ever smaller, seemed endless. Around a bend, on a broad rocky flat, we came upon the confluence of three streams of approximately the same size. We stopped, unsure of which branch to follow. We could see that one tumbled down from a cliff face in the Drug-di range, another came from a slope leading up into the Sag-ri. The third, slightly larger but only slightly, flowed between the two.

Which to take? Where did the principal source lie? I felt in all logic the answer could be found only at the end of the central torrent that rushed between the two ranges. In all probability it would lead us to some sort of a pass or would extend beyond the mountain face from which the other two streams rushed.

Half an hour later the sun had begun to set, casting the long shadows of our horses on the gravel while a golden light grazed the rocky hills. As we began to rise, following the central stream, the landscape slowly opened outward, and then, looking up, I saw the crescent-shaped slope mountaineers call a saddle—a ridge that links two ranges.

The river was now reduced to a bubbling stream barely a yard and a half wide, and yet it seemed that it would extend forever. We followed it up for another mile and a quarter; and then, right before me arose the saddle, whose lowest point was marked by a cairn. We had reached the foot of the pass, the Rupsa-la (perhaps derived from *Nubsa,* which means "sunset"), and indeed the sun now shone in our face, its yellow rays combing the barren ridges around us. The stream was very small, and it now fanned into three rivulets. Looking down, I saw that the stony ground was pale green with moss and short grass into which the rivulets merged and vanished. Above the green fan all was stony and brown, and then above that was the golden, darkening sky over the pass. Here just below the pass, in the fanlike bowl of a spring field, the water ended, or rather began. Here was the mythical line marking the existence, the birth site, the source of the easternmost and longest of the many branches of the uppermost extremity of the great river. Here at the foot of the Rupsa-la we had found the principal source of the Mekong.

Our first impression was one of surprise at being neither awed nor impressed. Dismounting, I slowly strode up the steep hill that formed the northern rim to the little green amphitheater from which the three rivulets ran. I saw before me how the rivulets from the spring field united to form the torrent that would become stream and then river, the river that roared across Tibet and burst through the Himalayas; the river that ranged across Yunnan before skirting the border of Burma and rushing between Laos and Thailand; the river that cut Cambodia in two with its brown and powerful breadth; the river that would finally explode into nine dragon's tongues before commingling with the vast and deep salt waters of the South China Sea.

Ling and Sebastian and I were filmed by Jacques as we inspected the spring field, examined our discovery: the long-secret source. It was amazingly unimpressive, but we had not come for theatrics. The source of the Mekong was as discreet as it had been elusive.

It was past six-thirty on my watch.

There was suddenly a lot to do. With Sebastian I photographed the site, snapping all four cardinal points as we examined the perimeter of the spring field. Then I took an altitude reading (4,975 meters, or 16,322 feet); and, most important of course, the exact latitude and longitude.

Lat. 33° 16′ 534 N.
Long. 93° 52′ 929 E.

On the surface these numbers were the entire purpose of our venture, the figures necessary to be able to pinpoint the source on any map of the world. This was what geography and exploration were all about. Just a few numbers, yet what a struggle to record them—how much bloodshed, tears, and sweat so that what had been spelled out in 1866 as the goal of the Mekong Committee of the French Société de Géographie could at long last be fulfilled. Suddenly it became important to record the day, September 17, 1994. Twenty-five years after man had set foot on the moon, here we were recording for the first time the source of the third-largest river of Asia.

As I stood there in contemplation, I began to appreciate that the struggle and the turmoil were over, and that we were living a very special and important moment. The spring field, the little trickles of water, the pass, the surrounding mountains—this was a truly magical place, for centuries the focal point of the dreams of millions of people.

A slow delight and excitement seized us, and even Ling, generally so dour, was literally bubbling with enthusiasm. Here we were at last, we had made it, we had conquered, we had reached that spot where water, earth, and sky met and merged, where myth was one with reality.

In spite of everything our expedition was a success. Only now did I realize how much I actually cared about getting here. Maybe it was more important, I thought, than I had anticipated.

We took photographs of each other straddling the little rivulet. Since leaving Paris we had discussed rather idly what we might place at the source if we found it. We had thought of flags, but then the question arose: what flag? The French, the Chinese, or the British? Sebastian was actually Anglo-Irish. Just in case, and partly out of curiosity, we had tried to buy a Chinese flag in Beijing, but that had proved not only impossible but embarrassing. Although the city was festooned with them in celebration of China's independence day, none were for sale. We tried to persuade a shopkeeper to take one down from above his stall, but this was instantly construed as an unpatriotic gesture. We finally gave up, as we had no English or French flags either, and we were reminded that the source was technically part of greater Tibet, not China. Moreover, the whole flag-planting proposition reeked of Victorian nationalism. Still, I now felt we should do something to mark the occasion. The obvious answer was a *katta*, the white ceremonial silk scarf Tibetans exchange as a sign of respect and friendship. I had one such *katta* in my saddlebag. I found myself panting as I went to fetch it, for now we were nearly 16,500 feet high.

I deposited the scarf at the juncture of the rivulets where the river was born. Jacques filmed the scene against the low rays of the setting sun, which sparkled on the clear bubbling water.

Much to our delight, Sebastian produced a can of beer and we toasted each other over the Mekong. I was really, really happy and grateful to all.

Only then did I notice it was already seven-thirty, a fact that quickly brought me back to reality. We had to head back and quickly, since our camp was so far away. We had been in the saddle since eight in the morning, practically ten hours, discounting the brief stops. Our return would be a long march in the dark; how long and how difficult?

1 2

EXPOSURE

⌘

Having taken a last long look at the source, I grabbed the reins of my pony and swung into the saddle, and the pony lurched forward, as frisky as ever. At that moment the girth slipped and the horse bolted, and threw me to the ground, causing the saddle to slide under its body. Somehow the saddle remained attached, bumping into the pony's legs and frightening it so that it darted off and eventually broke the heavy cast-iron Chinese stirrup before everything else came apart, and the pony finally stopped and stood still, snorting in anger. I had fallen heavily but fortunately felt no harm. More time was now wasted as the horse was caught, the saddle repaired, and a makeshift stirrup rigged out of nylon webbing.

A bitter wind began to blow down from the pass as we trotted and then galloped before finally settling down to a fast walk down the river. Our spirits were high, and we were filled with that virtuous contentment of accomplishment. We were all still a little amazed inasmuch as it seemed both too grand and unbelievable that we had actually discovered the principal source of the Mekong.

We were too busy to assess the full meaning of our claim or the complications and discussions that would surely arise later as experts lined up to challenge our discovery.

For the moment our only goal was to get back to camp, and quickly. The sun was hidden, but it was still light when we reached the foot of the ridge and the camp of our nomad friend who had pointed us on our way. I chose not to ride up and see him, preferring, lest it get any darker, to follow the great bend of the river so that we could travel every inch of its course. This led us in no time to the deep valley between the Sag-ri range and the Drug-di range near the steep hill that marked the confluence with the Drug-di stream leading to the sacred source. Riding around the hill as daylight dwindled, we finally reached the flat plain where the Mekong flowed into the broad rocky bed that we knew would take us to our camp.

Realizing that we would save precious time in the race against darkness, we decided to listen to our guide and leave the river to cut across the uneven bumpy surface of the dried-up marsh.

At first all went well. The horses, agile as ever, managed to pick their way through the lumpy sod, which, by some odd effect of the thaw, no doubt better understood by experts, was raised in hard little mounds as obstacles to our progress.

I was now confident in the wisdom and directional sense of our Khamba companion; as night began to fall, I had little reason for concern, I told myself. Then, faster than expected, it was pitch black. Shouldn't there have been a moon? What about the brilliance of the stars that on certain nights I had found so dazzling as to hurt the eye? Looking up I saw that there were no stars at all, just the slow knitting of clouds, black on black, those familiar clouds that we knew would bring hail.

Of course by now we felt immune to hail, as we had been pelted by plenty of it already. Our immediate problem was that the horses were stumbling on the half-frozen mounds on which they were obliged to step. Under our weight these clods would frequently crumble, causing the horses to lurch rather unpleasantly. After a short while I dismounted and so did the others, all of us relieved, in part, to be getting off our saddle sores. Walking proved even more difficult, however, in that the ground was hard to see and the rough tufts of sod constantly made us trip along with our mounts. In fact, it was a bit of a mystery how we could walk at all in the dark over the obstacle-strewn ground. It seemed we might be lost when suddenly, there, straight ahead of us, confirming the sixth sense of our Khamba muleteer, we saw a flash of brilliant light: Our camp lay straight ahead in the distance. It was now ten-thirty.

We were all exhausted, plodding on in disorder. I got back in the saddle with the others, and very soon our convoy was stretched out so that I couldn't see who was who or where anybody was. Sebastian and Ling had miner's lights that each occasionally turned on, though they were of little use in actually lighting our way. We had no choice but to abandon ourselves to the excellent night vision of our horses.

Toward eleven came the first rain, followed by the all-too-familiar sputter of hail. Dismounting, I donned my waterproof gear. Up in the saddle again, panting, I pulled my head into my shoulders as the little grains of ice bounced into my face and simultaneously froze my hands, since I had forgotten where I had put my gloves, somewhere deep in my backpack.

Looking up, I couldn't see the others. I shouted out to Sebastian, asking everyone to wait and stay together. I knew how easily one of us might stray and get lost, a potential disaster in the paralyzing cold of our situation. At this hour, in a freezing storm out in the open in terrain void of any shelter, getting lost could prove fatal. Straining my eyes for hours I had yet to see the light of our camp again. What could be the matter? Surely we should be able to see the light again by now. But no, the horizon was jet black. My heart sank as I imagined that somehow we had gone too far.

I decided to call a halt to assess the situation and talk with our guide. We clustered together in the dark: Jacques, Sebastian, Ling . . . but the Khamba muleteer had vanished.

We shouted into the wind and it took our voices across the plain—no sign of the man. We knew he had a light, the little light I had given him that he had charged all day on his cap under the sun. I knew it worked, as he had used it that very night. Where was he? Why had he gone off?

There are moments when everything comes into focus with a cold lucidity. I was now faced with two unpleasant facts: Our guide was lost, or had abandoned us, and we ourselves were lost. I had no compass with me, nor had I any idea where we were or where our camp was located. In the howling storm the best I could do was to turn to our right and, hopefully keeping a straight line, run into the Mekong again. Once there we would have to choose to travel either downstream or upstream.

A word kept on running through my mind: exposure. Exposure, that fatal moment when the body gives up from fatigue after struggling too long to keep warm. We were all exhausted, all of us freezing cold. How long could we roam on like this?

I had always been lucky in life, walking away from car wrecks, surviving the open sea in a dugout canoe, shooting Himalayan rapids by hovercraft, traversing unexplored jungles, mountain ranges, and deserts, flirting with armed guerrillas, and crossing strategic borders in disguise. Now for the first time I was aware that luck sometimes runs out, and I suddenly felt a mortal fear rising from deep within me.

The storm's hail had turned to freezing rain, the ground was slippery, the night as dark as ever without the slightest sign of a light. Maybe we had seen a nomad and not our camp at all. Where was our guide? Why and to where would he have fled?

As we advanced I saw a dark mass loom up to my left and realized it was a clifflike step in the plateau; perhaps we were nearing the river, having cut across the large bend. I had my flashlight accessible and shone it at the mud wall. It was pouring water and hail, and the torch lit up every drop as silver. Through this screen, who did I see cowering against the cliff but our muleteer, holding on to the reins of his horse?

I wanted to shout at him and demand an explanation, but being too weary I said only, *"Dro,"* or *"Go."* Looking sorry for himself, soaking wet, he got into the saddle, and once again we headed east, stumbling in the dark, our eyes hurting from scanning the void ahead for the slightest light or glow. The muleteer himself had given up trying to lead us.

Should we go back? Had we overshot our camp? Where exactly was the course of the Mekong? By my watch it was close to one o'clock, and I was too cold, too tired, and too worried to figure out how long we had been in the saddle. It had been such a long and momentous day on which all had gone so well, too well. Our having chosen the right tributary to lead us to the Rupsa pass, our meeting the nomad who knew the names of the smallest streams, the fact that the Japanese had not been up to the Rupsa pass and the end of the Mekong basin.

Everything had been in our favor. From now on I made sure everyone rode close together. There was little we could do to avoid exposure, no possible shelter, nothing like a cave or bush here. Fortunately the hail and rain soon stopped, but the night was just as dark and cold. I remember getting off my horse, too tired to spur it on, too cramped after what must have been over fourteen hours in the saddle. Would we make it till daybreak and survive?

My thoughts had sunk to the point of despair when suddenly there was an unmistakable flash of light ahead of us. It was our camp. The light blinked and swooped as if searching; we could see the wall of the mess tent. It was one-thirty, and we were finally home.

Few people could have been happier as we stumbled into the vast and comfortable windproof tent. In the glow of candles we ate, drank, and celebrated our victory over the Mekong and our having pulled through the long march in the dark.

⌘

Our original plan, after finding the source, was to turn around and travel down the Mekong as far as Nangchen Dzong and Nangchen Gar, the ancient fortress and capital of the nomad kingdom. This now conflicted with our natural immediate desire to make public our find. As I have said, the definition of discovery encompasses the duty to publish. As we set off back down the river we were torn as to what to do next, to carry on or run back and "inform the world." We decided to continue our research as planned, including a further study of the Nangchen thoroughbred horse in preparation for a larger equine expedition I was planning for the following year.

As we set out we were not yet fully aware of the toll our rush up the Mekong had exacted. Exhilarated, we began the long walk and ride all the way back to our jeeps, praying that rain and snow would not block the high passes that separated us from Zadoi.

We were never able to figure out whether our chief muleteer was a crook or was simply overwhelmed by having to lead "dog-faced" strangers to the source of a river where he had never been himself. Though I believe he was basically honest, I was nevertheless puzzled by the official in Moyun who, upon our return, tried to get Mr. Ling to pay for the three runaway horses without offering any explanation as to what had become of the man who had disappeared with them. Ling agreed to pay for one of the horses out of QMA funds.

Too happy to worry, we set off back through the Dza-Nak Lungmo pass, which we could now rightly claim had been for decades mistakenly identified in countless atlases as the watershed of the Mekong. Because of our research, the Mekong now extends a full degree west of this pass, sixty miles or more into the heart of southern Qinghai.

For years the location of the Dza-Nak Lungmo pass itself had been recorded in quite the wrong place, at Lat. 33° N, Long. 93° E (in the *Encyclopaedia Britannica*, for example), instead of where it actually is, at Lat. 33° 5′ N, Long. 94° 1′ E, a full degree off course.

(The *Times* atlas gives a better reading: Long. 33° 4′ E, Lat. 93° 55′ N.) By coincidence these mistakes placed the Dza-Nak Lungmo pass and source of the Lungmo River just south of the Mekong's true source, an ironic mistake revealing the relativity, or perhaps futility, of it all.

Crossing through the pass, once again surrounded by kiang, marauding wolves, gazelles, foxes, and wild sheep, I understood now that man was no different here than elsewhere, except that here the nomads—and I—felt closer to our very nature, to that biological expectancy we all carry in our genes—an expectancy that encompasses our spiritual aspirations and being, and an inherent state in which body and soul are fused, and both are as real as the feet we walk on.

In spite of the progress of science, we are still reluctant to attribute the origins of such behaviors as nobility, kindness, or love to our genetic structure and internal chemistry, even though we seem ready to accept the notion that aggression can be linked to specific genes and hormones.

At the source of the Mekong I realized that good and evil are complementary, and that both are essential elements of human nature.

After two harrowing days of driving through the mountains, we pulled into Zadoi. The main street, with its outdoor billiard tables, its general store stocked with sweets, batteries, and other marvels, its walled-in garrison and government depots, appeared to us like some huge capital.

It was a dismal capital, also a reminder of the fate that had befallen the whole country. While contemplating the garrison town as if for the first time, it came to me I was back where I had started, and as Eliot said, "know[ing] the place for the first time." Zadoi, the tiny garrison on the upper Mekong, was just like Paris, New York, or London in relation to the values of the nomads, whose world was without constraints, without objects, without police, without shops, and without money. Theirs was a world in which everyone is, in most ways, self-sufficient, free of the material wants we consider necessities, and free also of the thousand encumbrances that such needs and wants create—the chains that make us affluent slaves, men and women driven to pawn our time and our minds and bodies for a salary to purchase bowls of instant soup, international travel, and electronically illustrated storytelling machines. Slaves through onerous taxes paid to governments that are supposed to protect our goods from the greed of neighbors and protect our rights from the greed of merchants. Governments, who school our children to have the correct wants and needs in a world in which all and everything is for sale. To be civilized, in our terms, is to be controlled from within and from without, making a civilized gentleman, in many ways, into a domesticated animal.

Only rarely can we perceive in ourselves and in others behavior that isn't preconditioned, harnessed, or regulated. We are educated to respect the law, to believe in what is written in this or that book, to acquiesce to this or that social order, with the result that man has become tame and has traded freedom for easy access to shelter, food, and comfort.

Therein lies the dilemma that has caused us anguish in our cushy lives, spent on sofas before television sets.

"Man is not made for comfort just like the goat is not made for the plains."

Our very nature is opposed to what is sold to us by our merchant princes as the compulsory adjunct to happiness. Men are not made for comfort any more than we are made to spend our lives working for others, whether our employers be the state or the shareholders of some corporation.

Men are born to love freedom and independence; born to be masters of their own destiny; born to find pleasure in the struggle for survival; born to experience the delights of the chase and the fulfillment of what nature has established as our role and place in creation.

Only now that I was about to leave the upper Mekong did I clearly understand why modern Western myths of freedom and salvation are set in Tibet, on what was still a lost horizon as far as we were concerned. This was a world where men and women are still free to live out their destiny as nature intended. We Westerners, on the other hand, have lost the paradise that haunts our dreams, that Garden of Eden from which we long ago banished ourselves in the name of comfort, greed, and maybe also laziness. The Garden of Eden is still here in our midst, but maybe there's no going back to it. Maybe we're simply too tame to face the hardships of the wilds for which we were originally conceived. By this I don't wish to make noble savages of the Khambas and the other Tibetan nomads. I believe we are all noble and savage deep inside, and that it is only the debilitating effects of "civilization" that has undermined our nobility.

But aren't we now too numerous and too domesticated ever to achieve again the nobler ideals to which we aspire? What are we to do? Forfeit comfort for happiness or happiness for comfort? Few of us have a real choice, and so we must resign ourselves to live in a world cursed by the gods, and bearable only if one believes in a better life after death. The great irony lies in the fact that paradise on earth is a land of hardship, that only in discomfort can we find happiness.

In the meantime, slowly and inexorably, on the ultimate frontier in Tibet, as once occurred in North America and Mexico, the last free men are being hunted and exterminated or drawn into the net of civilization at the gates of a paradise already theirs.

Of course most of us believe sincerely that there is no turning back, that there is no solution because there are so many of us, and it seems we can do nothing about it. Instead, we turn over our responsibilities to divine providence, to the socialist welfare state, or to the whims of some modern prince. Few of us are able to understand that the world in which we live was made by man and not determined by fate. It is now up to man, not to God, to make the necessary changes to our society. The Eskimo, like the Tibetans themselves and so many of the people of our planet until recently, were masters of their own and their children's destiny. Their social system provided them with the means for survival through the ages. Shouldn't we once again meet our obligations to our descendants and, for instance, take whatever birth control measures might be required to allow our children to live a life closer to their aspirations? In thirty years China's ballooning population—Mao's biggest mistake—could reduce itself by half through rigorous birth control. But Mao exhorted the Chinese to have many children, and, now, like many another modern leader, he must take the blame for the slums and misery that have arisen as a direct result of an irresponsible ideology.

As we set out for Nangchen I knew exactly why it was that for several millennia the nomads had overrun the city states surrounding them: Their intimate convictions of what was right and wrong and their disregard for hardship allowed them to prevail both physically and morally over the self-doubting, comfort-loving, civilized nations.

It is strange to think that the British and French colonial powers were able to conquer the world because of the spartan nineteenth-century education they had received, which taught them to despise comfort, love effort, and draw a very straight line between right and wrong. The last barbarians of Europe were the colonials—the singularly stubborn, rugged, and unflinching schoolboys, with their black and white certitudes. Maybe as one of them I had become the last explorer, the last true barbarian.

It is likely that the coming millennium will see the disappearance of the last nomads of the upper Mekong, as a civilization of urban squalor and miserable masses is firmly established everywhere. This will certainly happen unless there is a reemergence of a race of men determined to fight, and to live free once again according to human nature.

⌘

In Zadoi we met Mr. Wu Jian Sheng of the travel office of the Chinese Academy of Science, who had organized the Japanese party composed of six members from the Agricultural University of Tokyo, under the leadership of Dr. Nakanishi Junichi, assisted by Dr. Kitamura Masayuki. We were told that they had not been looking for the source of the Mekong after all—a piece of news we would have preferred to hear at the outset. This was not the last we were to see or hear of Mr. Wu Jian Sheng of the Academy of Science, who had suddenly become most interested in our activities.

It took us two days to reach Nangchen Dzong from Zadoi. En route we visited the small Nyingma-pa–sect monastery of Chos-ling overlooking the Mekong. Thirty-five monks were busy repairing and restoring the main chapel, which had been destroyed in 1957 in the course of the fighting between the Khambas and the People's Liberation Army. That same night we slept in the huge Gelug-pa monastery of Nangchen, home to over one thousand monks whose parents are all nomads. According to the abbot, this monastery is the largest of all Tibetan monasteries in number of monks. We were proudly shown by my friend the abbot the chapels and assembly halls, built upon the ruins of the old monastery.

"I receive no money from either the Chinese or the Dalai Lama," explained the abbot with firm emphasis. The cost of his massive enterprise was paid for by the nomads, who are both highly religious and rich—because, devoid of needs and wants out on the tundra, they have no use for the money they get for their sheep and yaks.

It should be mentioned that although in certain parts of Tibet the Red Guards are to blame for the destruction of the monasteries, in Amdo and Kham it was the People's Liberation Army and the Communist cadres themselves who closed and destroyed the religious buildings between 1953 and 1959 during the Khambas' armed rebellion against the Communists.

These monasteries are now once again the schools and universities of Tibet, offering the study of medicine and animal husbandry along with theology, philosophy, and yogic arts. The monks pay for their own upkeep, with money given them by their families, or with what they earn working for the monastery, or for other monks, or by performing ceremonies for the laity. If they should choose to leave the monastery where they've started their studies, the monks can go on to another one (or quit completely if, for instance, they should wish to marry). They receive university-like academic degrees that are separate from any religious rank they might wish to attain, beginning with novice and rising to *Khempo*, or senior abbot. Each rank is accompanied by vows renouncing such things as drinking and eating meat.

Two days' driving from Zadoi, as the sun was setting, we came across the Mekong once again. Here, less than two hundred miles from the source, it was already a great, broad river whose banks, at twelve thousand feet, were bordered by fields of barley and the first villages of the local Nangchen farming community, which supplies the nomads with grain.

In Nangchen Dzong we tried in vain to hire horses, combing the bazaar, Jacques with his stethoscope searching to take the pulse of the local steeds. Everyone was dragging heels as we felt the aftereffect of our high-altitude marathon. In the end we drove yet more impossible roads to reach Nangchen Gar, the ancient capital. There we collected more information about how Nangchen was established as a kingdom in the eighth century, and how Mila Repa, the great Tibetan sage and poet, visited the realm.

The wealth of Nangchen was built on the export of horses to the Ming emperors in the fourteenth century. The nomads welcomed the lamaist Buddhists, and at their height seventy-two monasteries flourished on the remote plains of Nangchen's twenty-five tribes.

This bears a marked contrast to the region just south of Nangchen, which remains today the fiercest stronghold of the pre-Buddhist Bon-po religion—a region still largely unexplored, as we were soon to find out.

As much as we wished to investigate further the Nangchen region, ten days after reaching the source we were so exhausted that we announced to a delighted Mr. Ling that we would at last be heading back to Xining, six hundred miles away. The time had come to reveal our discovery to the outside world.

We all felt good about our achievement and had imagined that somewhere it might be appreciated. It was with great care that I worded the letter I faxed to the French embassy in Beijing from the post office in Gonghe, the last town on the high plateau before Xining. In the note I proudly communicated our discovery to the counselor, recounting how the quest had been started in France in 1866. I asked him to advise the ambassador. That done, we returned to Xining exactly one month after having left it.

In our eagerness, we had expected if not a full-fledged triumphal return, at least a little enthusiasm. Of course, given that we were no longer in the Age of Exploration, our reception was bound to be mixed, to say the least. The French embassy didn't bat an eye. In fact, the counselor seemed to have kept the information of my fax completely to himself.

Back in Beijing we wrote two press releases, and, to our satisfaction, several newspapers around the world echoed the news in tiny print. The immediate result of these dispatches was a visit, to our hotel, by Mr. Wu Jian Sheng of the travel office of the Academy of Science. With one of his colleagues in tow, he informed us rather crossly that we should have asked the Chinese Academy for permission to discover the source. Having said that, he explained that, for a price, the Academy of Science would be glad to arrange our future expeditions. We thanked Mr. Wu for his advice and informed him that we had been officially allowed into the region by the QMA.

Later, upon my return to Paris, I received a visit from Professor Cai Zongxia, a member of the Geographical Institute of the Academy of Science of China, to whom I gave a map of our findings.

Thinking it the correct thing to do upon reaching Paris, I advised the Institut Géographique National de France of our find, and received back a very brief letter thanking us for the information and congratulating us for the discovery. In the second paragraph, however, we were advised that we should communicate our finding to the National Bureau of Cartography in Beijing, as a record of the source of the Mekong was none of their business.

The Royal Geographical Society was more enthusiastic, and its director and secretary, Dr. John Hemming, wrote us a letter that was both warm and encouraging.

"Many congratulations on your achievement in reaching and locating the source of the Mekong River." He asked for further details.

In the meantime, *Paris-Match* printed a six-page article on our find in its December issue; this was followed by articles in *Liberation* and *Le Figaro.* The last of these was written in a slightly skeptical tone, with one expert (who had never been to Asia) declaring that modern geographers preferred to consider a cluster of sources rather than a single source for major rivers, and a grumpy general (who had written a paper on the Mekong) asserting, "No doubt other expeditions would be necessary, perhaps with a little more means, to register precisely all the sources of the river." No doubt he was right, but in the meantime we had paved the way for others.

By the end of December it seemed that everyone had forgotten us, and we were left to mull over the sad fact that the days of territorial exploration were no more. Our achievement had been met with only the slightest bit of public recognition and much disbelief.

Here our journey would have ended on a rather low note—we were frustrated by the thought that those who had failed before us were given heroes' welcomes, but we had received not so much as a handshake.

Suddenly, however, as if by magic, we ceased to be invisible. An article appeared in April 1995 in the *Geographical Magazine,* and then an item in the prestigious *Geographical Journal* started a wave of interest worldwide. It was as if we had discovered the Mekong all over again. With the tacit approval and publicity of the Royal Geographical Society, the skeptics were convinced at last.

A Reuters dispatch, followed by a dispatch from France-Presse, triggered a whole series of articles, not the least of which was a front-page article in the *New York Times* on the seventeenth of April, titled "In Wild Asia, Caravan to a River's Source." The piece was written by Marlise Simons and featured a photograph of me straddling the unspectacular baby Mekong. This was followed by a front-page article in the *International Herald-Tribune* the next day. Then came a flood of articles from Australia to Zanzibar, our find being declared by some as "the solving of the last great geographic enigma of the planet." The *Sunday Times* of London titled their piece "Guinness Heir Wins Mekong River Race," while the *Independent* hailed a "New Era of Exploration."

For once a story involving the Mekong had a happy ending. The Chinese press reported our discovery, and, unlike the case of the Nile and so many other rivers, there was no challenge by any other party. Many awoke to a fact that I had known and believed all along, that there is, indeed, something left to explore on our planet if the spirit is there.

Of course we were aware that others could probably have done a better job. But at the end of the day, I confess, there is nothing quite like being the first. When Sebastian and I addressed a full house at the Royal Geographical Society, we were overwhelmed at the crowd's enthusiastic response.

Our true reward, however, was the privilege of having reached the place where dreams and reality meet. Having done that I felt vindicated for the thirty-seven years I had spent roaming the remoter parts of a very often indifferent planet.

This book should end here, but as is the case with growing leeks or playing the stock market, in exploring, tomorrow is another day, and explorers just have to carry on.

POSTSCRIPT:
A LIVING FOSSIL

⌘

The film of our Mekong expedition made from Jacques's ten hours of videotape had not yet aired in the United States, when, putting the Mekong aside for a while, Sebastian and I prepared in September 1995 to set off again for Tibet, this time with a larger party to study the Nangchen horses.

My idea was to have a zoologist who specialized in equine physiology make a study of the Nangchen horse. We wished to examine in detail the horse's specific adaptation to high altitudes. I hoped, too, to be allowed to bring some of these horses back to Europe or America. Sebastian was the first to join the project.

As I boldly announced to David Smadja, our young and enthusiastic sponsor, we would travel this time from Lhasa to the remotest northeastern province of occupied Tibet. There, on the southern borders of Qinghai's Nangchen district, we planned to purchase the finest specimens of the Nangchen horse, and then to drive and ride the horses six hundred—odd miles across the whole of central Tibet all the way back to Lhasa. Having done all that, we would have horses at our disposal for further study and eventual export.

En route, the equine specialist of our team would perform a study of the horses under stress at various altitudes. This involved, among other tests, the monitoring of their heart rates before and after climbing through passes. As with the preceding expedition, this one would be filmed, but not by our friend Jacques Falck; Jerome Nouvelle, a professional cameraman, would be assisted by Sylvain Carellas. Both men were selected by our sponsor.

Dr. Harris of the Animal Health Trust in Newmarket, one of the world's foremost research centers specializing in equine physiology, recommended that we take along a brilliant young researcher by the name of Dr. Ignasi Casas.

Dr. Casas, who had worked for years with the Animal Health Trust, was Catalan. My son Jocelyn, just out of university in Barcelona, joined our party as a photographer, with the interesting result that four out of six of us spoke Catalan, a language nearly as esoteric as Tibetan. Sebastian and I had learned ours over the course of many summers in Cadaques, a coastal town north of Barcelona where we both had summer houses.

As I was researching this expedition, one of the first things that struck me was how little was known of the north-central part of Tibet, by virtue of the fact that it lay outside the two major trade routes that linked Amdo and Kham with Lhasa. I could find no account of a journey into the region by Europeans, Americans, or Japanese. It seemed travelers in the past had nearly always stuck to the major trade routes. It never occurred to me that there may have been an excellent reason. Not being very good at listening to other people's advice, I was going to have to learn the hard way.

"The area is inhabited by wild men," Rinzing, our Tibetan assistant, advised us on our arrival in Lhasa. Although he had never been there himself, he was aware of the ferocious reputation of the people of the area, on the one hand because they were Khambas, considered by the Lhasans as aggressive if not outright wild, and on the other hand because they weren't Buddhists but believers in Bon—in other words, they were primitive heathens. They had resisted conversion to lamaism for fourteen centuries.

I laughed at such warnings. I had spent years among the Khambas, and I felt I had nothing to fear. That said, we set off on the first leg of our long journey, a rugged 750-mile drive to the extreme northeast of Tibet, a region officially closed to all foreigners, and our jumping-off point. It had taken me two years of lengthy negotiations with the authorities in Lhasa to secure permission from the Chinese military to travel to the area. I was particularly interested in the prospect of exploring virgin territory. There was no telling what we might encounter.

Our first surprise was that the Indian summer we had hoped for failed to materialize. Two days out of Lhasa it began to snow as we left Nakchu-ka heading east along the Trans-Tibetan Highway linking Lhasa to Chengdu, the capital of Chinese Sichuan. This strategic route across Khamba territory was carved through Tibet in 1954 and played a key role in the suppression of the Khamba uprising. Forty years later, still a narrow dirt road, it took us slowly across snowbound pass after snowbound pass toward Sogchen, the site of a huge fortress and monastery that mark the limits of Buddhism on the frontier of Kham. Beyond Sogchen lay the land of the heathen Bon people.

The third day out of Lhasa our truck and two jeeps reached the remote Serchu valley, dotted with little hamlets composed of clusters of flat-roofed houses. Here, in the last week of September, the barley had been harvested and the fields were covered with a stubble of straw. Hundreds of the finest Nangchen horses we had ever seen were grazing happily all around. Nangchen itself and the upper valley of the Mekong lay just beyond the northern ranges from which we were overlooking the Serchu valley.

With great satisfaction I witnessed Dr. Casas's enthusiasm at the sight of "our" Nangchen horse. I was afraid that I might have been a little bit carried away in the manner in which I had been extolling its unique conformation and qualities to him since the time of our first meeting weeks before.

Upon leaving the valley and driving two days farther east, we noticed that the horses were getting smaller and less remarkable. A day's drive from the monastery of Riwoche, we decided, therefore, to stop our quest and go back to the Serchu valley and make it our base.

At Serchu we were in the heart of Bon territory, but we didn't realize at first what that meant. The local Khambas looked like tall, handsome "red Indians," and wore their hair long in braids intertwined with red silk threads. They cut fine figures on their elegant mounts, and we weren't shy about telling them that we were interested in renting and buying horses. We were also looking for men to accompany us on our long way south to Lhasa, we explained.

The day after we pitched our tents, our camp was surrounded by farmers with horses for sale. Obviously the crafty locals thought they could pull a fast one on us, as most of the horses were ugly and many were lame or blind in one eye.

Dr. Casas weeded out the animals with major defects and established that we were not to be taken in so easily. In spite of the many horses offered to us, none were as fine as the ones we had seen in the fields. The farmers said all the good horses belonged to relatives who didn't want to sell. When I singled out one particularly elegant mount I was told by the owner that he would not sell it for less than two thousand yuan (four thousand dollars), an exorbitant price considering that the average local horse was worth two or three hundred dollars. But the man wasn't joking. Just to test him I bid up to six thousand dollars, a sum with which I might have been able to buy up much of the hamlet where the farmer lived. Still no sale.

"They are our pride," the Khamba said forcefully, at which I was moved to recall that not so long ago in Europe not everything was for sale either, although it seems to be today.

The sedentary pagan Khambas were just as aggressive and arrogant as the nomads of Nangchen. Like the nomads, they lived for the annual fair that attracted the region's best horses to Serchu to compete in races and displays of skill. To own an excellent horse was to be famous, envied, feared, and respected. No one would part with their finer animals.

We soon discovered that the proud villagers were also unwilling to accompany us south, we thought because they were busy plowing their fields and threshing the harvest. We were quite oblivious to the fact that the journey we planned to take was dangerous, if not outright impossible.

We had already purchased three horses, which I now had to sell back to their former owners at a loss as we decided to seek better fortune in the town of Dengchen, a day's drive east. In Dengchen there was a large Chinese garrison and with the help of the local officials, we were at last able to hire the appropriate horses to take us on the road south. These horses were prime examples of the Nangchen breed, and Dr. Casas set about immediately to study their heart rhythms.

Four hours out of Dengchen, we began a steep climb, and two hours after that we staggered up to the snow-covered summit of a 16,600-foot pass. Neither the pass nor its altitude figured correctly on our maps. From that moment on, our journey became a strange and painful plunge into a hostile unexplored world. Now we knew why no one took this northern route to Lhasa.

The moment we descended the great pass we entered a new world. After camping at the foot of the pass we pushed on through bushes and trees that eventually formed a forest. None of our maps had alerted us to the presence of a forest here in the heart of the barren tundra. By a strange phenomenon, humidity had managed to seep all the way up from the tropics of Burma through the deep mountain gorges of the Salween River, traveling over twelve hundred miles like a submarine current, bringing right into the very heart of the dry, damp-free tundra the humidity of the tropics. Thus it was that we were entering great forests whose trees were shrouded in moss, an island of vegetation as unexpected as it was unique. There were tall pine trees side by side with willows and birches and a whole array of thorny trees reminiscent of the parasol-like trees of the African bush. The forest's microclimate came with a whole range of animals and insects. Without a road leading to this place, and, surrounded as it was by tundra, it had not yet been touched by the axe of the Chinese loggers who are elsewhere making short work of the other Tibetan forests.

In keeping with the gloom of some of the forest, the local people were a dour and primitive lot. We were now deep in the heart of the land of the Bon-po, a region so remote and primitive that even the Bon scriptures of the rest of Tibet forbade these people from becoming heads of religious institutions. We were in the heart of the land of the "wild ones," as the Tibetans themselves call these people.

After six days of painful riding, through every kind of weather, over a total of four passes, catching only now and then magnificent views of forested peaks reminiscent of the Rockies, we finally reached the Salween River. This great river, though far less famous than the Mekong, the Yangtze, and the Yellow River, is nevertheless formidable—it stopped us dead in our tracks. Described as "one of the wildest and most picturesque streams in the world" by Sir James George Scott, KCIE (Knight Commander of the Indian Empire), author of the *Upper Burma Gazetteer*, it drains most of central and northern Tibet and is the fourth-longest river in the region.

As in the case of the Mekong, its course across Tibet and northern Burma cuts a gorge so deep that it can't always be followed, and so it too remains a mystery. We found ourselves on a steep rocky cliff above the turbulent waters where a suspension footbridge built by the Chinese Army spanned the river—a bridge too crude to allow the passage of any animals but those horses and yaks especially trained for the purpose. Thus, on the north bank we had to abandon all our horses. It then took us the better part of half a day for one yak and a pony to shuttle our baggage across.

Before the bridge was built, it had been impossible to cross the swift current at this point. One had had to travel about sixty miles farther east, where the current relented a little so as to allow the crossing of yak-hide coracles and the hardiest of horses brave enough to swim.

We were soon to find out that the Salween wasn't the only formidable obstacle on our route. We continued on south once we were able to hire more ponies and some mules. Having lost all of our Nangchen horses, we had to make do with local ponies, a rather nondescript lot of what the Tibetans call *rong-ta*, or valley horses—ponies of mixed blood without distinction.

Beyond the bridge we began to climb the narrow and gloomy forested gorge of a tributary of the Salween. Hugging a trail along a slender ledge, we penetrated deeper into the evergreen moss-draped woods that clung to the sheer mountainside. For two days we rode in the gorge, eventually emerging at a snow-covered pass that led us down into a secluded wooded valley where small mud-colored villages punctuated patchworks of gray harvested fields. We were heading for Pemba, or rather Palbar as it is written out, what today is one of the most isolated of Chinese garrisons in Tibet.

Yet another pass, 15,900 feet high, gave us a frightening view of what lay ahead. The entire horizon was blocked by a sheer crenelated barrier of snowy peaks, a mighty range whose northern face barred our route. I wasn't at all sure that we would manage to cross *this* formidable obstacle.

Eleven days after leaving Dengchen we reached Palbar, exhausted but happy to have made it in spite of the rain and snow and the slippery and dangerous trail. Our arrival created considerable commotion.

"You have no right to be here," we were told by a Chinese police official, who then confined us to barracks until the local military commander could be alerted. That evening, all the local Chinese authorities, in red-bordered caps with gold braiding, examined our documents, and no amount of protest or waving of permits on our part seemed to make an impression on them.

It was announced again that the area was forbidden to all foreigners. Moreover, it was explained that the passes through the great ranges to the south were closed and the road to Lhasa would be impassable until the spring. The local Tibetans confirmed this last bit of bad news.

There was no use arguing. We could see for ourselves that the passes were buried in snow. But what could we do? There were no roads south to Lhasa, or west or north for that matter—no roads, it seemed, to connect us again with the motor road by which we had come. Couldn't we ride west until we reached a road? The answer was no, the entire zone was restricted, and our permit was only for the trail to Lhasa.

There did nevertheless exist one small dirt road that supplied the garrison at Palbar by truck. This trail ran east until it joined the highway that led north to Chamdo, the capital of eastern Tibet, five hundred miles away. But the road in question and Chamdo itself were strictly out of bounds to foreigners.

For a moment I was worried that we might be forced to backtrack on foot or on horseback, providing the passes were still open. In the end, faced with no other alternative but to let us travel east, the exasperated officials allowed us to go to Chamdo, although no one among them would take the responsibility of granting us an official permit.

Our way back to Lhasa was to be a long, rough, eight-day drive. First it would take us two days to reach Chamdo, then five days from Chamdo to Lhasa via Riwoche and Dengchen, the town from which we had set out for Palbar. This would be a journey of more than twelve hundred miles, most of it through restricted territory, a large part of which had never been visited by foreigners.

We were all disheartened by our setback, by our inability to blaze a new trail to Lhasa, and, more particularly, by our failure to secure any Nangchen horses. But there it was, the unexpected is to be expected on any true exploration.

Yet more surprises lay ahead as we started on our long journey across the remoter regions of Kham. Successively we climbed up and down the near-vertical gorges of the Salween and then the Mekong River nearing Chamdo. Sebastian and I eyed the Mekong with a certain complicity; had we not seen it as a mere trickle, known it at its birthplace? Our route to Chamdo had been across dry, barren, treeless country until we reached the deep gorges. Chamdo itself, the second-largest town of Tibet and the capital of Tibetan Kham, was a large Chinese-dominated town with all the attendant squalor a huge garrison can assume. It was here that the Tibetans had capitulated to the Chinese invaders in 1950, and here that Nawang Nagbo, the traitorous minister of the Dalai Lama's government, had blown up the town's arsenal rather than put up a fight.

In Chamdo we were treated as suspects of the highest order, and were not allowed to photograph or film this "forbidden city." Accordingly, we were pleased to leave the following day, climbing out of the gorge of the Mekong to head for one of its main affluents, which led us to Riwoche.

Riwoche was where I had originally planned to begin this journey because it was the Tibetan province closest to Nangchen. What happened on our way to Riwoche was to change our expedition from a semifailure into a success. True to the dictum that exploration is, above all, a venture into the *unknown*, it was by sheer accident that we discovered in Riwoche a fascinating breed of horse, never before recorded by Westerners.

We had been driving for six hours when we reached the foot of the Gung-la, the principal access to the main Riwoche valley. I was seated in the front of the truck with Jerome Nouvelle, the cameraman, and Dr. Casas. In the back the rest of the team were dozing on the floor of the truck. We had entered a forested region of large pines, broken up now and then by alpine pastures. The atmosphere here was very different from the dark forest on the banks of the Salween. Above us, the peaks rose to nineteen thousand feet, granite rocky crags up the sides of which climbed mighty pines. I was familiar with this kind of forest, a continuation of the sort found just east of Nangchen Gar. The forest was known for its white-lipped deer and also for the presence of two breeds of macaque monkeys and some rare members of the shrew family.

As we drove down into the shady valley, I sighted a small herd of horses grazing under the trees. It had become a reflex for me to look at horses carefully, and as I observed them in detail, I was struck at how short and stocky they were. I asked that we stop the truck. Getting out, I took a couple of snapshots of them with my camera from the roadside and then decided to walk toward them. I managed to reach two young horses with a third horse that may have been their mother. One of these was a pale coffee color with a dark stripe running down its back and, to my surprise, two brown stripes at the top of its fore and hind quarters. Such stripes, recalling the markings of wild asses, are occasionally found on feral horses that have returned to the wild. Looking at the two small horses I was struck by something particular in their bodies, although at first I couldn't say exactly what it was.

I called out to Jerome and Ignasi to join me. Jerome arrived with the camera and began shooting. With Ignasi I tried to approach the young horses and get within reach, but one swung around and tried to kick me. Were they wild? I didn't think so, as they wouldn't have let us get so near if they were. I now noticed nearby under the trees some rather elegant wooden shelters—the huts of herders from the villages below.

Ignasi pointed out to the rest of us that the horses looked primitive to him, and then suddenly everything fell into place. We were looking at a strange archaic horse. There were some twenty in all in the little herd, which had scattered at our approach. They all seemed to share the same general conformation. They were small—twelve hands (four feet) high at the withers—with truncated, triangular heads and very bizarre narrow nostrils and slanted eyes.

The horses resembled no others I had ever seen in Tibet, or anywhere else. What could they be, I wondered? They were all the more amazing for the fact that we were so close to Nangchen, and yet these animals were so different from the horses we had ridden there. Since I had begun my research on Tibetan horses, I had recorded eight breeds, the smallest being the Tsaidam pony inhabiting the marshy wasteland of northwestern Qinghai. But the Tsaidam too was a pony very different from these, with a much more "normal" horse's face.

We took many photographs and continued on down the valley. Here and there we sighted other horses and noted that they were all similar to those we had first observed near the pass. On arriving in the garrison of Riwoche we were excited about what we had seen, and we decided to investigate further. On learning that a veterinary station was attached to the garrison, Dr. Casas and I immediately paid a visit to it, while Rinzing set out to hire horses for the following day, so that we could comb the countryside for more horses and get an idea of their distribution.

What was particularly interesting was that this breed, if indeed it was one unto itself, seemed to fit into the well-contained local wooded alpine ecosystem with its unique deer and macaque monkeys. Could it be, we wondered, that the local horse was a leftover— a survivor—of some very ancient breed? A horse that somehow got locked into the Riwoche valley complex and was preserved from mixing with breeds in adjacent valleys?

We were told that all the horses of the region were similar to those we had seen. They all had slanted eyes, barely marked chins, and odd-looking noses.

Dr. Casas was eager to round up more horses for a closer look. The following morning we were presented with an odd bunch of mounts, hired from the police to take us to search out more of the little beasts.

Overnight, everyone had become rather suspicious of our intentions. Even our companions from Lhasa began to show concern: as tired as we were, they wanted to return to Lhasa. Dr. Casas declared that we should make sure to obtain a blood sample of this new breed to see if it had an anomalous chromosome.

Normally all horses except the wild Przewalski have the same number of chromosomes. Could this horse be an "intermediate" species? Only blood tests could prove that. But I couldn't give Dr. Casas permission to conduct the tests, for I myself had been expressly forbidden to take blood samples of the Nangchen horses. I explained the problem to Dr. Casas, whereupon he decided to act according to his "scientific conscience."

In the meantime we rode off to examine more horses. We immediately found that the accompanying policeman—a narrow-minded sort—had no intention of letting us wander into the wilderness, which meant that we were reduced to examining only those horses we could find just off the main road.

A few miles out of Riwoche we found a half-dozen fine specimens grazing, and we filmed and photographed them from every angle. We were now utterly convinced that the "Riwoche horse" was not only a breed apart, but that it was no doubt very, very ancient. In my mind's eye I saw the horses of the Stone Age cave paintings.

I was right, in fact: When we returned to Europe we were able to show that the little horse we'd come upon was the spitting image of the horses depicted in detail in the Chauvet cave found in southern France in 1994. The drawings in this cave have been estimated to be thirty-four thousand years old.

European prehistoric cave paintings, as has been said, consistently show two types of horse, one easily identifiable as being a Przewalski horse due to its white donkey-like muzzle, and the other, the mysterious horse number two, characterized by slanted eyes, a duck-billed nose (just like the "odd-looking" nose of the Riwoche), a straight face, a weak jaw, and a small rump.

Could the Riwoche horse be the famous archaic horse number two? The sheer isolation of the Riwoche region—the high passes closing off its valleys from adjoining areas—seemed to confirm what the horse's shape alone demonstrated: It was related to horses that roamed the world thirty-four thousand years ago.

On our return to Europe, blood samples were sent to Dr. Steven Harrison, an equine geneticist at the Royal Agricultural College, Cirencester, England. Unfortunately, we had only two samples, and neither one showed chromosomal anomalies or variations, so that little could be learned on that front.

It is important to remember that every existing animal or human being alive today traces back to the beginnings of time. "The Riwoche horse," as we had gotten used to calling it, was no exception. The key question, then, is simply this: How much, or how little, had the horse evolved over the years? Only pictures from ancient caves could give us the clues we needed and prompt us to say that it was very like the famous horse number two, which had been thought to exist only on the walls of those caves.

For centuries equine specialists have been wondering which breeds or types of horses were first tamed. Archaeological studies to date indicate that the first domesticated horses known are preserved in the six-thousand-year-old skeletons found in a tomb at Dereivka Sredri Stog in the Crimea. These skeletons show the wear marks of a bit on their teeth and are of a very small horse, much smaller than the Przewalski; their size—a coincidence?—matches that of the Riwoche horse. It thus seems quite clear that the first of the wild horses to be tamed were not, as some have long believed, descendants or crossbreeds of the wild Przewalski, but were a smaller horse, the famed horse number two from which the Riwoche—and possibly all other tame horses—now seemed to us to be descended. It is my belief that the Riwoche is a living fossil of the original "noblest conquest of man," the horse that man first dared ride some six thousand years ago. Perhaps domesticating horses was a small step for man, but it was without doubt a huge leap for humanity. When man domesticated the horse he changed the world forever. The ugly little, flat-nostriled Riwoche was rapidly to give way around the globe to the thoroughbreds raised by man for sport and war, the horses that ended up leading entire nations and their heroes on the paths to conquest and to greatness.

Our finding the Riwoche horse in 1995 was to have repercussions at least as great as our discovery of the source of the Mekong River.

Perhaps more important than our discoveries, as far as I was concerned, was the realization that the last years of this century, far from putting an end to a long tradition of exploration and discovery, can still lead us into a new era of scientific inquiry on what remains, even now, an exciting and mysterious planet.

INDEX

ACKNOWLEDGMENTS

I would like to thank, for their generosity, kind assistance, and encouragement, Gian Franco Brignone and Loel Guinness. I would also like to thank the staff of both the Royal Geographical Society and the Qinghai Mountaineering Association for their help in preparing and carrying out our expedition. I am also particularly grateful for the labors of Jonathan S. Landreth, the editor of this book, who pursued me around the globe and worked for months to ensure that it might appear in a language akin to English.

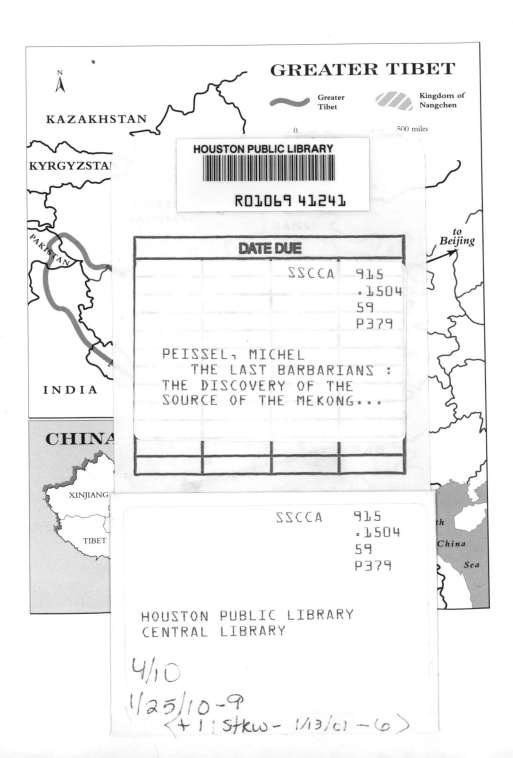